Tom Phillips is the former editor of Full Fact, Britain's leading independent fact-checking organisation. Previously he was the editorial director of BuzzFeed UK. Tom's first book, *HUMANS: A Brief History of How We F*cked It All Up*, was published in 2018, and has since been translated into more than 30 languages. Tom's second book, *TRUTH: A Brief History of Total Bullsh*t* was published in 2019 and has so far sold in 20 territories.

Jonn Elledge is a regular contributor to the *Big Issue* and the *New Statesman*, a less regular contributor to other titles such as the *Guardian* and *Wired*, and an almost constant contributor to the weekly *Newsletter of (Not Quite) Everything*. He was previously assistant editor of the *New Statesman*, where he was responsible for launching and editing the urbanism site *CityMetric*, hosting the Skylines podcast and writing a lot of angry columns about the housing crisis. He lives in the East End of London. Jonn's first book, *The Compendium of (Not Quite) Everything*, was published in 2021.

Praise for the *Brief History* series:

'Uproarious . . . [Phillips and Elledge] pair the abundant good humour of this book with a warning about the corrosive effects of conspiracy theories'
The Times

'This book is brilliant. Utterly, utterly brilliant. Apart from the epilogue which is idiotic'
Jeremy Clarkson

'In dark times, it's reassuring to learn that we've always been a bunch of clueless f*cking nitwits'
Stuart Heritage

'A light-touch history of moments when humans have got it spectacularly wrong... Both readable and entertaining'
Telegraph

'If you find yourself looking at the news and wondering how humanity has got so many things wrong, over and over again, this book is a very funny answer to just that question'
Mark Watson

'Witty, entertaining, and slightly distressing but ultimately endearing . . . And if you care to avoid orbiting the earth in a space-garbage prison of your fellow humans' design, you should probably read [this]'
Sarah Knight

'Tom Phillips is a very clever, very funny man, and it shows. If *Sapiens* was a testament to human sophistication, this history of failure cheerfully reminds us that humans are mostly idiots'
Greg Jenner

'Chronicles humanity's myriad follies down the ages with malicious glee and much wit . . . a rib-tickling page-turner'
Business Standard

'*Humans* is Tom Phillips' timely, irrevent gallop through thousands of years of human stupidity. Every time you begin to find our foolishness bizarrely comforting, Phillips adds another kick in the ribs. Beneath all this book's laughter is a serious question: where does so much serial stupidity take us?'
Nicholas Griffin

CONSPIRACY

A History of Bⓧllocks Theories, and How Not to Fall For Them

TOM PHILLIPS
& JONN ELLEDGE

WILDFIRE

Copyright © 2022 Tom Phillips and Jonn Elledge

The right of Tom Phillips and Jonn Elledge to be identified as the Authors of
the Work has been asserted by them in accordance with the
Copyright, Designs and Patents Act 1988.

First published in 2022 by
WILDFIRE
an imprint of HEADLINE PUBLISHING GROUP

First published in paperback in 2023 by
WILDFIRE
an imprint of HEADLINE PUBLISHING GROUP

5

Cataloguing in Publication Data is available from the British Library

ISBN 978 1 4722 8340 5

Infographic © 2021 Abbie Richards

Typeset in Parango by CC Book Production

Printed and bound in Great Britain by Clays Ltd, Elcograf S.p.A.

Headline's policy is to use papers that are natural, renewable
and recyclable products and made from wood grown in well-managed forests
and other controlled sources. The logging and manufacturing processes
are expected to conform to the environmental regulations
of the country of origin.

HEADLINE PUBLISHING GROUP
An Hachette UK Company
Carmelite House
50 Victoria Embankment
London EC4Y 0DZ

www.headline.co.uk
www.hachette.co.uk

Jonn dedicates this book to Agnes.

Tom dedicates this book to his parents, Don and Colette.

Additionally, we both dedicate it to our secret overlords.

Contents

Contents

Introduction

On 6 January 2021, a man stood behind the desk of the Vice President in the United States Senate and led the chamber in prayer.

There were several clues that the man in question was not, in fact, the Vice President. One is that leading the Senate in prayer is not generally the sort of thing VPs do. Another is that the man was speaking through a bullhorn and was armed with a spear, to which he'd attached a US flag.

Perhaps the biggest giveaway was that the man's face was covered with red, white and blue paint, and his chest with tattoos inspired by Norse mythology. These were visible because he was naked from the waist up, except for a furry hat with horns sticking out of it. This was Jake Angeli, a one-time US Navy seaman who had been born Jacob Chansley but who, by 2021, was better known by the label 'the QAnon Shaman'. The people he was speaking to weren't senators, either, but a coalition of Donald Trump supporters, activists and conspiracy theorists, plus a few uncomfortable-looking police officers.

This was not how things were *supposed* to go. The Senate
Chamber was supposed to be full of, well, senators, who
were supposed to be confirming Joe Biden as the 46th
President of the United States. But they had fled, for their
own protection. So had the actual Vice President, Mike
Pence, whose job it was to oversee the Senate's confirmation. So, too, had the fourteen Republican senators and 140
Republican members of the House of Representatives who
had made it clear that they would be voting *against*
confirming Joe Biden and were, in fact, on roughly the same
side as the protestors. As the sack of the Capitol Building
continued, pretty much everyone who worked inside it was
either hiding or running.

This was a reasonable response to the arrival of several
thousand people intent on preventing the confirmation by any
means necessary. Many of the protestors were armed; one was
carrying eleven Molotov cocktails. Out on the Mall, mock
wooden gallows had been erected, to cries of 'Hang Mike
Pence!' Over the course of the day, multiple journalists
covering the protest were attacked; fifteen police officers were
hospitalised. An officer assigned to protect the Senate, fifty-
one-year-old Howard Liebengood, would die by suicide several
days later. One of the rioters, a thirty-five-year-old former
US Air Force officer named Ashli Babbitt, was shot in the
shoulder while attempting to break through a door in the
Capitol, and died from her wounds.

With the world watching agog on live TV, a mob was
trying to overturn the results of a democratic election – yet at
least some of its members were sincerely convinced they were
trying to *save* democracy. Later, many were just as sincere in
their shock at learning that this was not, in fact, how the
justice system saw things.

So why did several thousand people – citizens of a country whose democracy is core to its sense of self – attempt, in the sight of the world, to launch what was, if not quite a coup, at least coup-adjacent?* The answer lies in a conspiracy theory. Or, more accurately, in a number of conspiracy theories – most of them false, and one of them basically true.

The main *false* theory was most pithily expressed by President Trump on 4 November, the morning of the election. 'We are up BIG,' he tweeted, with his customary commitment to the shift key, 'but they are trying to STEAL the Election.'[1]

There were lots of theories about exactly how the Democrats planned to 'STEAL the Election', most of which ... didn't really fit together. Bags of ballots had been thrown out, it was claimed, or suitcases of fresh ones mysteriously found. Mail-in votes were supposedly rife with fraud. Illegal immigrants and dead people were said to have voted in droves. Many claimed rigged voting machines had fiendishly switched Trump votes to Biden ones. Six months after the election, a spurious 'audit' in Arizona was still microscopically scanning ballot papers for traces of bamboo, in an effort to prove they'd been shipped from China.[2] (That the allegations mostly centred on major urban areas with large non-white populations – despite the fact that Trump largely increased his vote share in these places, while losing in the suburbs – may provide a hint about what was fuelling some of these claims.)

And *why* were the Democrats stealing the election? The answers here ranged from your basic hunger for power, to Marxist takeovers, to the belief that the President had been fighting a one-man war against a Deep State cabal of

* There's a bit of an academic debate about this, which basically boils down to 'How are we defining coup?'

cannibalistic, Satan-worshipping paedophiles, possibly operating out of a pizza restaurant basement, and that they
needed to rig the election to avoid their imminent date with
justice. This last idea stemmed from QAnon, the sprawling
conspiracy theory based largely on a series of anonymous
messages on the troll-infested website 4chan, to which Jake
Angeli, in his horned hat, had subscribed.

At any rate, conservative America's fears about the election,
nurtured by decades of overstated or baseless claims of electoral fraud, had been brought to the boil by months of
assertions from President Trump that the Democrats were
trying to steal the win. (This was, after all, a man who four
years earlier had insisted that an election he'd *won* had been
rigged against him.) This was amplified by the widely antici-
pated 'blue shift' during the night of the election, as the
running count began to include different types of votes from
different types of area. None of this was unexpected.[3] But if
you were the sort of person who simply couldn't conceive of
how the President could lose – which, it turned out, a significant minority of Americans were – it all looked pretty
suspicious. A poll in May 2021 found that a majority of
Republicans believed the election had been rigged, that
Donald Trump was still the true President, and that the
Capitol riot was led by left-wing protestors trying to make
Trump look bad.[4]

The thing is, there was fairly compelling evidence that
somebody was conspiring to steal the 2020 presidential
election: the guy who lost. That the Trump camp had planned
to declare premature victory and cast doubt on the election –
whatever the result and whatever the evidence – had been
reported well before election day.[5] In the aftermath, the
President openly discussed his expectation that the Republican

majority in the Supreme Court would help hand him victory; in addition, his campaign and sundry hangers-on had filed over sixty separate lawsuits in an attempt to overturn the vote in various states, while state election officials were pressured, sometimes directly by the President himself.[6] It all culminated in early January, with the novel legal theory that the Vice President – the real one, not the guy in the furry hat – had the power to unilaterally reject the election outcome and declare himself still the Vice President. We know this part because, helpfully, they wrote the plan down, in clear violation of the Stringer Bell rule about whether you should take notes on a conspiracy.[*]

So, that was the true conspiracy theory – the one about a real conspiracy that relied on a slew of other conspiracy theories, which would end up with over 400 people being charged with federal crimes and a man with no shirt leading the prayers in the United States Senate.

Several things are worth nothing about this story. One is that the Trump camp's conspiracy theories – whether they genuinely believed them or not – look surprisingly like the real conspiracy between the President and his fellow travellers. Another is that conspiracy thinking, so often dismissed as the preserve of outsiders, weirdos and the generally

---

[*] In *The Wire*, Idris Elba's economics-minded drug gang consigliere Stringer Bell attempts to introduce modern management techniques to Baltimore's crack and heroin trade. This is misinterpreted by an enthusiastic underling, who starts keeping minutes during a meeting between rival gangs. The rule isn't stated explicitly, but can be inferred from Bell's comments as he snatches the notepad away: 'Is you takin' notes on a criminal fuckin' conspiracy? What the fuck is you thinking?'

disenfranchised, was being propagated by the actual President of the United States.

The third is that conspiracy theories have real consequences. People died, and for the first time in its history – which included one election held *during an actual civil war* – the United States failed to have a completely peaceful transfer of power.

All of which raises the question: how the hell did we get here?

There's no doubt that the conspiracy theories that helped drive the Capitol insurrection were a product of the modern age, born in the fever swamps of 4chan, popularised through YouTube and Facebook, and spearheaded by a President who ruled by tweet and got his intelligence from cable news. And it has sometimes felt, over the last few years, that conspiracy theories are playing a bigger role in the world's politics than ever before. Social media has made it easier to propagate theories, while algorithms designed to keep people clicking or watching videos have doubled as conveyor belts to pull people towards more radical viral content.

But while Donald Trump may be the most famous head of government to use and spread conspiracy theories to achieve his goals, the recent history of Viktor Orbán's Hungary or Jair Bolsonaro's Brazil are a reminder that Trump is hardly unique. And all this was true even before the Covid-19 pandemic kicked off, and we all had to come to terms with the fact that a bat in central China had coughed and millions had died as a result (with the rest of us stuck inside for over a year and left unexpectedly celibate, unemployed or simply getting really into sourdough).

If it sometimes feels like we are living through a golden

age of paranoia, though, it's important to remember that conspiracy theories have a very, very long history. They were present in the politics of Ancient Athens and Rome.[7] And while many historical conspiracy theories have been lost in the mists of time, some have endured: as we'll see, many of the theories that motivated the Capitol rioters have lineages that can be traced back centuries.

Indeed, the very American democracy that was threatened by conspiracy theories that day in January 2021 was originally founded on conspiratorial thinking. Several historians argue that the Declaration of Independence – with its dark warnings of covert British plans for imminent tyranny, and its long list of supposed 'abuses and usurpations' – didn't so much *include* a conspiracy theory as it, in itself, *was* a conspiracy theory.[8] Conspiracy theories may be having A Moment right now, but that doesn't mean they are new.

These theories rarely spring from nowhere. Very often, they're adapted from earlier versions, updated and adjusted to fit new social contexts. Sometimes the villains, whether individuals or institutions or entire ethnic or religious groups, change over time. Sometimes – as many Jewish people who have tried living in Europe over the last thousand years or so could probably tell you – they do not.

The stereotype of conspiracy theories often says that they're something that the masses believe about society's elites – a backlash of the powerless against the powerful. And sometimes that's true. But, as we'll see, conspiracy theories are often spawned and spread by elites themselves. The patronising view that they're the sole preserve of the left-behind, the under-educated and the ill-informed, couldn't be further from the truth. Among the conspiracy believers we'll meet in this book are monarchs and political leaders, lawyers and businessmen, mathematicians and chemists, eminent physicists and pioneering inventors. There are plenty of military officers, and a fair few priests. There's one Nobel laureate who'd feature on any decent list of 'smartest people of the twentieth century'.

And none of us – whether we're on the political left, right or centre – are immune from believing in conspiracy theories. Our brains are built to see patterns in the world, and do it so well that they sometimes see patterns where none exist. At the same time, our world is often shaped in profound ways by unseen forces that can seem like the product of conscious design – from social change to patterns of disease to the effects of the market.

Many of these forces are, as Adam Smith wrote in *The Wealth of Nations* in 1776, 'not originally the effect of any human wisdom', but simply a 'consequence of a certain propensity in human nature'.[9] All our lives, we're constantly pushed, pulled and prodded by invisible hands. Is it really surprising that, sometimes, we imagine those hands must be attached to somebody? Conspiracy theories allow us to put a face to those forces, to give a name to the most primal fears and deepest anxieties that haunt us. They give us someone to blame.

There's one other thing it's worth stating outright before we get too far into the weeds here: sometimes, conspiracy theories are true.

Sure, we can be pretty confident that the Earth is a globe, that the 'chemtrails' left behind by planes are harmless condensation, not some kind of bioweapon, and that Bill Gates has not been using vaccination programmes to turn humanity into his personal slave army. But in 1956, the British and French governments really did secretly coordinate an

Israeli invasion of Egypt, so they could march in as peace-keepers and take control of the Suez Canal. The US Department of Defense really did draw up (though didn't carry out) plans to commit terrorist attacks on US soil as a false flag operation. And the US Public Health Service and the Centers for Disease Control and Prevention really did leave several hundred African-American men with untreated syphilis for decades while telling them they were healthy, just to see what would happen. You could write a whole other book just on the conspiracies that may once have been dismissed as crazy talk, but turned out to be absolutely real.

Just because you're paranoid, that doesn't mean they're not out to get you. They're just *probably* not.*

So, if we're going to understand the role that conspiracy theories play in our societies – how they affect our politics, our culture, and how they can draw our loved ones down obsessive rabbit holes – we need to understand their history. We need to understand where conspiracy theories come from, why people believe them, why they're more likely to pop up in some circumstances than others, and what it is about our brains that makes us prone to believing them.

In the first part of this book, we'll dive into the theory behind the theories: what *is* a conspiracy theory, what are the different types, and why do our brains seem irresistibly attracted to them? Then we'll look at the history of conspiracy theories that try to explain specific events – from revolutions to assassinations, from UFOs to pandemics – many of which teeter on the boundary between the implausible and the all-too-plausible.

---

* But they might be.

After that, we'll look at the theories that expand their scope and, in doing so, become increasingly detached from reality. These are the ones that suggest that our world is not as we know it, that global events have been maliciously engineered, and that everything is controlled by shadowy groups, who may be the Illuminati or possibly aliens. We'll see how these have developed over history – and confront the possibility that history itself may be a lie.

We'll finish back in the present day, as we return to look at our modern age of conspiracies – and, finally, we'll suggest some helpful tips on how to avoid falling down the rabbit hole yourself. How can you tell the difference between a bullshit theory and an actual conspiracy?

There are a lot of conspiracy theories in this book. Sometimes they link up; often they don't. And the further in we get, the more we'll find that people have found ways of connecting them, all the same. Along the way, we'll see both how conspiracy theories have helped create the world we live in, and how they often reflect our societies and ourselves back at us. We'll learn that the Illuminati really did want to change the world in secret, but that this wasn't as scary as it sounds, and anyway they weren't very good at it. We'll see that, sometimes, conspiracies spring from nothing more than the excitement of deciding that everything you know is wrong. We'll discover that many of them are weird; some are funny; others are terrifying. And we'll find that none of us is immune from believing them.

But first, we need to ask: what exactly *are* they?

Part I

Theory about Theories

In which we attempt to work out what a conspiracy theory actually is, and ask why our brains love them so.

1

What Is a Conspiracy Theory?

I t was early in the morning on the Saturday of Holy Week in the year 1144 when the dead boy was found in the forest. Actually, he was found several times: because reporting a death would lead to no end of hassle, the first few people to discover the corpse decided to let it be somebody else's problem. So a peasant and a nun both saw the dead child and passed on by, before eventually the peasant told the forester, and the forester had to acknowledge that this was in fact his problem, because he was in charge of the forest.

The boy's name was William, and the forest was Thorpe Wood, which covered a large swathe of ground to the northeast of Norwich. Several centuries of deforestation means there's less woodland there today than there used to be, and the exact location where young William's body lay is lost to history. But still, a few miles out from the city centre – somewhere off the A1024, probably just across from the Homebase and the DFS – is the spot where a twelve-year-old boy was found dead at the foot of an oak tree. This is where one of the most enduring and destructive conspiracy theories in all of history began.

William's death would become the origin of the 'blood libel' – the utterly fabricated claim that Jews practise the ritual murder of Christian children, supposedly so they can use their blood in religious ceremonies. In the years that followed, this theory would spread out from Norwich across medieval Europe and beyond. It would be embraced, denounced and exploited by monarchs, politicians and clerics, and it would become embedded in the belief systems of cultures across multiple continents. It would fuel individual accusations and notorious trials, and contribute to centuries of religious persecution, ethnic cleansing and genocide. It remains widely believed to this day, and echoes of it can be heard in contemporary conspiracy theories, from the Satanic panics of the eighties and nineties to the QAnon theories that drove many of the Capitol insurrectionists on 6 January 2021.

Nowadays, the blood libel is most commonly called something other than a conspiracy theory – it's a 'myth' or 'folklore' or an 'anti-Semitic canard'. It is all those things, of course. But that can seem to suggest it's something eternal, inevitable; that it simply emerged fully formed from our ancient collective well of prejudice and superstition. As we'll see, the specifics of how the blood libel was created – a story involving a grieving uncle, a dissolute knight, and an ambitious monk – show that this simply isn't true.

The blood libel spread because it was a theory about a conspiracy.

The term 'conspiracy theory' gets chucked around an awful lot these days. Twitter threads about celebrity gossip are

introduced as conspiracy theories. Completely standard interpretations of history are branded as conspiracies, usually by
people who don't like those interpretations. Politicians will
angrily denounce basically any criticism directed at them as a
conspiracy theory, and bemoan with serious faces the decline
in standards of public discourse. The term is applied to
everything from scandalous rumours whispered in schoolyards
to emailed urban legends about sinister hitchhikers. Not only
is the phrase used extremely loosely, but a lot of energy is
expended arguing about who and what deserve to have that
label – almost always pejorative – slapped on them. *You* are a
conspiracy theorist; *I* am just asking questions.

But given this is a whole book about them, it's worth
asking: what exactly do we mean when we say 'conspiracy
theory'?

This is one of those areas where the seemingly simple
quickly gets pretty complicated. As the phrase itself helpfully
indicates, a conspiracy theory has two key components. No
prizes for guessing. But while a conspiracy theory obviously
needs to be a) a *theory* about b) a *conspiracy*, looser uses of the
term often lack one or the other.

Most often, they don't involve a group of people working
together in secret. 'Conspiracy theory' is often used to mean
any kind of previously unknown truth, be it celebrity gossip
or the existence of aliens. But unless it involves people actively
working to keep that truth hidden, it's not a conspiracy. You
can't have a conspiracy if nobody conspired.

You wouldn't necessarily know this from the way the
media uses the term, however. To pluck just a few examples
of things described as 'conspiracy theories' recently: 'the Loch
Ness Monster is real' isn't a conspiracy theory, it's just speculative biology; 'the actress Anne Hathaway is actually the

reincarnation of Shakespeare's wife Anne Hathaway' is not a conspiracy theory, it's just being confused about how names work; and 'Anna and Elsa's little brother is Tarzan' is not a conspiracy theory, because Anna and Elsa are fictional characters in the movie *Frozen* whose relationship or otherwise to the fictional character Tarzan is entirely a matter for the imagination.*

That said, 'a bunch of people doing stuff in secret' isn't quite enough to qualify as a conspiracy either. There needs to be some attempt to affect the wider world – to gain some advantage, to screw someone else over, to shift the course of history. If you suggested that, say, every meeting of the British cabinet ends in a secret orgy, then ... well, that's a disturbing and horrifying image, but it doesn't really rise to the level of a *conspiracy*. Conspiracies need some kind of tangible and deliberate impact outside their own boundaries. Otherwise they're less a conspiracy, more a private members' club.

Another unexpectedly thorny aspect of defining a conspiracy as 'people doing stuff in secret' is what, exactly, we mean by 'secret'. To do something in secret suggests more than simply not doing it in public – that's just *private*, and it's where all of us conduct large parts of our lives. 'Secret' implies that you're actively taking steps to conceal what you're doing.

Claims that something was 'secret' are central to conspiracy theories – and to why we find them compelling – because, as any tabloid editor knows, you can make almost anything sound sinister or salacious if you call it 'secret'. ('Secret love

---

* Anyway, Chris Buck – who directed Disney's 1999 *Tarzan* and also co-directed *Frozen* – has said that he agrees Tarzan is indeed the younger brother of the *Frozen* sisters. So there.

nest' sounds so much more exciting than 'the flat you share with your partner'.) We love finding out stuff we weren't supposed to, and promising to reveal behind-the-scenes information is a sure-fire way to get people to pay attention. But just because *you* didn't know something before now doesn't mean anybody was actively trying to keep it secret. During the Covid pandemic, a number of vaccine conspiracy theories suggested they were revealing secret information . . . which had literally been publicly released months earlier by the organisations involved.

What's more, the boundaries between what's public, what's private and what's secret are fuzzy, and we often can't agree about exactly where they should lie. Many things that affect our lives, in ways large and small, happen in those ambiguous spaces where nobody's watching. Bad things can sometimes happen behind closed doors. But so too does a huge amount of everyday life. Our difficulty distinguishing between the two is one reason we sometimes see conspiracies everywhere.

It didn't take long after William of Norwich's death before the first accusation of a conspiracy came along.

According to William's mother, the boy was last seen alive entering the house of a local Jewish family, with a suspicious man who had claimed to be offering the lad a prestigious job working in the archdeacon's kitchen. How reliable the mother's testimony was is open to question, as it appears to have been based in large part on a dream she had in which some Jews were attacking her. But still, that single piece of evidence soon expanded as people speculated about what might have happened behind that closed door; before long, accusations were being levelled against the entire Jewish community of Norwich.[1]

In this, it followed a familiar, dispiriting, path: they were a small group of recent immigrants (indeed, the accusation is virtually the first historical evidence of the community's existence), and as such were subject to all of the usual suspicions and resentments. Such issues were magnified by the social context of the time: the Jews were seen as wealthy, and they were strongly associated with the Norman elites who had come to England with the conquest less than a century before. In 1144, both England and Normandy were in the middle of the brutal, two-decades-long war of succession known subsequently as 'the Anarchy', which divided communities, resulted in a widespread breakdown of order, and created a pervasive atmosphere of suspicion and paranoia. Additionally, a wave of anti-Jewish sentiment was rising up across much of Europe in the 1140s, fuelled in part by the Crusades, which both fostered a general atmosphere of religious violence, and forced crusaders to take on debts to equip themselves for their mission. At least some of those debts were owed to Jewish lenders.

While William's mother may have been the original source of the accusation, by far the loudest voice accusing the Jewish community of responsibility for the boy's death was his Uncle Godwin, a local priest. At the annual synod, he demanded that the Jews be brought before an ecclesiastical court and subjected to trial by ordeal. It's striking that, even with a respected community figure advancing this accusation, many of his peers remained sceptical; the trial never happened, and while his oratory did stir up local sentiment against the Jewish population, the sheriff – a Norman named John de Chesney – took the community under his protection until things simmered down.

Which they did, remarkably quickly. The most notable

thing about the original accusation is how rapidly it subsided: it just doesn't seem to have been an especially big deal. People had bigger things to worry about. Outside of his family, most people had largely forgotten about William within just a few years.

But then a debt-ridden knight murdered his creditor, and needed a legal defence.

The knight in question was Sir Simon de Novers, and he was bad news. Quite why he was so heavily in debt isn't known for certain, but in her book *The Murder of William of Norwich*, historian E. M. Rose suggests that the most plausible explanation is that he had been involved in the Second Crusade – a catastrophic failure that saw many minor nobles returning home in the late 1140s to a pile of debt, no spoils of war with which to pay, and the distinct absence of a hero's welcome.

Whatever the reason, in 1149, Sir Simon had the man to whom he owed money ambushed and killed on the road in the woods outside Norwich. The victim was one of the wealthiest men in the city. He was also Jewish.

Even by the standards of the time, and even in the midst of a civil war, there was no way that was going to be allowed to slide. The Jewish community demanded justice, King Stephen had to show that law and order had not completely collapsed, and Sir Simon did not help his case by apparently making little secret of the fact that he definitely did it. His trial before the king in 1150 should have been an open-and-shut case, were it not for a devious ploy cooked up by de Novers' counsel, the local cleric Bishop William Turbe.

Faced with a flimsy defence, Turbe decided to instead go on the attack, by reviving Godwin's claim regarding his nephew's death. Entirely baselessly, Turbe asserted that the dead man had in fact been the ringleader of the Jewish community's murder of William of Norwich. Sir Simon had not been trying to avoid paying his debt; he had merely been delivering justice! Turbe didn't need to make an especially convincing case (which was lucky, because he didn't); he just needed to throw out enough accusations and sow enough uncertainty to turn the straightforward trial of an errant knight into what Rose calls a 'double trial', in which the Jews of Norwich were suddenly facing judgement, too.

It worked. Presented with what was now an unexpectedly confusing and complex case – and in no political position to offend any of the interested parties, lest he lose their support – the king and his advisers decided to simply ... not deliver a verdict. They stuck the case in a drawer, and never took it out again. Sir Simon was free to spend the rest of his life being a dick in the Norwich area; meanwhile, the accusation of child murder against the Jewish community was allowed to fester in a grey zone of permanent suspicion – unproven, yet unrefuted.

The accusation of conspiracy had shown that it had staying power, and that it could be wielded by powerful people for their own ends. But it wasn't until an ambitious monk came along that the claim of conspiracy would turn into a full-fledged theory.

Actual conspiracy theories have been around a lot longer than the term 'conspiracy theory'. That's a relatively recent invention, and there is, naturally, a conspiracy theory about the origin of the term 'conspiracy theory' itself, which holds that it was invented by the CIA in 1967 to discredit criticism of the Warren Report into the JFK assassination. It wasn't, of course: the document cited as evidence for this, in which the

CIA describe accusations made against them as conspiracy theories, simply reflects that the term was already in common use.[2]

But what we mean by conspiracy theory has changed over time. When the phrase was first used in the press, in the late 1800s, it didn't convey quite the same meaning that we understand it to have today. In fact, it was a lot closer to the accusations of conspiracy that had been hurled at Norwich's Jewish population centuries earlier. A crime had been committed, the newspapers would report, and the police investigating it had a 'conspiracy theory', much as they might have an 'arson theory'.[3] It was only decades later, largely from the 1950s onwards, that our modern use of the term took off.

The change comes down to our understanding of the second element of conspiracy theories – namely, the 'theory' bit. We take this to mean not just a suggestion of 'I reckon this thing happened', but something that explains it more fully: placing it in a framework for understanding the world at large. Crucially, it also suggests that there are rival theories – there needs to be an 'official narrative' that the theory provides an alternative to.

You can see this reflected in how our attitude to conspiracy has changed over time. Fears of conspiracy were almost universal among the elites of late medieval and early modern Europe, beset as they were by religious schisms, regular wars and all manner of courtly intrigue. But that's unsurprising, because in those societies – lacking as they were in many of the trappings of modern democracies, like 'being able to criticise the king without getting your head chopped off' – conspiracy was also pretty much the main way of getting things done. So while the dukes and barons of sixteenth-century courts might have seen conspiracies everywhere, their beliefs about them weren't quite the same as our modern notion of conspiracy theories, because they weren't necessarily presenting an alternative to a rival narrative. When everything happens behind closed doors, there's not much to distinguish conspiracy from business as usual.

A belief doesn't necessarily have to have a fully worked-out explanation of every detail to count as a conspiracy theory: as we'll find out, many of them really, really don't. But it does need to propose some kind of joined-up alternative reading of the facts. You can't just go around shouting random claims: 'Harry Styles is secretly dead!' 'Cows are robots in disguise!' 'The sun is actually just a cleverly positioned cylinder!' That just makes you a bit odd. For a proper conspiracy theory, you have to offer some kind of explanation. You need to delve at least some way into the 'how' and the 'why' of the situation.

Without that, what you have is – at most – a conspiracy hypothesis.

Thomas of Monmouth was a Welsh monk who had become obsessed by the story of William of Norwich, and who, over time, would turn a simple accusation into something grander. He provided the theory to explain the conspiracy. It's Thomas who, more than any other single figure, is responsible for the dissemination of the blood libel, thanks to his work *The Life and Passion of William of Norwich*, a lengthy tome that he spent two decades writing, starting in the year of de Novers' trial.

Significantly, Thomas wasn't an eyewitness to any of the events he documented. He wasn't even in Norwich when William actually died: he only rocked up some years later, in the late 1140s. His interest in William was probably sparked by the realisation among the ecclesiastical population of Norwich that Bishop Turbe's claims in the trial – initially intended only to get Sir Simon off the hook – could serve a second purpose. If a good Christian child like William had indeed been murdered in a gruesome religious killing, then that made him a martyr. And if he was a martyr, then he could be made a saint.

Norwich was England's second largest city at the time, a major hub of both trade and learning. It didn't have a saint, though. Lots of other, lesser places had a saint. This stuff really mattered when it came to status, and the lack of a saint would have been keenly felt; so Thomas decided to devote himself to being the champion of William's saintly cause.

To do so, he filled out what was missing from the family's initial accusations, and from Turbe's defence of de Novers: he added the *how* and the *why*. The religious rites of the Jews, he claimed, called for the sacrifice of a Christian child at Passover; and so in the days before Easter, they had chosen William for that purpose, torturing him with a parody crown of thorns before 'in mockery of the Passion of the Cross, sentenc[ing] him to be crucified'.[4] Thomas also expanded the conspiracy outwards – not only did they conspire to murder William, he suggested, but the local sheriff de Chesney was in on it, having been bribed by the murderers to protect them from the consequences.

Thomas's book may have been written more than eight centuries ago, but it has many of the hallmarks of the conspiracy literature being published today. While much of it is devoted to assembling a list of supposed miracles linked with William's remains (another crucial component of the sanctification process), the sections about the murder itself set a template that would become very familiar. It includes florid descriptions of events that took place behind closed doors, of which the author couldn't have had any knowledge. And it piles up reams of 'evidence' for its thesis: no single piece is convincing on its own; but the effect of them all together, read in the context of the already-asserted truth of the conspiracy, creates a sense of certainty entirely unjustified by reality. Thomas also casts himself in the role of the dogged lone investigator hunting down the truth, visiting the crime scene and spotting vital clues. (Indeed, one academic has suggested that it can be read as one of the earliest examples of the 'peculiarly English genre' of detective stories 'in which the investigator is an amateur without official standing'.)[5]

If it was simply a case of Thomas spending twenty years writing a book slandering Norwich's Jewish population in order to promote the sainthood of a child whose death had been all but forgotten, then we probably wouldn't be talking about it now. But when he expanded the conspiracy accusation into a conspiracy theory, he made it reproducible. What served as an explanation for one event could serve as the explanation for other events, too. And as the news of William's provisional sainthood spread, people began to wonder whether their own small local tragedies might also be candidates.

In the following decades, Thomas's theory would be repeated elsewhere, first in other parts of England, and then overseas. The spread was underway. The blood libel's long, deadly journey had begun.

Conspiracy theories are not all the same. What Thomas initially wrote was one thing: a narrowly focused theory about one specific incident. What it became – a sprawling, mutating belief that was used to explain and justify a vast number of terrible things over the course of many centuries – was something very different. By 1903, when another infamous anti-Semitic conspiracy theory was published – *The Protocols of the Elders of Zion*, a crude forgery that pasted together text plagiarised from multiple sources to depict a Jewish plot for world domination – it was clear that conspiracy theories had become something else again.

There are a lot of potential ways you could carve up and label the conspiracy universe, but space is short, so we'll focus on two of the most interesting.* One of the most useful ways of categorising and understanding conspiracy theories was introduced by political science professor Michael Barkun, in his 2003 book *A Culture of Conspiracy: Apocalyptic Visions in Contemporary America*. He divides them into three basic types: event conspiracies, systemic conspiracies and superconspiracies.

Event conspiracies

Event conspiracies are the basic form of the conspiracy theory – an attempt to explain a single event, or a closely linked series of events, by positing a secret conspiracy as its true cause. A plane crashes, a government falls, a disease rips through a population, a princess dies in a car accident: what could be explained by random chance, by a confluence of complex social factors, or even by the publicly acknowledged actions of known figures, is instead explained as the machinations of a hidden group manipulating events for their own ends.

One distinguishing aspect of such theories is how they respond to the question, 'What do the conspirators want?' Event conspiracies tend to offer a relatively simple answer to this. The plotters have a clear, limited and understandable

---

* What are we hiding, hmm?

objective – whether that's to perform a religious rite, gain a political advantage, or murder two Supreme Court justices so that the court will be more likely to rule in favour of plans to drill for oil on a protected nature reserve in Louisiana. These plotters can set goals, hit milestones, and have well-defined success metrics. Their annual review process, if organisations of shadowy puppet-masters have such a thing, should be quite straightforward.

Because of their relatively narrow focus, it's possible to believe in an event conspiracy theory without it having much impact on the rest of your worldview. After all, some events really *are* explained by secret cabals of people plotting behind closed doors – this doesn't imply that everything else is a conspiracy as well.

Systemic conspiracies

These are bigger in size and scope: rather than trying to explain a discrete set of facts or events, these theories credit the conspirators with a wide range of events, in multiple locations, across a long span of time, in different areas of life. The conspiracy isn't just limited to a narrow set of actions, but is viewed as an organisation that infiltrates and influences many institutions and walks of life – the government, business, academia, media and so on.

The supposed goals of systemic conspiracies are both more ambitious and often vaguer than those of event conspiracies: the plotters are often said to want something as broad as 'power' or 'control', often with some overarching ideological or religious motivation.

Because of their sweeping nature, systemic conspiracy

theories can have a significant impact on the worldview of believers. It becomes difficult to fully understand many aspects of the modern world without understanding the reality of the conspiracy. Dealing with the conspiracy is likely to be an overwhelming priority; large swathes of politics and culture might get reframed as a battle between the conspirators and those trying to resist them. As Richard Hofstadter put it in his classic essay, 'The Paranoid Style in American Politics', in this view, 'History is a conspiracy, set in motion by demonic forces of almost transcendent power, and what is felt to be needed to defeat it is not the usual methods of political give-and-take, but an all-out crusade.'[6]

Superconspiracy

The final type of conspiracy theory is the superconspiracy, which is what happens when a lot of different conspiracies join up and have a party. Superconspiracies aren't fundamentally different from systemic conspiracies in their form; it is their scale that sets them apart, as they combine multiple different theories into one. In the superconspiracy world, there is no longer a single conspiratorial organisation, but a vast network or hierarchy of conspiracies, becoming ever more secretive and malign as you get closer to the centre of the web. The Illuminati are working for the aliens, or maybe the aliens are working for the Illuminati; or perhaps they're both working for some mysterious hyper-powerful third party. It's the Marvel Cinematic Universe of conspiracies, filled with crossovers and connections and interweaving plot threads.

The impact of superconspiracies on the worldview of believers is almost total. At this point, virtually everything about the world can only be understood and explained with reference to this network of conspiracies. Conspiracy is the overwhelming driving force shaping the world around us, and virtually any person or institution may be suspected of being in on it in some way.

One important thing to note about this classification system is that things have a tendency to escalate. This can apply to an individual's journey into conspiracism, with the simple conspiracies acting as a gateway drug into more complex ones. And, as we'll discover, it can also be seen in the way conspiracy theories evolve over time: what began as basic event conspiracies grow into systemic ones, as later theorists build on the work of earlier conspiracists. Superconspiracies have only really taken off in recent decades (Barkun traces their explosion to the 1980s), but now make up a significant proportion of what we commonly understand as conspiracy theory culture.

This approach to classifying conspiracy theories rests on descriptions of the theories themselves. It only incidentally says anything about how plausible the theories may or may not be.

If you want that, you're better off taking our other major approach to conspiracy classification, which was introduced by American researcher Abbie Richards in a TikTok video in September 2020. Unlike Barkun's classification, Richards' 'Conspiracy Chart' doesn't look at what the theories them-selves are describing, but at how the theories relate to reality. It takes the form of an inverted pyramid, divided into segments, with 'Grounded in Reality' at the bottom and 'Detached from Reality' at the top.

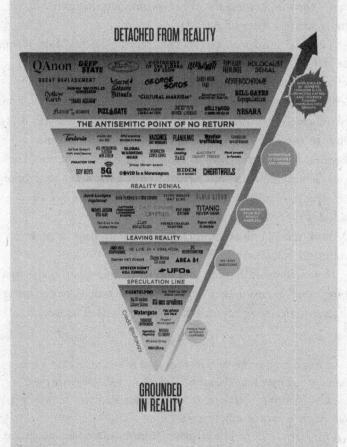

The lowest level is devoted to 'Things That Actually Happened' – conspiracy theories that are verified facts, such as MKUltra* and COINTELPRO†. Across the 'Speculation Line', we find theories that aren't backed up by evidence, but wouldn't fundamentally break reality if they turned out to be true – theories around the JFK assassination, for example, or the secretive nature of Area 51.

The next escalation crosses the 'Leaving Reality' line, where we start to find theories that don't just lack evidence, but actively contradict what we know about the world. These become more dangerous as they become more detached – from the relatively harmless, like alien abductions or Elvis still being alive, to the more harmful, like anti-vaccination conspiracy theories. Finally, the theories cross what Richards terms 'The Anti-Semitic Point of No Return', where she notes that 'once you believe one, you usually believe most'. This upper tier includes theories such as *The Protocols of the Elders of Zion*, QAnon, the Illuminati, and the existence of slave colonies on Mars and Nazis on the moon.

If you compare Barkun and Richards' frameworks, the first thing you'll notice is that – despite the fact that they're using different criteria – they match up pretty well. The lower,

---

* An illegal programme of CIA experiments involving LSD, brainwashing, attempted mind control, Canadians and other out-there things, which readers may recognise from Jon Ronson's *The Men Who Stare At Goats*, among other works.
† A fifteen-year illegal FBI program targeting 'subversive' groups and individuals – responsible for events including the effective assassination of Black Panther leader Fred Hampton, and a dirty tricks campaign against the actress Jean Seberg that may have led to her suicide.

more reality-based levels of Richards' pyramid tend to have a lot of straightforward event conspiracies; as you move up, you find more systemic conspiracies, and by the time you're at the top, you find the beliefs that make up the superconspiracy pantheon. As Barkun suggests and Richards explicitly says, there comes a point where belief in one conspiracy theory predisposes you to believing virtually every conspiracy theory. When taken together, what Barkun and Richards provide is a journey plan for the route many conspiracy believers take: a map of the rabbit hole that people fall down.*

So, how can you tell that you're looking at conspiracist thinking, as opposed to someone simply describing a real, actual conspiracy? That you're talking to someone who's been down the rabbit hole, rather than merely someone who once met a rabbit?

One of the big clues is how they react to contradictory evidence. As a general rule, our brains are not keen on being wrong. When confronted with evidence that conflicts with our beliefs, our most common approach is to simply ignore it. We merrily breeze past inconvenient truths and carry on cherry-picking only the evidence that supports our views. Conspiracist thinking, by contrast, provides ways to confront contradictory information head-on.

---

* A couple of other schemes for dividing the conspiracy universe in brief: Jesse Walker of *Reason* magazine has proposed dividing them up by the nature of the enemy: outside, within, below, above, or, in a few rare cases where there is no enemy at all, benevolent. The economic historian Murray Rothbard, meanwhile, instead contrasted 'shallow' conspiracies, that simply jump to conclusions based on who stands to benefit, and 'deep ones', which start with someone having a hunch and proceeding to do their own research.

For starters, you can often simply change your theory. Conspiracy theories tend to move extremely flexibly around one fixed certainty – that immovable point being the thing that believers most want to be true. The fixed quantity could be the outcome of the events ('the election was rigged!'), or it could be the motivation behind the events ('they want to reduce the population'); a lot of the time, it's the nature of the culprits ('it's not entirely clear what happened, but whatever it was, the Illuminati were definitely behind it'). Around this fixed point, everything else can be retconned to accommodate new evidence and fresh narratives. What was done, who did it, why they did it and how they did it can all change if it serves the central purpose of the narrative.

And if that doesn't work, you can always fall back on the classic of conspiracy literature: claiming that any evidence against the conspiracy theory is in fact part of the conspiracy itself. This is how conspiracy theories render themselves unfalsifiable – it's an essential part of how successful theories sustain themselves over time. If nobody can ever prove you wrong, because anybody who does is part of the plot, then you're laughing.

Of course, both changing your theory to fit the evidence, and questioning the validity of that evidence, are generally seen as good things. They're basically critical thinking 101. Compared with our normal tendency to simply ignore information we don't like, it seems almost laudable. And indeed, one of the more counterintuitive markers of conspiracy literature is that it absolutely loves evidence – or at least, stuff that *feels* like evidence. The conspiracist, as Hofstadter puts it, 'carefully and all but obsessively accumulates "evidence"',[7] all of it dutifully sourced and footnoted.

The problem comes with a failure to apply that critical

thinking back to your own theory. Conspiracists may accumulate evidence, but rarely evaluate it. They may change their theories to accommodate new information, but those fixed certainties are untouchable. And questioning evidence becomes something very different when it allows you to dismiss anything you don't like as lies. At that point, it's just cherry-picking by another name.

And this is also why the theories themselves tend to grow over time and consume ever larger swathes of the believer's reality. As every source of confounding evidence gets rolled up and accused of being part of the conspiracy, more and more of the world becomes folded into the plot. (Remember, it's what Thomas of Monmouth did, when he asserted that the sceptical sheriff who pushed back against the original accusations was also in on the plot.) It's how the escalation in both Barkun and Richards' frameworks happens: how a simple event conspiracy turns into a systemic conspiracy, and how what starts as reality-based speculation gradually leaves the anchoring of reality behind and enters the realms of fantasy.

This is one reason that it becomes harder and harder to get off the conspiracy ride the longer you stay on it: the more all-encompassing the theory is, and the more evidence you've had to dismiss, the fewer opportunities there are for reality to reassert itself – at least, without experiencing the psychological pain of admitting you were totally wrong.

This doesn't just make it hard for people to abandon conspiracies. It also provides a route down the rabbit hole for people who weren't previously conspiracists but simply believed something that turned out not to be true. The world is full of ideas that aren't themselves conspiracy theories, but become increasingly hard to sustain in the face of over-whelming evidence – *without* believing that there's a conspiracy to suppress the truth. It's something we'll call 'implicit conspiracism', and we'll encounter it plenty of times throughout this book. One example: it wasn't a conspiracy theory to have believed in the early stage of the pandemic that the true fatality rate of Covid-19 was likely to be around 0.1 per cent rather than a higher figure like 0.5per cent. But as the evidence to the contrary piled up, it became harder and harder to maintain that you weren't wrong without imagining (as at least one major newspaper columnist in the UK did) that the health authorities were fiddling their own statistics in order to exaggerate a pandemic.

It turns out that, when the incentives are lined up in a certain way, and they're faced with a choice between admitting error and becoming a conspiracist, a worrying number of people will choose the latter path.

Speaking of being wrong, there's one issue that's worth addressing briefly: do conspiracy theories have to be false?

After all, that's how the term is commonly used. When a politician dismisses an allegation about them as a 'conspiracy theory' they're trying to suggest to the listener that it's nonsense (even if they might be carefully avoiding an outright denial).

We're not here to tell you off for using the term in that way. We are not the Conspiracy Police.* But in this book, we'll take a more neutral approach – if it tries to explain something about the world as the result of a group of people secretly collaborating to achieve a goal, then it counts as a conspiracy theory, regardless of whether it's true or false.

---

* Or are we?

Mostly this is for the very practical reason that, a lot of the time, it's hard to be definitive about what actually happened. Uncovering the truth is a tricky business, and especially for events buried deep in the past – but also plenty in the present day – there simply isn't enough evidence to conclusively say that the theories are wrong. Waiting around for proof that may never emerge before you can decide if something counts as a conspiracy theory seems rather limiting. We'd be here forever.

But there's also a sort of circular logic to insisting that it's only a conspiracy theory if it's wrong – especially because the term is so often used pejoratively. You end up getting trapped in an endless loop: 'How do you know it's wrong?' 'Because it's a conspiracy theory.' 'How do you know it's a conspiracy theory?' 'Because it's wrong.'

Given that one of the common traits of conspiracy theories is bundling up everything you disagree with and insisting that they're all part of the same phenomenon, we think it makes sense to avoid doing that with conspiracy theories themselves. It's also useful, because thinking about what counts as a conspiracy theory in this way can throw up some interesting revelations.

Take crop circles. We'd guess that if you were asked, 'Are crop circles a conspiracy theory?', there's a decent chance you'd answer 'yes'. (Both of us did when we were listing things we might write about in this book.) After all, they're a fairly kooky fringe interest, heavily associated with the explosion of paranormal and UFO-related conspiracy theories in the 1990s, and all manner of bizarre concepts have been proposed to explain them: they're messages from aliens; they're produced by the mystical conjunctions of ley lines; they're caused by ball lightning; they're the Earth itself trying to talk to us and ask us to ease up on the climate change.

But as entertaining as they are, none of these explanations are conspiracy theories. They're theories, yes, but not one of them involves much in the way of conspiring. In fact, there's only one explanation of crop circles that actually counts as a conspiracy theory – which is that they're hoaxes, deliberately produced by groups of people secretly flattening wheat in the night with some rope and a few planks.

In other words, in this case, it's the boring, sensible, mainstream, rational explanation which is the conspiracy theory. We're going to go out on a limb here and state with some confidence that, for reasons we'll get into later, it's also the *right* explanation. Apologies to any ley line fans.

If we struggle to admit that we were wrong, we also struggle to admit that there are things we just don't know at all.

In reality, the mystery of how poor William of Norwich died will never be solved, and speculation is all we have. It's not as if a violent death at that time needed any kind of special explanation: there was a war going on, accompanied by a breakdown of law and order. Killings by soldiers or brigands were not uncommon; plenty of them were accompanied by outbursts of sadistic torture and mutilation that match up pretty well with the supposed injuries that William suffered, which would later be interpreted as a parody of the cruci-fixion. Equally, as is often the case, he could have been killed by someone he knew, for whatever small, dark reasons such murders take place. Or he may not have been murdered at all; in her book on the subject, Rose suggests that it's also plau-sible he could have taken his own life. The vehemence of his relative's accusations of murder could be a natural reaction to the strong religious taboos around suicide at the time.

Such speculation isn't narratively satisfying. Reality often isn't. As tempting as it is to go all 'true-crime podcast' on it ('That uncle who was very keen to point the finger elsewhere seems a bit suspicious, wouldn't you say?'), that's exactly the temptation we need to resist.

But we also need to resist the temptation to label all of this as purely irrational, a product of nothing more than superstition or hatred. As William's story shows, conspiracy theories often begin as nothing more than an attempt to explain reality based on incomplete evidence. Yet they grow and survive because they fulfil some need we have: to increase power, to deflect blame, to make the world make some kind of sense. As Rose writes: 'This supposed "irrational", "bizarre", "literary trope" was the product of lucid, cogent arguments, thoughtfully and carefully debated in executive councils, judged in detail by sober men who were not reacting under pressure to thoughtless mob violence.'[8]

This book will cover many, many conspiracy theories, a lot of which will strike you as utterly bizarre. It's worth remembering that all of them will have begun somewhere, and those beginnings may be very far removed from the fantastical places in which the theories ended up. They just escalated, because escalation is kind of built into the nature of conspiracy theories.

The next question, of course, is why we're so drawn to explanations of this sort in the first place.

2

Psyche!

The enthusiasm of the crowd was so great that the motorcade was running late. Just as the open-topped limo entered Dealey Plaza, Nellie Connally, the wife of the governor of Texas, turned to John F. Kennedy and said, 'Mr President, you can't say Dallas doesn't love you.'[1]

Kennedy, with all the understated modesty that had allowed him to seduce Marilyn Monroe, is reported to have replied, 'No, you certainly can't.'[*]

They were the last words he ever spoke. A few moments later, three shots rang out from the windows of the Texas Book Depository, and the President lay dying in his wife's arms. The knowledge that he was about to be shot, that

---

[*] These last words come from Jackie Kennedy's testimony to the Warren Commission, although she admitted her recollection was hazy ('I don't know if I remember it or I have read it'); she can be forgiven for having other things on her mind that day. Governor Connally remembered a similar comment, but worded differently ('"That is very obvious," or words to that effect').

Dallas would be forever famous as the place that killed JFK, makes it impossible to read those last words without them seeming quite horribly ironic.

But everything about JFK's last fateful moments now feels freighted with such ironies, and watching the silent Zapruder film, your mind is inevitably filled with questions.* Why was an unknown woman standing on the grass between Elm and Main Streets wearing a Russian-style headscarf, earning her the nickname 'Babushka lady'? Why, in blazing sunshine, is there a man carrying an umbrella? Why does he open it as the President's car passes by? What does it *mean*? The brain simply can't cope with the possibility that the people watching the car pass had no idea they were about to witness a major moment in history. As Arthur Goldwag wrote in his 2009 book, *Cults, Conspiracies and Secret Societies*: 'When something momentous happens, everything leading up to and away from the event seems momentous too. Even the most trivial detail seems to glow with significance.'

There's a similar psychological impulse at work in much of the theorising that followed: an urge to impose a satisfying narrative on an otherwise meaningless jumble of events. Kennedy is still the youngest man ever to be elected US president, only forty-three when he took office, and his victory was framed as the passing of power to a new

---

* It is, incidentally, extremely weird that anyone with an internet connection and a smartphone can choose to watch one of the most famous murders in history, complete with Jackie Kennedy's agonised reaction, whenever it suits them. Though perhaps not quite as weird as the fact that the algorithm, in its infinite wisdom, chooses to follow up this video with 'Five things you didn't know about *Star Wars*'.

generation.* So quite apart from the trauma that would accompany the death of any national leader, the fact that Kennedy could be cut down in his prime just felt *wrong*: a decision taken by one man did not feel like sufficient cause for a shock on that scale felt by millions. 'Caught up in the press and stress of a catastrophe,' Goldwag continued, 'we grope for a significance that's proportionate to the gravity of the events ... Even years later, long after the dust has settled, the impulse perseveres.'[2]

This chapter is about two questions: why we believe in conspiracy theories, and who is most likely to fall for them. One of these, it turns out, is a lot easier to answer than the other.

It's possible that, courtesy of online discourse or some TV show or another, you have a mental image of a conspiracy theorist. He – it is probably a he – is a bit of a mess. He's badly dressed, not in great shape. He needs a haircut, even if he's losing his hair. He spends a lot of time on the internet, probably in a house owned by his parents. Perhaps he struggles to make eye contact when he talks to you, and addresses most of his comments to his shoes.

It's comforting, this image: it suggests that conspiracy theorists are other, are *them*. But they're not: a lot of the time, they're us. More than half of all Americans believe that the government concealed facts about 9/11; a third believe there was some truth to the 'birther' conspiracy theory (the idea Barack Obama was secretly born abroad);[3] and a fifth believe

* Teddy Roosevelt was actually a little younger, but wasn't initially elected: he assumed the office after President McKinley was assassinated six months into his second term.

that aliens crash-landed at Roswell, New Mexico.[4] In the mid-1970s, as many as eighty-one per cent believed that more than one person had been involved in JFK's assassination, but even in less paranoid times that number has never fallen below fifty per cent: this, remember, is the very definition of a conspiracy theory, and it has consistently had the support of a majority of Americans.[5] That's not to say this tendency only affects Americans: a 2018 survey found that sizeable minorities believed the government was hiding the truth about immigration figures in Sweden (twenty-nine per cent), Britain (thirty per cent), France (thirty-two per cent), Germany (thirty-five per cent) and Hungary (forty-eight per cent).[6]

So, of course, conspiracy theorists don't all resemble the Comic Book Guy from *The Simpsons*. They mathematically couldn't: there are conspiracy theorists of every age, race, political tendency and gender.[7]

There's another problem with making sweeping assumptions about the profile of conspiracy theorists: we know a hell of a lot less about them than you might think. A lot of the academic work on this is surprisingly new, and some of the research seems to contradict the other research. Getting embroiled in a conspiracy theory seems to require an openness to new ideas; while sticking with it seems to involve a rejection of such things. Some evidence suggests people with higher levels of education are less likely to fall into conspiracism; some shows that intelligent people may actually be more susceptible because they're better at rationalising their beliefs. To make matters worse, what research there is has often been misrepresented by the press, with correlations framed as causes, or trends found in the aggregate used to describe individuals.[8]

And of course, there's the thorny question of what counts

as a conspiracy theory, or at least a false one. One question used in research asks how much a person agrees with the following statement: 'Even though we live in a democracy, a few people will always run things anyway.'[9] That's something lots of conspiracists would no doubt sign on to, but you could also read it as a fairly straightforward description of representative democracy or the simple realities of modern centralised states. Another study from 1999 was taken aback by the 'surprisingly strong belief' among African Americans in the 'conspiracy theories' that they 'are harassed by police because of their race and that the criminal justice system is not fair to Blacks'.[10]

None of which is to say that there aren't some trends we can identify. But as far as we can tell, the most visible effect of demographics is seen in *which* conspiracy theories someone is likely to believe. So African Americans are more likely to believe that the government was responsible for the AIDS epidemic or the rise of inner-city drug culture, while white Americans are more likely to think it wants to take away their guns in preparation for a socialist one-world government.[11] Left-wingers are more likely to blame evil corporations, right-wingers a liberal academic establishment.[12] And so on.[13]

While many people have at some time believed in one conspiracy theory or another, people with certain traits do seem more suggestible than others. Political extremists are more likely to believe them than those with less strong views – which may be related to their propensity for believing there are 'simple solutions to complex political problems'.[14] Surveys of Americans have found that people who distrust their partner or government are more likely to believe in conspiracy theories as well. Perhaps unsurprisingly, gun ownership or a belief that the end of the world will happen in their lifetime seems to correlate with conspiracism, too.[15]

In 2013, a trio of psychologists from Goldsmiths, University of London, tried to impose some order on all this. One of the things that the research had managed to demonstrate beyond reasonable doubt was that people who believed in one conspiracy theory were more likely to endorse others, including those which contradicted their existing beliefs, or which had been made up on the spot by researchers. This suggests that a belief in conspiracy theories is 'not exclusively a result of rational evaluation of the evidence relating to each specific conspiracist claim': rather, some people were just more likely to look at the world and see conspiracies than others. The Goldsmiths team termed this trait 'conspiracist ideation'. What's more, they noted, a tendency to fall prey to conspiracism did indeed seem to be linked to certain other personality traits, such as low interpersonal trust, paranoia and receptivity to other unusual beliefs.[16]

And so, they came up with the Generic Conspiracist Beliefs Scale (GCBS). By asking someone to agree or disagree with a series of generic questions that don't relate to specific conspiracy theories ('A small, secret group of people is responsible for making all major decisions, such as going to war'; 'New and advanced technology that would harm current industry is being suppressed'), the GCBS makes it possible to quantify roughly how susceptible a person is to conspiracist thinking.*

But – there's always a but – the GCBS can only highlight correlations. And correlation, as any fool knows, is not

---

* We both took this test. One of us is slightly below average susceptibility for conspiracy theories; one of us slightly above average. We are not telling you which was which, because the latter doesn't trust you.

causation. 'The psychology of conspiracy theory beliefs is not yet well understood,' the paper that first outlined GCBS begins: researchers cannot yet explain why you and your brother had the exact same genetic inheritance and upbringing, yet he spent the whole of 2020 convinced he was receiving personal messages from Q, while you spent it edging slowly away and wondering if you could block his access to YouTube.

If science is still trying to work out why some people are more prone to conspiracist thinking than others, it's made rather more progress when it comes to working out why human brains are so prone to conspiracy theories in general. There are a number of well-attested mental shortcuts and psychological biases that make us prone to believe things about the world that are not in fact true.[17]

Two of the most important are the ones that afflicted those trying to understand the assassination of JFK. One is **hindsight bias**, which, if its name wasn't clear enough already, also goes by labels such as 'creeping determinism' or the 'knew-it-all-along' phenomenon. That's the tendency to read history backwards, to perceive inherently uncertain or contingent events as having been more inevitable, and thus predictable, than they actually were.

This bias is so strong that it can distort someone's memories of how much they actually knew beforehand. What's more, if an event was predictable, it's not a huge leap to assume *it must have been predicted*. And if this leads you to believe that the rest of the government must have known that Kennedy's life was in danger, then the question becomes: why didn't they save him? The only logical answer to that is that somebody, somewhere, didn't want to.

Related to this is **proportionality bias**: the way that, in the words of Rob Brotherton, one of the creators of the GCBS, 'When something big happens, we tend to assume that something big must have caused it.'

In the case of JFK, it didn't seem enough that so much harm could be caused by one angry, armed loser. Therefore, conspiracy theories have tended to add other factors, in an attempt to balance the scales. In the weaker versions – that is, those that are *technically* conspiracy theories, but in a small-scale, not-requiring-vast-numbers-of-secret-connections kind of way – this generally means another gunman standing on the grassy knoll, a sign that other people must have been involved. In the stronger ones, it might extend to vast networks involving Russia or Cuba or multiple government agencies, all conspiring to dispose of a president who might have prevented the war in Vietnam. Either way, a single man with a gun just didn't feel like a proportionate cause.

Proportionality bias can apply in situations where there was a real conspiracy, too. Several dozen members of al-Qaeda really did conspire to fly planes into the World Trade Center, the Pentagon and other targets. But even then, this didn't feel like a big enough deal to explain over 3,000 deaths at the heart of the world's only superpower – so some became convinced there must have been something else going on. Someone in government must have passively let it happen, or even actively *made* it happen, for their own reasons (like wanting a big war). The idea that shadowy forces inside the US state did this on purpose is somehow far less frightening than the possibility that the mighty US government could have been caught unawares by something so big – or that New York might be vulnerable to attack.

Michael Shermer, the American science writer and founder

of the Skeptics Society, has coined two more terms* to describe cognitive biases that make the brain open to conspiracy thinking. The first is **patternicity** – the tendency to find meaningful patterns in meaningless noise. If you've ever started to predict the next dice roll in a board game based on the last few numbers, or started spotting faces in inanimate objects like coat hooks or burned toast, then you've fallen prey to patternicity.

There are evolutionary reasons why the brain should play such tricks. Being able to spot patterns – the face in the bushes that might be a tiger; the change in the weather that means the storm is coming – provides a clear advantage in the battle for survival, and the small furry hominid that sees threats that aren't there is far more likely to pass on its genes than the one who misses those that are. But while paranoia made for a good survival strategy on the plains of East Africa, it can translate to reactionary views or crappy decision-making today. Instead of jumping at some leaves we've mistaken for a tiger, in modern society, the patternicity bias can lead to us seeing conspiracies where there is only coincidence.

What's more, experiments have found that many people are more likely to spot patterns in noise when made to feel powerless or out of control in some way. This may explain why conspiracism seems to go through the roof in times of pandemic, disaster or economic crisis. The more anxious we are, the harder we find it to stop looking for a tiger.

This would perhaps not be so bad were it not for the

---

* Both are actually subsets of 'apophenia', a term taken from German that means 'a tendency to perceive connections between unrelated things'. We're not saying Shermer's terms are better, but at least we can actually pronounce them.

other cognitive bias Shermer identified: **agenticity**, 'the tendency to infuse patterns with meaning, intention, and agency'. It is not merely that we see patterns: it's that we assume that someone must be responsible for them.

Shermer credits this to our theory of mind – our ability to understand that others have desires and motivations just as we do, a vital tool for understanding the world and predicting what might happen.* But it means that, in our attempts to understand a complex and uncaring world, we sometimes wrongly imagine someone pulling the strings. Once, natural disasters or plagues were attributed to the anger of the gods. As the world has become more secular, the disasters have continued – but suddenly, there's nobody to blame them on.

Which, as you may have guessed, is where the conspiracy theory comes in: instead of angry gods, disasters caused by abstract forces can instead be attributed to the actions of a group you don't like. Pandemic killing dozens in your village? Perhaps outsiders poisoned the water supply! Economy destroyed by the ineffable tides of changing technologies and international capitalism? Why not blame the Jews?

In other words, the agenticity bias, the belief that someone, somewhere, must be in charge, can slip over into imagining that bad things only happen because bad people will them to. The tendency to treat a dizzying range of

---

* Oddly enough, agenticity doesn't literally have to mean invisible forces pulling the strings: it can be seen, too, in the way children instinctively draw smiley faces on pictures of the sun or moon; in the way objects associated with death or disaster are treated as somehow cursed; even in the way certain suggestively shaped foods – such as bananas or oysters – are, unscientifically, assumed to have aphrodisiac properties.

groups – from the Freemasons to the Bilderberg Group to, well, the Jews again – as the true power in society starts with the assumption that there must be a true power, somewhere.

In a strange way, there's something almost comforting about this. Agenticity is not just at work in the belief that the gods are watching over us, or that there are dark forces manipulating everything from wars to viruses to the food supply, but also in the strangely persistent belief that government could fix everything if only our politicians weren't so lazy, venal and corrupt. If the only thing standing between us and utopia is some bad people, then utopia exists and there is a path – however appalling – that leads to it.

If, on the other hand, bad things happen because the world is simply a cold and cruel place – if your life can be ruined because it was cheaper and easier to hire workers in Mexico, or because of the mutation of a virus carried by a bat in China – then nobody is in control at all. And isn't that terrifying?

From this point of view, conspiracy theorists are simply people whose sense of cause and effect is just a bit too developed. In Michael Barkun's telling, conspiracism is a worldview in which 'nothing happens by accident', 'everything is connected' and 'nothing is as it seems'.[18] To Goldwag, meanwhile, conspiracy theories offer 'a vision of a world that, however terrible, is always purposive'.[19]

So when we're tempted to mock conspiracy theorists, we shouldn't just remember that we're all prone to a little conspiracism: we should remember that it's driven by the same mental shortcuts that enabled our ancestors to survive to build the civilisation from which we're mocking such tendencies in the first place.

* * *

There is no single, grand unified theory that can explain why every conspiracist believes in every theory: the human brain is complex and messy, so our psychological biases are, too. But we should at least glance meaningfully at a few other reasons that people fall down the rabbit hole, and are then reluctant to climb back up again.

Dissonance

Cognitive dissonance is the psychological discomfort you experience when your actions clash with your sense of identity, or when new information contradicts a carefully constructed belief system. You know how uncomfortable it is to think about how much you loved playing with your friend's micropig while you're tucking into a bacon sandwich? Or how it feels to fact-check your belief that your chosen football team is the best in the world against its actual, demonstrable record? There you go.

The brain has a number of tricks to deal with this dissonance. One of them is **confirmation bias**: the tendency to dismiss the difficult information and cherry-pick the stuff that fits our preferred narrative ('Well, to be fair, the team's had a lot of bad luck recently'). Another is **self-justification bias**, the ability to construct coherent narratives to convince ourselves that, really, our actions were for the best and we almost certainly behaved in the best way we could ('Well, it's not the same *kind* of pig, and these bigger ones would certainly eat *me* if they got the chance').

These can be useful psychological defences: imagine how much work it'd be if we had to completely rewrite our belief system every time something came along to contradict it. But they also make believers remarkably talented at explaining away information that might get in the way of what they already think.

Seventy years ago, a Chicago housewife named Dorothy Martin became convinced that aliens were communicating with her via automatic writing, and that the inhabitants of the planet Clarion were trying to warn her that a terrible catastrophe would befall the Earth on 21 December 1952. Aliens would be arriving in a flying saucer to rescue a select few the previous night – provided, of course, that they had no metal on their persons. The hours before midnight on 20 December saw a group – many of whom had ended relationships, quit jobs or sold their possessions – gathered at Martin's house, removing buttons, zips and anything else that contained metal. But no extra-terrestrial visitor was forthcoming. The next day (sorry, spoilers), the promised catastrophe failed to occur.

One might naturally assume that this would have under-mined Martin's followers' faith in her prophecies, and among some, so it proved. Others, though, became *more* convinced she was right, after she received a further message telling her that the 'God of Earth' had been so impressed by their group's simple faith that the end of the world had been called off. The demonstrable fact that Martin had been wrong was smoothly incorporated into a new, updated theory explaining how she had been right all along.[20]

This incident now seems darkly amusing.* Others – such as the recent spate of claims that mass shootings were actually 'false flag' incidents, thus proving the importance of the right to bear arms – do not.

---

* It may not have seemed amusing to anyone who'd broken up with their partner or sold their house.

The need to know

Sometimes we jump to conspiracies because we're trying to fill in the gaps of an incomplete narrative. The sociologist Tamotsu Shibutani suggested that rumours – which he described as 'improvised news' – are more likely to start when the public demand for news and information outstrips the supply available through regular, institutional channels.[21] The same is often true of conspiracy theories as well – which is unsurprising, given they're just a short way downstream from rumour.

This is why dramatic news events tend to act as a magnet for conspiracy theories: we crave information about them, but very often the amount of actual available, verified information falls well short of our desires. The unsolved murder of a child; a plane falling out of the sky; the spread of a new disease – they're all situations in which we're desperate to know the full story, but a complete narrative may not be available for years, if ever. It's like reading a detective story only to find out someone's torn out the last five pages: there's no way your brain isn't going to start making wild guesses about who did it.

The desire to feel special

Most of us are not, in the grand scheme of things, important. Most of us are not special. And much of what we do in life – whether it's following a faith, joining a political move-ment, conducting a string of ill-thought-through love affairs, or becoming an obsessive fan of a singer/sports team/TV show – is intended in some way to counteract this, to assert that our particular collection of proteins and processes in fact *matters*.

Now, imagine you are one of the few people in the world who knows about the real shape of the planet, or the existence of aliens, or the US government's extensive mind-control experiments. Suddenly you are special: you are one of the few who knows the truth.

We don't need to spell out why that would be a very seductive feeling – a way of giving you a sense of status you may otherwise lack. Indeed, if you're one of a ragtag army fighting corruption at the highest levels of the government, you're not just a truth-seeker: you're a hero.

What's more, some conspiracies act like cults, encouraging their followers to recruit friends and relatives, and to cut them out of their lives if they refuse. Even those that don't do this kind of thing can still supply their followers with new friends and partners and a social circle. Stop believing, and you aren't just abandoning the theory: you're saying goodbye to your friends. All this means that, once you're in, it can be hard to get out.

Primal fears

There are many fears that are virtually universal across human cultures: fear of spiders or the dark, for example. Then there are particular terrors that mould themselves to the cultures and social circumstances from which they emerge, whether that's the modern fear of spy cameras in your Airbnb, or zombi lore in slavery-era Haiti.

Not only do we have these fears, but we also have a really

powerful urge to express them and share them. Our brains seem to crave spooking themselves. Perhaps that's simply a mechanism to stave off complacency and keep our senses on alert; perhaps we find catharsis in the release. Probably it's both: in scaring ourselves, our fears get both exercised and exorcised. Either way, there's a particular pleasure to be had in realising that our private terrors are not unique to us, but are widely shared.

So conspiracy theories that play on some of these primal fears tend to be very successful at rapidly spreading. Fear of contamination; fear of outsiders; fear of harm to children – all are recurring themes in conspiracy lore. They often have remarkable long-term staying power, too.

Nostalgia and anxiety

Sometimes, conspiracy theories are very obviously driven by a simple anxiety about change, and represent nothing more than a desire to live in a familiar past over an uncertain future. This anxiety can sometimes become so great that it leads people to wish they lived in a past that was objectively quite grim, like ageing British Boomers looking fondly back on the three-day week because sometimes people fancied them and at least their backs didn't hurt.

In March 1991, several years into *perestroika* (reconstruction), the USSR held a referendum on a new treaty, amending the relationship between its various republics. The treaty passed overwhelmingly, but following a failed coup that summer, the Soviet Union collapsed anyway.

Or did it? The Soviet Citizens Movement, which has members across the 15 countries that once made up the Soviet

Union, maintains that the USSR never fell, and the treaty still holds.[22] In this alternative reality, the modern Russian Federation is less of a nation state than a private offshore company registered in Delaware. As of 2020, the Politburo was headed by a retired Moscow surveyor named Valentina Reunova, who was busy issuing government decrees to her 51,500 YouTube followers. (By 2021, government communications had been interrupted: the channel had been removed due to claims of copyright infringement.)

In other words, for a small but measurable proportion of the 300 million people who today live in the former USSR, post-Soviet capitalism has proved such a disappointment that they're prepared to deny the USSR ever fell at all. It's like the film *Goodbye Lenin*, except it's run for thirty years.

Brilliantly, this means that the American conspiracy theory that Vladimir Putin controlled Trump really is matched by a Russian one stating that Joe Biden controls Vladimir Putin.

Relatedly:

Comfort

In 2016, on both sides of the Atlantic, the forces of the progressive liberal left took quite a beating. In June, in part because of the votes of traditionally Labour working-class strongholds, the UK voted to leave the European Union. Just over four months later, in part because of the votes of similar communities in the Midwest, the US elected President Trump.

It wasn't long before conspiracy theories were attached to both these election results. In fact, it wasn't long before the *same* conspiracy theories were attached to both these election results: that an unholy alliance of the consulting firm

Cambridge Analytica and various shadowy puppet-masters had somehow swung the votes. As we'll see later, the evidence for these claims was patchier than you might think. So why did they get so much air time?

The obvious answer is: because it was a kind of comfort. It's traumatic to lose an election, and horrifying to face up to the fact that so many of *your people* chose to vote the other way. Much more comforting to assume that the majority was *really* on your side; it's just that dark forces somehow rigged the election against you. At least then you have an enemy you can fight.

Legitimising your worst impulses

Conspiracy theories can also appeal to us because they give us an excuse for indulging desires and behaviours that the system tells us we should suppress. After all, if *they're* not playing by the rules, then why should we?

One thing you notice when looking at the history of conspiracy theories is how often believers start acting in ways that mirror the conspiracies they claim exist. They'll organise in secret; they'll spread falsehoods because they think it will push people towards a greater truth; they'll try to suppress or purge ideas they believe to be dangerous. When you're faced with a powerful and deceitful enemy, all bets are off.

It's a familiar dynamic: if they're spreading propaganda, then so should we. If they're rigging the election, then we need to rig the election too. One recent study* of political

---

* A preprint, not yet peer-reviewed – so worth treating with caution.

partisans in America suggested a link between inaccurate beliefs about their opponents' support for political violence and their own attitudes.[23] Those who overestimated how many people on the other side were in favour of using violence to achieve their political goals were more likely to support the exact same thing from their own side.

On a personal level, this can mean people are drawn to conspiracy theories that legitimise their existing personal preferences (like, say, not wanting to wear a mask in a pandemic). On a national level, it's why authoritarian leaders find conspiracy theories to be useful ways to build support for repressive policies.

If the workings of the human brain have given us plenty of irrational reasons why people end up falling for conspiracy theories, it seems worth noting that the workings of the world mean there are sometimes rational reasons, too. One is that the authorities really don't always help themselves. The US patent system, for example, is set up in such a way that you could speculatively file a patent on an invention that doesn't actually exist yet. This means there are currently patents for everything from space elevators to spaceships, filed by entrepreneurial souls who hope to one day be able to claim millions in compensation from the people who actually do the hard work of turning theoretical science into actual stuff. Given that, it's no surprise that some people might have been duped into believing that such advanced technologies exist and are being hushed up.[24]

In addition, politicians sometimes act in a way that seems almost designed to inspire conspiracy paranoia. Richard Nixon famously recorded everything that went on in the Oval Office, and withheld documents from his own military chiefs, thus necessitating that staffers stole them just so that their bosses would know what was going on. A few years before that, President Johnson is known to have wanted the Warren Commission, which investigated the JFK assassination, to conclude that gunman Lee Harvey Oswald acted alone.

This was almost certainly because Johnson wanted to prevent the commission from digging into the nefarious things that the CIA and other security agencies really were involved in, such as their many attempts to assassinate Castro and their close links with the Mafia. But it was interpreted in some quarters as a sign that the President – who only held the job because his predecessor had been shot, and thus stood to gain more from the assassination than pretty much anyone – was in it up to his neck. The CIA's own chief historian concluded that the agency's evasiveness and withholding of evidence 'might have done more to undermine the credibility of the commission than anything else that happened'.[25] They may not have been involved in a conspiracy, but they certainly helped fuel the conspiracy theories. And, as we'll see again and again, a lack of transparency from governments often ends up with people believing much, much worse things about them than if they'd just been honest from the start.

The other factor that might explain why conspiracy theories sometimes evolve is one we've mentioned before, but honestly it's one worth stressing: sometimes, there are real conspiracies. Julius Caesar, Abraham Lincoln and Archduke Franz Ferdinand were all killed based on plans put together by enemies acting in the shadows. Watergate was a real conspiracy; so was Iran Contra; so was the attempt by the tobacco industry to hush up the fact that cigarettes cause cancer. The 9/11 attacks happened after a conspiracy by enemies of the state; the 1605 destruction of the English

Houses of Parliament by an organisation with links to the Spanish Empire would have come under that heading, too, had it not been foiled at the last minute.

There are undoubtedly conspiracies happening today that we'll only learn the full truth of in fifty years' time; there are surely people currently being dismissed as conspiracy theorists who, with the benefit of hindsight, will be at least partly vindicated. Sometimes, the conspiracies are real – and not everyone who sees it is simply a madman trying to come up with a comforting explanation for a terrifying world.

Part II

A Series of Unfortunate Events

In which conspiracy theories attempt to explain specific events, a grip on reality is at least partly maintained, and we are forced to acknowledge that, honestly, sometimes they may have a point.

Part II

A Series of Unfortunate Events

3

Panic! At the Discourse

In May 1776, a university professor in the Bavarian city of Ingolstadt formed an intellectual society with a handful of like-minded students. The professor, a man named Adam Weishaupt, had some novel thoughts about religion and humanity and society – and, in the long tradition of small-town college professors with big ideas, he wanted to do more than simply prepare his students for a life in the professional class. He wanted to ensure that when they went out into the world, into positions of power and influence, they would carry along with them the beliefs that they'd debated and refined in the halls of academia.

Weishaupt's ideas were certainly on the unusual side, although hardly out of place in an age of philosophical, theological and political upheaval, when bold new ideas were being launched into the world at a head-spinning rate. Four months before Weishaupt formed his society, Thomas Paine's *Common Sense* was published; the month after that, Adam Smith dropped *The Wealth of Nations*; just a few months later, the American Declaration of Independence would be drafted and ratified. Seized with the spirit of the age, Weishaupt believed that human society could be improved, and that humans were not condemned to live eternally as flawed, sinful creatures. He believed that through study and reason and the spread of knowledge, humans could be guided towards a state of perfection. As such, he called his group the 'Bund der Perfektibilisten': the Union of Perfectibilists.

This was a rubbish name. They decided to change it soon afterwards.

Weishaupt wanted to leave a legacy behind him, and on those grounds, he definitely succeeded. In the real world, his little collective collapsed in under a decade, torn apart by infighting, government suppression and a weaponised sex scandal, forcing Weishaupt himself to flee into exile. But in the popular imagination, his group has lasted into the present day, growing stronger with every retelling. The society has been blamed or credited for the rise and fall of governments, and for shaping the whole course of history to their whims. Their hidden hand has been seen at work in the background of almost every major triumph and catastrophe to befall humanity. They've been accused of the greatest crimes imaginable, and ascribed an almost inconceivable level of power.

It's tempting to wonder whether any of that would have happened if they hadn't rebranded with a catchier name than 'the Union of Perfectibilists'. The new name that Weishaupt chose for the group, you see, was 'the Illuminati'.

Yeah, them. Not just any 'them'; the ultimate *them*. A name we've come to use as a shorthand for every unseen group meddling in human affairs, every shadowy cabal of malign puppet-masters working the strings of suspected conspiracies over the course of more than two hundred years. This is no coincidence: the Illuminati of the paranoid imagination isn't just one of history's most famous conspiracy theories, it's the direct source for a vast range of modern conspiratorial ideas – including many that may not even mention the Illuminati at all.

When you think about the Illuminati – the version in the popular conspiracy theories and the Dan Brown novels and the phrase 'Beyoncé is Illuminati' – we'd guess that you picture a group of extremely powerful and influential people. You know that they're supposed to work under a cloak of absolute secrecy, never revealing their membership or the workings of the organisation publicly. And you might think that their aim is to infiltrate, subvert or supplant other powerful institutions – even national governments – to seek ever greater control over the direction of human society.

So. There are three things you need to know about Weishaupt's Illuminati:

1) Yeah, this was roughly their plan.
2) They absolutely did not achieve it.
3) It's also – perhaps, depending on your perspective – not *quite* as sinister as all that makes it sound.

To understand how we got from there to here means telling two stories. One is the history of the Bavarian Illuminati themselves, and the impressive amount of personal drama they packed into one messy decade. The second tale is more complex, tracing the evolution of an idea over two centuries of popular writing, during which the Illuminati myth grew as they got blamed for everything from the French Revolution onwards.

This is a story of how conspiracy theories rarely spring

from nowhere; instead, they are handed down the generations and passed from country to country, being adapted to fit local contexts and the anxieties of each new age they find themselves in. It's also a story of how many conspiracy theories don't serve only as an explanation of events, but are part of a broader battle of ideas: just as conspiracies let us put a face to invisible trends that shape our world, they also give us villains who personify the ideologies and cultural trends we consider dangerous. (In that sense, it's also a story of how conservatives have been freaking out over the issue of 'liberal professors on college campuses' for a lot longer than you might suspect.)

But before we get to all that, let's head back to Ingolstadt in 1776, where a young academic is about to make a series of increasingly poor decisions.

Adam Weishaupt was in his late twenties when he formed the Perfectibilists, at which point he'd been a professor of law at Ingolstadt for around four years. This meant both civil law and ecclesiastical law, a mixture of the political and theological that gives some insight into the society Weishaupt inhabited. This was before the modern state of Germany; Bavaria was part of the Holy Roman Empire, a loose and shrinking collection of largely autonomous semifeudal statelets, in which political power mostly resided in local princes, and churches held great sway over the everyday lives of the people.

What were the dangerous ideas that Weishaupt advocated, those beliefs so heretical and subversive that they would see the power of the state suppress his organisation? They're summed up by one modern academic as – brace yourself – 'free thought, republicanism, secularism, liberalism, and gender equality'.[1]

Good *god*.

As the name they eventually chose for the society suggests, the Illuminati were a product of the Enlightenment, and their outlook was broadly in line with the trends that had been shaping European thought for more than a century at that point.* Weishaupt was particularly taken with the philosophy of Jean-Jacques Rousseau, and the notion that the trappings of the modern state were a corrupting and oppressive influence, one that kept man from a natural state of happiness. As such, he opposed the authoritarian, absolutist power of the state and the Church, and dreamed of a future without either institution. He was concerned with notions of liberty and equality, and he believed that it was through the powers of reason, rather than superstition or dogma, that human society could be improved. Beliefs like this may have seemed radical to some of his contemporaries, but they were hardly unique. From our modern vantage point, they just read as vaguely laudable but rather mundane. They're basically the lyrics of 'Imagine'.

But a crucial element that marked Weishaupt out was the way he planned to bring about his utopian vision for humanity. He would form a secret society, which would aim to place believers in his philosophy into positions of influence. This society would have different levels, or 'grades', through which members could progress, starting at Novice

---

* It's worth clarifying that Weishaupt's Order of the Illuminati – *'Illuminatenorden'* in German – were neither the first nor the last people to use that name. Various groups had described themselves as 'Illuminati', or the French *'Illuminès'*, over the previous centuries, and would continue to do so in the years after. That's unsurprising, really; when people think up names that will make their organisations sound good, 'light' has always been a fairly popular metaphor.

and working their way up to Illuminated Minerval. Sworn to absolute secrecy, its members would have codenames, usually drawn from classical literature (Weishaupt was 'Spartacus'; another early member was 'Cato', and so on). Weishaupt would lead the society, with his orders being passed down through the hierarchy – although he'd hint at the existence of mysterious and entirely fictional 'superiors' at higher grades than himself, to give the instructions a bit more gravitas.

If this all seems like an odd choice for promoting your excellent ideas about how to run the world, then ... well, yes. But it's worth remembering a few things. Firstly, Weishaupt wasn't living in a democracy: it's not like he could stand for election on his platform. Using patronage and influence networks to place favoured people into key jobs was simply how things worked at the time.

Another thing to note is that, even though the Enlightenment age was all about the expansion of public discourse, people were absolutely mad for secret societies. Couldn't get enough of the bloody things. Masonic lodges were in a boom period, and new secret societies were springing up everywhere, all trying to occupy different niches in a competition for members, many inventing entirely spurious histories to connect them to the ancient world in an effort to seem fancy. Weishaupt was quite consciously piggy-backing on this fad in order to gain support. 'Whatever is hidden and secret has a special attraction for men,' he wrote in 1781.[2]

Perhaps most importantly, Weishaupt didn't believe that his ideal world would be achieved within his lifetime, or indeed several lifetimes. In large part, the purpose of the society was to ensure that the torch would be passed down through the generations as it attempted to nudge humanity in the right direction.

That was the plan, at least. But four years after it was formed, Weishaupt's little student group looked like a resounding flop. Despite gaining a few recruits in nearby Bavarian cities, it still hadn't expanded far beyond its Ingolstadt origins, and its membership could have all met comfortably in a fairly small room. This was probably at least partly due to the fact that Weishaupt was rather picky, not to mention snobby, about new recruits ('I don't like his walk,' he sniffed about one prospect in an early letter to a fellow Illuminatus, adding that 'his manners are crude and unpolished').[3] In the first years of the group's existence, the Illuminati were in no position to influence anything, never mind shape the course of global history. They were little more than a book group with notions.

That all changed when Weishaupt met Baron Adolph Knigge,* an orphaned minor noble whose late parents had bequeathed him a huge pile of debt. Knigge was still in his twenties when he joined the Illuminati in 1780, but he was an inveterate networker who had dealt with his diminished circumstances by studying law and remaking himself into a figure of influence, holding governmental positions in several courts across the Empire. (He's mostly remembered in Germany today as the author of a popular book on etiquette, rather than as a sinister puppet-master of human affairs.)

---

* To be precise, Knigge's title was actually 'Freiherr', a rank in the nobility of the Holy Roman Empire that roughly corresponds to that of Baron. Also, his name is frequently given as 'von Knigge'; the aristocratic 'von' seems to appear and disappear throughout his life, possibly according to the prevailing political winds.

Knigge was also a huge fan of the Freemasons: he disagreed with them on various intellectual matters, but loved their clubbable nature and deft way with an esoteric ritual. Weishaupt was initially opposed to Freemasonry, but he'd already discovered that creating a rival secret society from scratch was surprisingly hard, so by this point had given in and joined his local lodge. And in an age when patronage was the order of the day, Knigge had everything that Weishaupt needed to make his intellectual ambitions a reality: contacts, influence, a dash of nobility, and a knack for creating scenes people wanted to be part of. (In addition, unlike Weishaupt, who had been brought up in the Catholic religious order of the Jesuits, Knigge was a Protestant, which helped the Illuminists cross over Germany's religious divides.)

And so Knigge set about refashioning the Illuminati along more Masonic lines. He changed their initiation rituals to give them a more compelling, mystical, quasi-religious air. He started recruiting from his social circles – older and more influential figures than the students Weishaupt had been trying to get on board. In order to tempt prominent members over from other branches of Masonry, he drew up plans to expand the number of grades in the organisation's hierarchy, adding senior levels such as 'Priest', 'Prince' and 'Mage'. (Throughout their decade of existence, the Illuminati never come across as anything less than *extremely* full of themselves.)

It worked. Under Knigge's influence, the Illuminati grew dramatically in the space of a few years, at their peak claiming at least 600 and perhaps as many as 2,500 members. They attracted nobles and people of note, possibly including famous names like Johann Wolfgang von Goethe, the author of *Faust* and the foremost giant of German literature.* Suddenly, things seemed to be going very well.

But as any band can tell you, it's when you get a surprise hit after years of obscurity that everything falls apart. Weishaupt, the perfectionist Perfectibilist, was constantly embroiled in arguments with other members. He and Knigge increasingly found themselves at loggerheads over the group's direction. Weishaupt disliked the mystical turn that Knigge's Masonic leanings brought to an organisation intended as a beacon of rationalism, and he hated some of the people that Knigge was now attracting to the society, who he felt were hangers-on rather than true fans of his work. So, he tried to claw back the control he'd ceded to Knigge in return for his recruitment activities.

Weishaupt also seems to have discovered that running a secret society is an absolutely horrible job, writing later of how it led to 'hostility and hatred [from] my friends', gave him 'care-burdened, sleepless nights', and how 'very often, I wished no longer to exist'.[4] Knigge, for his part, seems to have found Weishaupt to be an insufferable, pedantic control freak and an overbearing pain in the ass, with worryingly Jesuitical tendencies to boot. He eventually left the group in the summer of 1784.

They also faced the basic problem that, the bigger a secret society becomes, the less secret it stays. Knigge's free and easy way with attracting members had meant that the Illuminati

---

* The game of 'was this person in the Illuminati?' is one that's beloved of modern Illuminati obsessives; thanks to their use of codenames, this often amounts to little more than guesswork and wishful thinking. Goethe was probably a member, but it's not 100 per cent certain.

were increasingly un-secret – and the group's rapid success at gaining influence meant that it was equally rapidly making enemies among those who felt they were being shut out.

Beset by internal division and external opponents, what happened next shouldn't come as any surprise: in short, the Illuminati got WikiLeaked. Somebody gave a bundle of their correspondence to the Bavarian authorities, who weren't hugely keen on the whole 'subvert existing power structures and dismantle the nation state' thing. The authorities raided several members' homes, and published a selection of their documents and letters designed to make them look as dangerous, corrupt and seditious as possible.

The exposure of the Illuminati created a huge scandal in the German world. This was partly because their ideas were shocking, at least to traditionalists. But as newspaper editors down the ages have known, if you want to hang someone out to dry, what you *really* need is a sex scandal. In Weishaupt's correspondence with his fellow travellers, the authorities found exactly that.

You see, the letters revealed that Weishaupt had got his sister-in-law pregnant, and had written to other members of the Illuminati asking for help in procuring an abortion. This ... did not go down well. It was all the evidence their opponents needed that the Illuminati were wicked and immoral to their core. Weishaupt mounted an impassioned and, to modern eyes, fairly reasonable defence: his wife Afra had died in 1780, and before passing had given her blessing to the notion that her sister Anna Maria should marry Weishaupt after she passed on. But such a marriage would need the permission of the Church authorities – which turned out to be a three-year-long bureaucratic nightmare, in which Weishaupt was supposedly advised that a pregnancy might actually help to hurry things along. Believing their marriage was just a few weeks from getting the go ahead, the couple were despondent to then be told they hadn't submitted all the correct paperwork – leaving them still unmarried and with an increasingly visible pregnancy. 'It was a lapse – that I do not deny,' Weishaupt would write, 'but few people have lapsed in more forgivable circumstances.'[5]

You won't be surprised to hear this cut little ice with Weishaupt's enemies. From 1784 onwards, laws were brought in banning secret societies in Bavaria, and Weishaupt faced trial. Before he could be jailed, he fled into exile in the duchy of Saxe-Gotha-Altenburg, where Duke Ernest II (who had been a member, and who remained sympathetic) offered him asylum. Most of the society's former members denounced it or distanced themselves from it; a few tried to keep aspects of the organisation or its philosophy going in some form, but they got little traction. By 1786, just a decade after it was founded, the Bavarian Order of the Illuminati was, for all intents and purposes, dead.

Of course, that wasn't the end of the story.

How did a small society, active for only ten years, with limited impact in the German-speaking world and virtually none outside it, turn into the Illuminati of legend?

The short answer is: in 1789, the French Revolution happened. The overthrow of the Ancien Régime, the executions of nobles, and the increasingly bloody aftermath as former comrades turned against each other had sent shockwaves through Europe, and left many countries' elites feeling decidedly nervous. It was an event so large and dramatic that conventional explanations seemed insufficient. So, an explanation that placed the blame on a malicious enemy (rather than, say, the fundamentally unsustainable nature of the social system) had an obvious appeal to those who liked things as they were and wanted to keep them that way.

But the conspiracy theories about the Illuminati didn't start in France. As is often the case, what eventually became global started extremely local.

If the Illuminati were a product of the Enlightenment, then the theories sprang from the burgeoning forces of the Counter-Enlightenment. This was a loose coalition of those opposed to change: royalists who defended the absolute power of kings; religionists aghast at a morality founded on rationalist principles rather than the word of God; property owners who weren't keen on some of the chat about equality. (They didn't call themselves the Counter-Enlightenment, of course; everybody insisted that their views were the true Enlightenment.)

In the German world, the Illuminati scandal provided a focal point for this Counter-Enlightenment to rally around. It spawned conspiracy theories even before revolution in France. One slightly baffling effort came from a chap called Ernst von Göchhausen, whose *Exposure of the Cosmopolitan Republic* in 1786 insisted that there was a 'cosmopolitan-Jesuitical' conspiracy, in which a small group of hidden intellectuals – 'cosmopolitans' – had worked throughout history to manipulate societies. The Illuminati were an instrument of that larger plot – which, Göchhausen said, was secretly controlled by the Catholic Church. (Göchhausen was a Protestant, natch.)

The theory that the Catholics and the Enlightenment secularists were in cahoots was ... weird. It was greeted mostly with bemusement, and is interesting mostly as an early example of themes that recur a lot in later conspiracy thinking. One is the tendency to see everyone you don't like as working together, even when they obviously can't stand each other. The other is his attempt to fill the massive plot hole this created – why would the Church want to promote the Enlightenment? His answer was simply that they wanted to create confusion and anarchy, which would cause people to turn back to the Church in their desire for order. This idea – that the prime goal of conspiracies is to create chaos in order to seize or cement power – is a trope that recurs repeatedly, notably in *The Protocols of the Elders of Zion*.[6] (It's a useful get-out clause for your theory not making sense. If confusion is the goal, then just about *anything* can be explained away.)

But the Illuminati conspiracies really got going in the aftermath of the Revolution. This period, and the backlash to the upheaval in France, was crucial in the formation of modern conservatism as a distinct ideology. In the German world, a central role was played by the earliest conservative periodicals – notably the *Wiener Zeitschrift*, which ran for under a year in 1792, and its slightly more long-lived spiritual successor *Eudämonia* in 1795. These publications were full-bore conspiracist; their central purpose was fervent opposition to the imagined machinations of the Illuminati.

Perhaps the most important figure in all of this is Leopold Alois Hoffmann, who founded *Wiener Zeitschrift*. Hoffmann was many things – a failed dramatist, a woefully under-qualified university professor, a part-time spy – but above all, he was a proto-journalist; a dirt-digger and polemicist in the no-holds-barred shit-flinging fashion. What he lacked in literary gifts he made up for with a dogged work ethic and a willingness to knock out pamphlets condemning Emperor Leopold's enemies in vitriolic terms at an impressive rate. Leopold was said to have considered Hoffmann 'as stupid as a donkey', but found him useful.[7]

Hoffmann loathed the Illuminati. This may have been more personal than philosophical: for much of the 1780s he'd run with an Enlightenment crowd, using his attack-dog style of journalism to call out conservative priests for problematic sermons. In fact, he nearly joined the Illuminati himself, and had scored a cushy university job, despite not being qualified, on the word of a prominent member. But whatever the reason for his estrangement from his former pals, he took up the anti-Illuminist cause with the zeal of a convert and the bitterness of an Olympic-standard grudge-holder. One of his first acts was to set up a secret society almost identical to the Illuminati, specifically to do anti-Illuminati things.

The *Wiener Zeitschrift* was an exercise in furious condemnation of everybody who held the wrong political opinions, and it saw conspiracy in even the mildest dissent. Liberals and free-thinkers were denounced in vituperative passages about the nation's 'intoxication with liberty', alongside demands that the 'voices of subversion be muzzled'. Fellow conservatives who questioned the tone or the factual accuracy of the periodical's wilder accusations would, likewise, be condemned as part of the conspiracy. A representative edition included a denunciation of the censorious nature of liberal public opinion (which had seen two conservative plays in Leipzig cancelled); praise of Leopold's new censorship laws to suppress subversive writing; support for the right of the government to open people's private letters; and calls for the government to prevent the Illuminati from opening people's private letters (something Hoffmann was convinced they were doing to him).[8]

After *Wiener Zeitschrift* folded, Hoffmann moved on to *Eudämonia*, which brought together a larger coalition of conservative figures – notably Johann August Starck, a cleric who was a major figure in German conservatism and a firm believer that the Illuminati represented an anarchist plot. The prim and proper Starck was a marked contrast to the vulgar-tongued Hoffmann, but that didn't stop them working together to expose the conspiracy that both perceived.

Starck provides us with an excellent example of how conspiracy theorists reach their conclusions before there's any evidence. In the summer of 1789, he was on holiday with a Counter-Enlightenment pal when news reached them of the storming of the Bastille. Despite knowing nothing else about what had happened, his companion reported that they turned to each other and said at the same time: 'That is the work of the Illuminati.'9

So, the conspiracy theory of the French Revolution started in the petty personal rivalries and culture wars of the German world. But it would take a French priest and a Scottish physicist to transport it to the international stage, in a pair of books published in 1797: *Memoirs Illustrating the History of Jacobinism* by Abbé Augustin Barruel, and *Proofs of a Conspiracy against all the Religions and Governments of Europe* by John Robison. It was these books – which drew on the work of Hoffmann, Starck and others to paint a picture of a grand plot, decades in the making, as the reason for the Revolution – that popularised the Illuminati theory, and sowed the seeds for centuries of conspiracy beliefs that are still with us today.

Of the two, it's Barruel's doorstop of a tome that is most frequently cited as the prototype of the modern conspiracy theory. It's an event theory, to the extent that its primary goal is to explain the Revolution. But it shares many characteristics of systemic theories: it has a vast cast of characters, covers a huge span of time, and attempts to fold in almost every political event in France over the course of many decades as the work of the plotters. It draws links between seemingly unconnected people, groups and incidents; alternative explanations and contradictory facts are dismissed or simply ignored. And what it lacks in quality of evidence, it tries to disguise through sheer *volume* of evidence. The effect is to overwhelm the reader – after a while, the natural reaction is to let your sceptical defences collapse and assume that at least *some* of it must be true. It's not simply a classic of the conspiracy genre: it set the template that many would follow.

To roughly condense 800-odd pages down to a few lines, Barruel's theory is that Jacobinism and the French Revolution were the end product of a decades-long conspiracy between three groups: the *philosophes* of the Enlightenment, the Freemasons and the Illuminati. Between them, he writes, 'in the name of their Equality and disorganising Liberty, they trampled underfoot the altar and the throne'. Each of the groups focused on a different branch of the conspiracy: the philosophers took aim at the religious order, the Freemasons targeted the monarchy, and the Illuminati worked to subvert the societal order as a whole.

Barruel is willing to grant that some of the participants in this supposed affair may have simply been misguided. But for the Illuminati, he has no such generosity, describing their moral degeneracy in sulphuric prose and introducing Weishaupt as follows: 'An odious phenomenon in nature, an Atheist void of remorse, a profound hypocrite, destitute of those superior talents which lead to the vindication of truth, he is possessed of all that energy and ardour in vice which generates conspirators for impiety and anarchy. Shunning, like the ill-boding owl, the genial rays of the sun, he wraps around him the mantle of darkness; and history shall record

of him, as of the evil spirit, only the black deeds which he
planned or executed.'

So, not a fan.

For all the vitriol thrown Weishaupt's way, though, the
book's main villain (if a book this sprawling can have such a
thing) is the great liberal thinker Voltaire – who Barruel
depicts as ultimately pulling the strings, setting plots in
motion, and directing the conspirators over the course of
decades. Now, Voltaire had been dead for eleven years by the
time the Revolution happened, so his alibi would seem fairly
solid. But the fact that Barruel casts him as the puppet-master
gives a hint of what he's really mad about.

Like Hoffmann and Starck (whose work he cites several
times) Barruel had been part of a Counter-Enlightenment
scene, centred around the periodical *Année littéraire*, which, for
years before the Revolution, had been spreading dire warnings
that the *philosophes* represented a conspiracy against religion
and monarchy.[10] This was less a conspiracy of shady meetings
in smoke-filled rooms, and more a conspiracy of ideas.
Specifically, ideas about society that went against Barruel's
vision of the natural order of things.

And even worse than coming up with these ideas in the first
place, it seemed, was the fact the philosophers attempted to
convince other people that those ideas were right. As the historian
Amos Hofman put it, Barruel's book is largely 'an attempt to
discredit "public politics", that is to say, politics based on the
support of public opinion'.[11] Barruel is explicitly opposed to
democracy – which he dismisses as 'the capricious fluctuations of
the multitude' – and he suggests the conspiracy was spread
through 'impious writings', by which the plotters would 'infuse
the poison of their writings into the minds of the people'.[12]

This all makes his theory a bit confusing, because he can't

seem to decide whether their crime was keeping their ideas hidden (as the Illuminati did) or making them public (as the philosophers did). In his second paragraph, he makes the remarkable claim that the conspiracy had two million supporters and 300,000 active agents in France at the time of the Revolution. That's more than seven per cent of the total population. Is it still a conspiracy if that many people are involved?

Naturally, because Barruel is also doing the 'assuming everyone I don't like is working together' thing, he completely ignores that many of the people he insists were conspiring didn't even agree with each other. (Voltaire, supposedly the architect of the decision to overturn the throne, actually supported a constitutional monarchy.) Enlightenment philosophy wasn't a defined political programme: it was more a rolling series of public arguments. If it had a common theme, it was simply expanding the category of things you could actually have public arguments *about*.

So Barruel's book, with its dire warnings of what the Illuminati did under that 'mantle of darkness', certainly set the template for centuries of theories about what people were getting up to behind closed doors. But really, the 'conspiracy' he was arguing against was any attempt to open those doors.

By contrast to Barruel's vast tome, Robison's *Proofs of a Conspiracy* is a shorter and slightly more focused work. Unlike the priest, the scientist Robison had been very much a creature of the Enlightenment. An eminent physicist, he'd been largely on board with the age's spirit of free enquiry until, plagued by ill-health and increasingly cranky in his later years, he turned against it. But those later years would see him leave his two lasting legacies on the world: in addition to helping to found the conspiracist view of history, at around the same time, he also invented the siren. Which is a brilliant thing to invent.

Like Barruel, Robison's main beef with the Illuminati is his opposition to their ideas, and their approach to spreading those ideas. He holds a conservative scepticism of utopian beliefs, a concern that revolution simply leads to chaos with no greener pastures on the far side, and an understandable fear of those who believe they are creating a society so perfect that any means would be justified to bring it about. He really doesn't like all this talk of equality, believing that such a 'dreadful equalisation' would permanently entitle 'the idle or unsuccessful' to strip 'the diligent' of the fruits of their labours.

A remarkably lengthy section is devoted to Robison's 'horror' at the Illuminati's proposal to involve women in their society, which he believes will lead to 'the corruption of the fair sex', and debase women from their natural role of being 'lovely'. As evidence, he points to the dreadful situation in France, in which women appear at the theatre, 'laying aside all modesty, and presenting themselves to the public view, with bared limbs'.

Aside from this denial of French women's right to bare arms, what's notable about Robison's book is that, for something titled *Proofs of a Conspiracy*, it is notably short on ... well, proofs of a conspiracy. As a sympathetic biographer would write a few years later, 'the alarm excited by the French Revolution had produced in Mr Robison a degree of credulity which was not natural to him', with the result that he took 'the slightest presumption as clear and irrefragable evidence'.[13] Large chunks of the book are cribbed uncritically from Hoffmann's partisan publications. Additionally, much of Robison's information came via Alexander Horn, a

Benedictine monk who was also a British secret agent, and whose surprisingly active social life led to one female acquaintance labelling him 'a good young man but a bad monk'.[14] Horn was a firm believer in the Illuminati theory, but sadly for Robison was perhaps not an entirely reliable source. 'It is difficult to persuade one's self,' wrote his biographer, 'that the original documents from which Mr Robison drew up his narrative were entitled to all the confidence which he reposed in them.'[15]

Robison ends with a call to 'discourage all secret assemblies' and reject any political notions that could stir in the populace 'hankerings after unattainable happiness' – a road that would inevitably lead to 'the vile tyranny of a profligate mob'. In this, he got at least part of his wish remarkably quickly.

A year after *Proofs* was published, the Irish Rebellion of 1798 spooked the British government into believing they could face a repeat of the events in France. So it passed the Unlawful Societies Act, banning groups like the United Irishmen outright, and outlawing any society in which members were required to take an oath or the list of members was kept secret. The text of the Act begins by warning that 'a traitorous Conspiracy has long been carried on ... [to overturn] every existing Establishment, Civil and Ecclesiastical, both in Great Britain and Ireland'. The conspiracy theory view of history had become embedded into law.

Robison was hardly alone in succumbing to credulity when faced with the massive upheavals that were occurring in France and beyond: the Age of Revolutions, which started in the late 1700s and continued into the first half of the nineteenth century, was a breeding ground for conspiracy theories of all kinds. For supporters of the status quo, it was inconceivable that such seismic shifts could be occurring without a guiding intelligence manipulating events – the idea that they might reflect genuine popular discontent was unthinkable. For those who looked to overthrow the old systems, every setback they faced might be a conspiracy, bolstering their paranoia and fuelling their cause – more proof of how powerful the establishment was, and of why revolution was necessary.

And so, the Indian Rebellion of 1857 against the rule of the British East India Company was long interpreted as a conspiracy by both opponents and supporters. (The historical evidence suggests that the leaders who supposedly planned it were actually taken by surprise, and in fact their first response was to try to stop it.)[16]

In Cuba, there were duelling theories over the 'Conspiracy of La Escalera' – a supposed plan for a slave revolt in 1844, which led to violent reprisals by the authorities known as 'the Year of the Lash'. One side argued the revolt was a real conspiracy; the other that it was a false flag used to justify repression. (The historical consensus says a revolt was indeed being planned, with the backing of an abolitionist British consul.)[17]

Such theories could have real consequences. One of the reasons Texas joined the United States when it did was because of a conspiracy theory spread by the pro-slavery Secretary of State John C. Calhoun. In 1844, with Texas newly independent from Mexico, Calhoun promoted a theory (based on little more than the paranoia of a former US consul in Jamaica) that the British were engineering slave revolts so that an influx of freed slaves into the American South would 'poison the minds of the Negroes' and spark a race war. Calhoun used this theory to stir up fears about emancipation in both Texas and Washington, convincing both sides to open secret negotiations to annex Texas into the Union.[18]

It's understandable that revolutions prompt conspiracy theories. Almost by definition, revolutions require *some* degree of coordination in order for them to happen. A load of angry people don't just turn up outside the Bastille one day simply by chance. And revolutionaries aren't wrong to believe that they are opposed by powerful forces; of course they are!

But the conspiracy theories of revolutions are a classic example of agenticity in action. They work backwards from effect to cause, seeing every event that may have led to an uprising as therefore having been *intended* to produce that result. They simplify complex situations down to the actions of a few key villains; they assume that domestic discontent must have been seeded by foreign powers; above all, they massively overestimate the extent to which chaotic events can be directed at all. No revolution is entirely unplanned; but no revolution is entirely planned, either.

Beyond that, there's also the same basic impulse that animated Barruel and Robison – a tendency to view your political opponents as inherently conspiratorial. If you scratch the surface of many conspiracy theories down the ages, underneath the dramatic accusations of secret meetings and hidden coordination, you'll often find a fundamental discomfort with the idea that people whose politics you disagree with appear to be actually trying to achieve their political goals. These theories both personify our anxieties about the direction of society, and cast our opponents' ideas as not just wrong, but as essentially illegitimate.

Both Robison and Barruel's books found a ready audience of people looking for exactly that. The first edition of *Proofs* sold out almost immediately; it went through four editions in total, a massive hit by the standards of the time. Barruel's theories were also widely cited, being reprinted in newspapers and repeated in sermons across the country. While it was far from universally accepted, for several years the Illuminati theory was given widespread credence, particularly in conservative and traditionalist circles.[19] Edmund Burke – who I think we're legally obliged to describe as 'the father of modern conservatism' – certainly appears to have bought into it. In a fan letter to Barruel, he pronounced himself 'delighted' by the first volume of *Memoirs*, praising the Abbé's proofs for their 'juridical regularity and exactness', and adding that he himself knew for a fact that several of the supposed conspirators had been working on the French plot for decades.[20]

Which prompts the obvious question: it may have been popular, but was any of it actually true?

Robison's book, as we've noted, was based on a slew of dodgy sources, as was evident even to a sympathetic biographer just a few years later. Barruel's book is likewise riddled with errors, evidence-free assertions and wild over-interpretations. No serious modern scholars now give it much credence as an actual historical description of the Revolution ('a farrago of nonsense' is how one historian of secret societies describes it).[21]

That's not limited to modern scholars. Even at the time, plenty of Barruel's contemporaries (including those who basically agreed with him politically) pointed out its flaws. Among others, *The Anti-Jacobin Review* – which probably can't be accused of harbouring secret pro-Jacobin sympathies – accused him of paranoia, and said that Barruel's theories were 'not warranted by the facts'. His claims were described as 'foolish' by Joseph de Maistre,[22] a leading opponent of the

Revolution and someone who, like Burke, is frequently described as a father of modern conservatism.[*]

Many of Barruel and Robison's assertions simply don't hold up. Both men have to deal with one fairly obvious objection – that the Illuminati literally didn't exist by the time the Revolution happened. Their solution is simple: the society did not collapse, it just went underground. They suggest it carried on in two ways: it was spread to France thanks to a 1787 visit to Paris by a prominent Illuminatus, Johann Joachim Christoph Bode, who planted the seeds of revolution; meanwhile, in the Holy Roman Empire, it was resurrected in the form of a front organisation called the German Union.

But the idea that Bode's Parisian trip was the wellspring of rebellion doesn't make the slightest sense. For one thing, Bode helpfully kept a secret diary, which was rediscovered in the twentieth century, and is notable for the complete lack of entries like: 'Plans for fomenting revolution going well; French Freemasonry now entirely converted to Illuminati principles.' His actual reason for visiting Paris was to try (unsuccessfully) to sort out one of the interminable petty squabbles in the Masonic world at the time.

Of course, Barruel and Robison can't really be faulted for not having read Bode's diaries – but there were plenty of critics who explained where they'd gone wrong at the time. Most notable was Jean Joseph Mounier, a centrist politician who played a key role in trying, unsuccessfully, to strike a compromise in the early days after the Revolution. He was well placed to judge the accuracy of the allegations, thanks to his courtside seat for several key events, and his acquaintance

---

[*] Yes, conservatism has two daddies.

with many of the supposed conspirators – for whom he held no particular fondness, after being forced to flee France in 1790. His conclusion was that it was piffle. 'To causes extremely complicated have been substituted simple causes, adapted to the capacity of the most indolent and superficial minds,' he wrote in 1801.[23]

Mounier points out that the real purpose of Bode's visit was well known to anybody familiar with Parisian Masonry, and that the individuals named in the theories either had nothing to do with the Illuminati, or nothing to do with the Revolution. Moreover, he makes clear that the conspiracy theory *didn't make any damn sense*. Bode had nothing to offer the people whose minds he supposedly turned. He couldn't tempt them with power or influence or jobs, because they were already the great and the good of Paris. Nor was he likely to impress the intellectuals of France with a philosophy that was little more than reheated Rousseau – indeed, the parts of Rousseau's theories that Mounier notes 'had not been fashionable for a long time'. The idea that Bode could spend a couple of weeks sipping coffee in the Café Procope, being all, 'Hey, you guys should do a revolution,' and the philosophers of Paris would suddenly be like, 'Oh shit, we hadn't thought of that – cool idea, thanks Germany,' is laughable.

The notion that the Illuminati continued under a front organisation, in the form of the German Union, doesn't hold up any better. The German Union was a real thing: the brainchild of a terrible theologian named Carl Friedrich Bahrdt, whose obnoxious personality had seen him forced out of a string of university jobs, and who'd managed the impressive feat of producing a translation of the Bible so unpopular that the supreme court of the Holy Roman Empire had banned him from ever publishing a work of theology again.

Trailing a string of unpaid debts and at least one pregnant mistress, his reputation so dire that people would literally cross themselves when they passed him in the street, Bahrdt was impoverished and reduced to running a pub when he hit upon a brilliant scheme to form a secret society: the German Union. Like the Illuminati, much of the business of this society would be devoted to reading the improving books of the Enlightenment. But there was an important twist: Bahrdt's vision of a perfect world was one in which a monopoly on printing those books would be held by ... Carl Friedrich Bahrdt. Ker-ching!

This was such a transparent scam that the German Union collapsed even quicker than the Illuminati had. It was also brought down in a very similar way, with an anonymous pamphlet published in early 1789 exposing all the society's secrets to the public. Bahrdt was arrested shortly afterwards.

This presents a few problems for the theory that the German Union was a continuation of the Illuminati, enabling them to direct the French Revolution. One is that the German Union *had also collapsed* by the time the crowds stormed the Bastille. Another is that we now know who wrote the anonymous pamphlet that brought down the German Union.[24] It was ... Johann Joachim Christoph Bode.

You can see the problem here, right? If Bode was the agent who continued the Illuminati's work, and the German Union was the front organisation for its continued existence, then why did the former expose the latter? It can be one or the other, but it can't be both, despite Barruel and Robison's claims.

Of course, you don't really need to debunk the details of the Illuminati conspiracy theories to see why they're wrong, because the fundamental point is that the Illuminati really weren't a revolutionary organisation. He may have been a pompous, secrecy-obsessed pedant with dictatorial tendencies, but Weishaupt was a gradualist, who believed that his ideal society was probably many centuries away – that, after all, was the whole point of the society in the first place.

As we'll see later, many subsequent conspiracy theories would claim that the Illuminati were the ideological forebears of every left-wing movement to spring up in the following centuries. But while Weishaupt was on the progressive side of his age, his particular slant on the intellectual interests of the Enlightenment was neither especially radical, nor terribly influential. In fact, in many ways, it was Weishaupt's *lack* of radicalism – his failure to imagine a future that could be very different to the society he lived in – that sowed the seeds of both his group's downfall and their subsequent legend.

As with many utopians, his liberal impulses were undermined by a controlling paternalism; humanity could not travel the road to perfection under its own light, but instead would need to be guided there by wiser minds (i.e. him). That's why he tried to play the system rather than challenge it, to exploit the closed networks of power and influence that were already starting to fray across much of Europe – the very thing that led to the backlash against them, and allowed the Illuminati to be painted as sinister manipulators. The problem was that Weishaupt was too much a product of the society he came from, not that he was too opposed to it.

This was a point made across the Atlantic by then US Vice President Thomas Jefferson in an 1800 letter to Bishop James Madison,* in which he suggests that Weishaupt's actions were

---

* Confusingly, not the same James Madison who would be president after Jefferson. The US had too many James Madisons.

a result of the fact that he 'lived under the tyranny of a despot & priests'. Jefferson writes: 'If Wishaupt [sic] had written here, where no secrecy is necessary in our endeavors to render men wise & virtuous, he would not have thought of any secret machinery for that purpose.' [25]

Jefferson was writing because the US had become gripped by a flurry of Illuminati panic. Accusations were hurled back and forth across the political spectrum; the preacher and geographer Jedediah Morse railed against the Illuminati, and was accused in return of being Illuminati himself.[26] Jefferson was also accused of being a member, which must have come as something of a surprise – as his letter makes clear, the first he'd heard of the Illuminati was when he read Barruel's book, which he dismissed as 'the ravings of a Bedlamite'.

The American Illuminati panic was an example of how far the conspiracy theory had spread. But it was also one of the final outbreaks of its first wave. The works of Barruel and Robison had set a template for what was to come: for much of the nineteenth century, conspiracy theory would be a central part of how many people analysed politics. But the Illuminati theory itself would go quiet for quite some time – cropping up every now and then as an explanation of some event or other, but never making much of a stir. More sceptical voices appeared to have won the argument. Meanwhile, the rise of Napoleon had given Europe other things to worry about. Realistically, it's a bit harder to get worked up about the machinations of Bavarian law professors when the Grande Armée is marching down your street. For a long time, the Illuminati conspiracy theory seemed like it might become little more than a quirky footnote in history.

It didn't. The theory would be revived more than a century later, and would become more influential than Weishaupt,

Barruel or Robison could have ever dreamed. But that's a story for a later chapter. Instead, next we'll consider the other side of the phrase 'Beyoncé is Illuminati'. We need to talk about celebrities.

4

The Faults in Our Stars

You've probably never heard of William Campbell, but you've definitely heard his songs. 'Hey Jude' – that was a big one. 'Lady Madonna', that was another. 'Get Back', 'Let it Be', 'The Long and Winding Road' ... There were plenty more after he went solo – no one thinks they were as good, but even now you'd be lucky to make it through December without hearing 'Wonderful Christmastime' a good twenty or thirty times.

You'd recognise Campbell too, even if you didn't know his name. (There's actually some debate over that: he's also known as William Shears Campbell.) That's because he's the guy who, for well over half a century now, has performed under the name 'Paul McCartney'.

This is not just a stage name, to be clear: David Bowie may have started out life as David Jones, but the real Paul McCartney was always Paul McCartney. Billy Shears, as he might also be called, is not the real Paul McCartney, because the real Paul McCartney died in a car crash in November 1966. And so, mere days after the first Doctor Who, William

Hartnell, regenerated into Patrick Troughton, Paul
McCartney regenerated into William Campbell. Or Billy
Shears. Or possibly William Shears Campbell. Over the years
that followed, as the Beatles moved into their more experimental phase and produced some of their most famous songs,
fans could be forgiven for wondering whether Paul
McCartney had actually been that much of a loss.

If we seem to be glib about this, it's because a) the whole
thing is quite obviously a load of old Rutles, and b) Paul
McCartney – who is confident he didn't die in 1966 – has
been cheerily making jokes about it for two-thirds of his life.
Nonetheless, for a few weeks in 1969, the story of his 'death'
and the cover-up that followed was all over the world's music
press. And trawling through the 'clues' has been a fun pastime
for Beatles fans ever since.[1]

The story goes like this. In September 1969, the Drake
Times-Delphic, the student newspaper of Drake University,
Iowa, published an article with the headline, 'Is Beatle Paul
McCartney dead?' Its author, nineteen-year-old Tim Harper,
claims he wasn't a conspiracy theorist, or even, really, a Beatles
fan: he had just heard people discussing the rumour on
campus and decided it would make a good story.

His article outlined a whole load of 'evidence' that something terrible had happened to Paul roughly three years
previously. It noted that, at the foot of the *Sgt. Pepper's Lonely
Hearts Club Band* album cover, there lies a left-handed guitar,
of the sort McCartney would have played, on a sort of grave.
On the gatefold photograph, McCartney is wearing a black
armband featuring the letters 'OPD' – 'officially pronounced
dead'. On the back cover, he has his back to the camera, while
the other three look forward; George Harrison appears to be
pointing to the lyric 'Wednesday morning at five o'clock',
representing the time of death. The next Beatles album

released in the US was *Magical Mystery Tour*, on which three of the Beatles are dressed in grey walrus suits. The fourth is in black. 'The walrus is supposedly the Viking symbol of death,' Harper wrote.

That 'supposedly' is doing a lot of heavy lifting.

That may well have been that – it was just one article, after all – except that on 12 October 1969, Russ Gibb was hosting a show on a Detroit radio station when a caller phoned in to discuss the rumours with the world. He suggested playing the opening to 'Revolution 9' – the long, wordy, deeply unmusical interlude that people have been skipping on the White Album ever since it first appeared in 1968 – backwards. Suddenly the refrain of 'number nine' was reconstituted as something that, if you do the aural equivalent of squinting, sounds a bit like: 'Turn me on, dead man.' Which, if you do the *mental* equivalent of squinting, could be taken as a reference to the fact that someone involved in the Beatles was now dead.

Over the next few hours, Gibb discussed the rumour with callers, and found more clues, such as Lennon using the closing moments of 'Strawberry Fields Forever' to intone the words 'I buried Paul'. Two days later, another student newspaper, the *Michigan Daily*, ran another article under the headline 'McCartney Dead; New Evidence Brought to Light'. Most of that evidence came from the recently released *Abbey Road* album, whose famous cover shows the four Beatles using the pedestrian crossing outside the recording studio.* Paul is out of step with

---

* An early proposed title for the album had been *Everest*. It's a mark of how well things were going inside the band at this point that they decided they didn't want to travel further than the street outside the studio for their cover image photoshoot, and named the album accordingly.

the others, and barefoot, like he'd be in a coffin. The other three were all said to be dressed in the manner of a funeral procession: John in white like a preacher, Ringo in black like a mourner, George in denim like a gravedigger.

As the rumour spread, it gradually coalesced into something resembling a coherent story, constructed by taping together a load of otherwise disconnected Beatles lyrics. On one 'stupid bloody Tuesday' in November 1966, McCartney had 'blown his mind out in a car'. The surviving three had decided – rather rapidly, it must be said – to hush up the story, ensuring that 'Wednesday morning's papers didn't come'. To prevent public grief, they'd recast McCartney with the winner of a Paul McCartney lookalike competition. The opening track to their next album, *Sgt. Pepper*, concludes with the words, 'So let me introduce to you, the one and only Billy Shears'. The fact it was McCartney singing those words, and the character introduced as Billy Shears was played by Ringo, didn't seem to bother anybody.

In fact, several of the clues don't stack up, even on their own merits. Priests in England do not dress in white; gravediggers do not wear denim. The car numberplate on the cover to *Abbey Road* reading '28IF' was interpreted as a sign that Paul would have been twenty-eight years old, *if* he were still alive (he was actually twenty-seven – and also not dead). The 'officially pronounced dead' badge on Paul's uniform on the cover to Sgt Pepper actually read 'OPP', meaning Ontario Provincial Police, because it was one of their badges. And in the closing moments of 'Strawberry Fields Forever', John Lennon is definitely saying 'cranberry sauce', rather than 'I buried Paul' (although if no one ever argued this meant John had trussed Paul up like a turkey, we'd be amazed). More than that, recasting a band member with a lookalike is one thing.

Finding someone who sounds like the guy too, and will follow in his footsteps as one of the greatest songwriters of all time, seems just a tad unlikely.

By the end of October 1969, things had got so out of hand that the Beatles' label, Apple Records, was being bombarded with calls asking if one of the band was dead, and their press officer Derek Taylor was giving increasingly exasperated interviews explaining that, no, he wasn't. Eventually, *Life* magazine tracked the very-much-alive Paul down to his farm in the west of Scotland, where he was hanging out with his wife Linda and their growing family. The resulting interview made a cover story with the headline, 'Paul is still with us'.[2] The world was so obsessed with the question of whether or not McCartney was dead that it entirely missed the fact that he used the same interview to announce that the band had split up. That somehow remained under wraps for another six months.

There may be several reasons why this story caught fire, one of which is surely *when* it emerged. In the closing months of a decade that had brought assassinations, riots and the draft, US college campuses had become very paranoid places, beset by a sense that young and old were on different sides. If the government could lie about something as big as the Vietnam War, why would Apple Records hesitate to lie about the exact line-up of a band?

Another explanation is one we'll encounter again and again: not everyone who wrote articles discussing the 'evidence', or phoned into radio stations to discuss it, seriously believed a word of it. It was a laugh, a game, an attempt to fool the credulous. In a memoir for *Rolling Stone*, the novelist Richard Price tells of calling a radio phone-in to ask, 'You know what eighty-four per cent of all the coffins in England are made of? It might even be eighty-seven per cent ... Norwegian Wood.' The fact 'Norwegian Wood' was produced over a year before McCartney's 'death' didn't matter. Price was making it up.[3]

But perhaps there's another reason the story caught on, which wasn't about the mood of the times, or the urge to cause trouble, or even, particularly, about Paul McCartney. Perhaps it was because of the function played by celebrities.

Humans have always told ourselves stories in an attempt to explain the world, and conspiracy theories are just one version of that. The thing about stories, though, is that they need *characters*.

In older times, the explanatory stories we told ourselves certainly had characters: they were the mythic pantheons of gods and heroes, and the dramatic twists in the soap opera of their lives had effects in the mortal world. Why did a thunderstorm happen? Thor was having an argument. Why did the crops fail? Osiris was displeased with the quality of rituals lately, and we need another temple.

Modern conspiracy theories often have a very similar quality to these ancient tales of bickering gods. They try to explain events in the world around us by saying they're the result of the actions of distant, all-powerful individuals with inscrutable motives and a penchant for the dramatic. But for these kind of tales to work best, for them to spread far and resonate with many, they need a widely recognisable cast of characters. 'You know who's behind all these floods recently? It's Gary,' doesn't really work if the most common response you get is, 'Who's Gary?'[*]

---

[*] Fucking Gary.

Hardly surprising, then, that many conspiracy theories feature a famous face as their lead character. Some of these people seem to attract conspiracies like a flame attracts moths. Who created this global pandemic? Why, it's Bill Gates, the man who made your computer update itself a lot over the course of several decades. Who's giving the marching orders to every social-justice movement, from Black Lives Matter to trans rights? Naturally, it's famous 1990s currency speculator George Soros. Figures like Gates and Soros crop up again and again in conspiracist lore, which rivals Hollywood for its propensity to recycle storylines and bring back villains for the sequel, even if it doesn't make any sense from a plot point of view.

This need for a shared cast means that conspiracy theories often swirl around celebrities, because – by definition – they're the figures that most people know about. Granted, our modern celebrities may lack some of the more impressive powers of their counterparts from the pantheons of old. Very few have been responsible for the outcomes of wars; almost none have the power to make the harvest fail. Chris Hemsworth almost certainly can't control actual thunder, no matter how impressive his abs are.

But still, when *Guardian* columnist Marina Hyde coined the term 'Wagnarok' to describe the Instagram-based detective drama between footballers' wives Colleen Rooney and Rebekah Vardy, it was more than a nice pun: there is a sense in which celebrities now fill a narrative role once played by gods and heroes.[4] This particular use of the word 'star', after all, originates in the idea that those who left the realm of man to become immortal would reside in the heavens. In his poetry, Ovid writes about how Julius Caesar, declared a god by the Roman Senate, later appeared in the sky as a comet;[5]

more than a dozen centuries later, Geoffrey Chaucer coined the verb 'to stellify' to describe such an ascent. In this sense, stars quite literally inhabit the realm once occupied by the gods.[6]

Of course, most of the time we don't use the term 'conspiracy theory' when talking about the private lives of our favourite – or least favourite – celebrities. We normally just call it 'gossip'. But, as with its close cousin rumour, the lines between gossip and conspiracy theory can be a little fuzzy sometimes, and what may start as the former can, over time, grow into actual conspiracism. Both can be seen as forms of 'improvised news', filling a demand for information where reality has not supplied enough to satisfy our cravings, and both play important roles in how we understand our world.

Sometimes we obsess about celebrities' personal lives for fun; sometimes, there are other motives. Jennifer Aniston and Brad Pitt broke up over a decade and a half ago. Yet, as late as January 2020, *Vogue* writer Michelle Ruiz could look at a photo showing Pitt clutching Aniston's wrist as she walked away from him, and use it as the basis for a 'deep dive' into 'our obsession' with the relationship. 'I want Pitt to want Aniston,' she wrote, 'but ... I do not want her to want him back.' In her telling, Aniston had been recast as the every-woman, who deserved to beat her no-good cheating husband by moving on more successfully than he did. The fact she was not, in fact, the girl next door, but one of the most desirable women on the planet, is a reminder we are not dealing with mortals here.

At any rate, Ruiz argues, the world's decades-long obsession did not result merely from the glamour of celebrity soap opera. It was because those involved were not simply people any more: they were symbols, of our hopes and fears for ourselves and our friends. Where those looking for archetypes and shared stories once needed gods and heroes to provide the canvas through which universal themes could be explored and discussed, now we have the celebrity gossip pages to do much the same.[7]

So when fans began to fear that Paul McCartney had died and been replaced by an imposter, it wasn't just some bloke from Liverpool they were really worried about. It meant something more.

Something did change in the Beatles in 1966, but it wasn't the identity of the man they called Paul McCartney. In the first few years of their fame, they'd been a pop band, churning out two-minute songs with titles like 'I Want to Hold Your Hand'. Sure, they had more hair than their fans' parents might have liked, but they also wore suits and turned up on the *Ed Sullivan Show* or cracked jokes at the *Royal Variety Performance*. Compared to a lot of youth culture, they were unthreatening.

But 1966 was the year all that changed. In March, there was the infamous interview in which John Lennon said the band was more popular than Jesus: when the comments were picked up in the United States several months later, radio stations stopped playing their songs and their records were publicly burned. The band received death threats that summer in the Philippines, too, and – feeling that maybe this wasn't fun any more – decided to stop touring. Instead, they stayed in the studio, making increasingly psychedelic music that would never have worked live anyway. At the same time, they let their hair grow and, let's be honest, took a lot of drugs. As Bob Dylan is reputed to have said, when McCartney played him 'Tomorrow Never Knows', the last and weirdest song on the band's 1966 album *Revolver*: 'Oh, I get it. You don't want to be cute any more.'

Perhaps this is why the 'Paul is dead' theory got traction; why some were willing to believe the jokes had at their root something real. Fans had believed the Beatles to be one thing, a cuddly sort of boy band, then watched as, before their eyes, they became something more interesting, but more threatening, too. Perhaps the conspiracy theory was simply a very literal explanation for why the Beatles of 1969 were so different from the Beatles of 1963: they literally weren't the same people.

As to why it should be McCartney that the rumours had focused on, perhaps it was chance: there really had been rumours of a crash on the M1 involving McCartney in the winter of 1966–7, which a fanzine had felt obliged to rebut at the time. Or perhaps, as the Oxford English professor Diane Purkiss has suggested, it was because Paul was the one 'approved of by mothers'.[8] She compared the hoax to the myth of the 'changeling', a lookalike left by fairies in place of a real, kidnapped child. In the late 1960s, she said, 'I suspect lots of parents felt their own children had become strangers to them.' The 'Paul is dead' myth 'was a way for parents and teenagers to negotiate the feelings created by the new estrangement'. It had to be Paul, because he was the one parents might have been willing to recognise as their own in the first place.

Whatever the reason, the real McCartney had the last laugh. In 1993, he released a live album called *Paul Is Live*, whose cover featured the grinning singer being dragged across the Abbey Road crossing by a dog. In April 2019, Russ Gibb, the Michigan DJ who had done so much to spread the story, died, aged eighty-seven. McCartney had outlived him.

* * *

There's another reason to think there must be some deeper psychological explanation for the appeal of the 'Paul is Dead' myth: rumours of celebrity imposters have attached to dozens of other celebrities down the years. The 'Doppelganger and Identity Research Society' message board has been running since 2008, and includes lengthy threads with titles like (we're copying the punctuation exactly here) 'Sheryl Crow Was Killed on April 3, 1996', 'GOODBYE CHARLIE SHEEN', 'Marianne Faithful, Yes Even her!' Slight changes in appearance are taken – with, presumably, varying degrees of seriousness – as clues that a popular actress has been replaced by a double, a fake, referred to as, say, a Fegan or a Fangelina – rather than, say, a testament to the powers of good make-up or Hollywood's best plastic surgeons.[9]

Elsewhere on the internet, similar rumours have been attached to Miley Cyrus (who was replaced by her former body double after dying of an overdose and/or being killed by a corporation in 2010); Eminem (whose lengthy writers' block before 2009's *Relapse* is explained by the fact he'd died in a car crash organised by the Illuminati, who went on to replace him with a clone more amenable to the New World Order); or Taylor Swift (who may in fact be the clone of one Zeena Lavey, born in 1963, daughter of the founder of the Church of Satan, on the grounds that she looks a bit like her, but, let's be honest, probably isn't).[10]

The Paul McCartney Memorial Award for Celebrity Considered Most Likely to be Secretly Dead, however, must go to Avril Lavigne, whose passing was first mooted by a Brazilian fan page back in 2011. The Canadian singer, so the theory goes, fell into depression after the death of her grandfather, and died by suicide in 2003, having released just one album. This was obviously an inconvenience to a record company that had put a lot of effort into making people believe that skate punk was a thing,* so it persuaded her friend and body double Melissa Vandella to take her place.[11]

As the years have gone on, however, the guilt has taken its toll on Melissa, and so she's been dropping clues, such as changing her dress sense, or writing tell-tale lyrics in songs like 'Slipped Away' ('The day you slipped away/was the day I found it won't be the same'), or – bit obvious, this one – writing the word 'Melissa' on her hand. All of this is intended as a message to the fans, snuck past the greedy record company executives, to tell them that Avril is not who they think.

The funny thing is that the blog that originally put forward the 'Avril is dead' theory – a Blogspot with the do-we-really-need-to-translate-this-name of 'Avril Esta Morta'[12] – opened with the line, *'Esse blog foi uma forma de mostrar como teorias da conspiração podem parecer verdadeiras'*: 'This blog was created to show how conspiracy theories can look true.' It was part of a network of similar blogs, making similar cases regarding the death and replacement of Miley Cyrus, Selena Gomez, and – yes – Paul McCartney. These weren't a serious attempt to spread the idea that these various celebrities were dead: they were consciously and openly fictitious.

At first, Avril Esta Morta was taken in the spirit it was intended: the theory became a sort of in-joke on the Brazilian internet, but, since relatively few people can read Portuguese,

---

* One of the authors, who had a giant Avril Lavigne poster on their kitchen wall and also owned an Avril-branded skinny tie, would like to make it clear here that skate punk absolutely *was* a thing. The other would like to respond: nerd.

never made it any further. But then in 2015, Ryan Broderick, an American writer working for BuzzFeed, decided to tweet about it. One result was that a lot of Avril Lavigne fans were suddenly extremely angry with Ryan Broderick. Another was write-ups in titles including *Gawker* and *Vice*, and thousands upon thousands of social media shares.[13]

Each time the theory was repeated, it mutated a little, often in a way that moved it a little further from the crucial 'this thing is not actually true' stuff. And some fans, who wanted to believe they possessed secret knowledge of their heroine, took it seriously.

By 2019, the skate punk singer was just as dead as Paul McCartney.

If the world seems determined to prove that very-much-alive people are dead/lookalikes/clones/replicants, it's no less determined to prove that those commonly understood to be dead are actually still walking about. Elvis Presley has been spotted everywhere from Memphis International Airport on the day of his death, supposedly buying a ticket to Buenos Aires, to the background of a crowded airport scene in the movie *Home Alone*, to a 1984 photograph with Muhammad Ali.* All these sightings have been debunked: despite its name, there weren't any international flights from Memphis International in 1977;† even if you buy the idea that Presley might have

---

* It doesn't help that somebody got his name wrong on his tombstone, calling him Elvis Aaron Presley, rather than Elvis Aron Presley. It's like they wanted these rumours to spread.
† This is not as crazy as it sounds. Stratford International station in east London opened in 2009. At the time of writing, it has never been served by an international train.

decided to hide out in the background scene of a massive, internationally released Christmas movie, the extra was later identified as Gary Richard Grott;* the man in the photograph with Ali was later identified as sports agent Larry Kolb (although Ali reportedly didn't help the fact by identifying him to an interviewer as 'my friend Elvis').[14]

Other celebrities for whom rumours of their continuing life have been greatly exaggerated include Jim Morrison, Michael Jackson, Princess Diana and Kurt Cobain. Tupac Shakur was shot in Las Vegas in 1996 and died six days later, aged just twenty-five, but both the murder of his bitter rival Biggie Smalls a few months later, and the fact Tupac has somehow managed to release more albums dead than alive, have led some to believe he is alive and well and quite possibly living in Cuba.[15]

That anyone would believe a living celebrity had died and been replaced by a doppelganger is strange and unnerving and difficult to explain. That anyone would believe a dead celebrity was still alive is altogether more comprehensible. If we see celebrities as archetypes or avatars, characters in a story rather than flesh-and-blood people, then a normal, mundane human death doesn't feel like enough. The idea that Elvis died on the toilet, fat and depressed in early middle age, lacks the grandeur his rags-to-riches story seems to require: it doesn't *fit*, for the same reason that the notion that a lone assassin could wipe out Camelot doesn't fit.

---

* In 2016, a flurry of news websites breathlessly reported the *Home Alone* bit of the story, including the fascinating detail that the name of Macaulay Culkin's character, Kevin McCallister, is an anagram of the phrase 'I, Mr Elvis, act'. Not all of them seemed to have noticed that this was only true if you removed five letters, which is not actually how anagrams work.

There's another, even simpler, reason why so many fans would convince themselves their favourite singer was still alive: no one wants their heroes to be dead. Nobody wants to say goodbye.

Let's leave aside matters of life and death for the moment, and consider an altogether more important question: has Katy Perry been trying to lure the youth of America away from Christianity by publicly performing a series of rituals intended to honour the Illuminati and/or Satan? The evidence is compelling.[16]

Firstly: Perry is clearly aware of what the righteous, Christian, properly American path looks like. She was raised in a strict, born-again Christian household in which her mother called devilled eggs 'angelled eggs' and refused to let her children eat Lucky Charms breakfast cereal because the word 'lucky' reminded her of Lucifer. Perry also began her career as a gospel singer.

However, she only attained commercial success when she released her 2008 bi-curious anthem 'I Kissed a Girl'. The chorus of that song includes its title followed by the damning words 'and I liked it', in a quite frankly shameless transparent attempt to lure other impressionable young people to follow her away from the path of light.

Furthermore, in 2010, Perry married Russell Brand – *Russell Brand* – in a traditional Hindu ceremony. Not Christian, you note, but Hindu. In 2013, she released her fifteenth single 'Dark Horse', along with an Ancient Egyptian-themed video presenting her as Katy Pätra, the witch of Memphis. In it, she dismisses and disintegrates a series of would-be suitors, all the while surrounded by Illuminati imagery including the all-seeing eye, pyramids and birdcages, a symbol of mind-control, worn by the witch's blue-skinned slaves.

She also turns a man into a dog.

Additionally, Perry performed 'Dark Horse' at the 2014 Grammys, emerging from a bubble into a smoke-filled landscape of dead trees, dressed in robes, surrounded by backing dancers who were also dressed in robes, as well as mysterious horned figures, all of whom ended the song dancing around upturned brooms before the stage suddenly ignited. The conspiracy website Infowars covered the performance in a story with the headline 'ILLUMINATI PRIESTESS CONDUCTS WITCHCRAFT CEREMONY IN FRONT THE ENTIRE WORLD'. Infowars is very trustworthy and in no way unhinged.

Most damningly, when *Rolling Stone* asked Perry about all this the following August, she *didn't even deny it*. Instead, she replied, 'Listen, if the Illuminati exist, I would love to be invited! ... I want to be in the club!' The magazine headlined the subsequent story, 'Katy Perry: I Want to Join the Illuminati!'

Perry was still being dogged by such headlines half a decade later, when she attended the 2019 Met Gala in a red veil with the word 'witness' sewn into it in black material. 'Witness to what?' asked the YouTuber The Christian Truther in a video titled, 'Anti-Christian Katy Perry Embraces Satanic Beltane Ritual'. The same commentator noted that the 't' in 'witness' looked a lot like a cross, almost as if the anti-Christian and Satanic Katy Perry was mocking Jesus.*

And so on, and so on.

---

* On the upside, from the Christian right's perspective, the video for 'Dark Horse' also features a man wearing a pendant that seems to read 'Allah' in Arabic script, whom Katy Pätra cheerfully turns into sand, thus suggesting that the Witch of Memphis isn't all that sold on Islam, either.

To be fair to the conspiracists, Perry clearly did make a conscious choice early on in her career to move away from her Christian roots and begin selling herself on her own sexuality. And her videos and performances have clearly traded on distinctly pagan imagery. (Honestly, that Grammys performance is eerily reminiscent of that scene in *Harry Potter and the Goblet of Fire* where the death eaters resurrect Voldemort. Only sexier.)

But pop stars have been playing with such imagery for almost as long as there have been pop stars to do anything. The symbols in the 'Dark Horse' video are not Illuminati, merely Ancient Egyptian. As to what Perry was claiming to be a 'witness' to at the Met Gala in 2019, the obvious answer is 'her most recent studio album, which was called *Witness*'. She was also five days late for Beltane, which must raise some questions about the efficacy of any Satanic ritual held on 6 May.

Perry is far from alone in being linked to the Illuminati, of course. An incomplete list of other celebrities who've at some point been accused of links to that shadowy and currently non-existent body include Beyoncé, Jay-Z, Tom Hanks, Kim Kardashian, Lady Gaga, Rihanna, Lebron James, Lindsay Lohan, Selena Gomez, Jessie J, Madonna and the cast of *Boy Meets World*. What many of these people have in common, with the possible exceptions of Tom Hanks and the cast of *Boy Meets World*, are confident expressions of sexuality and consumerism. Their actual views on the perfectibility of humanity, the cultural debates of the late eighteenth century Germanic Enlightenment, and the philosophy of Jean-Jacques Rousseau are somewhat less clear; furthermore, it's debatable whether Adam Weishaupt would even have let them join, or whether he would have taken issue with their manners or their walk.*

As with the moral panics around video games, rock music, jazz music, the birth of the novel, or, if you go back far enough, chess, dice and chariot racing, what is really on show here is a panic that young people's social and moral development might be influenced by someone other than their parents or other traditional authority figures.[17] The fear that pop music is the domain of Satanists or the Illuminati is really the fear of the power that cultural figures have, of a generation gap, of the limits to our control over our children.

Although where Tom Hanks fits into that is anybody's guess.

Anyway. That's enough about pop starlets pushed by the music industry into trading on their own sexuality. Let's talk about Britney.

Comedians Barbara Gray and Tess Barker launched the podcast *Britney's Gram* in 2017, with the intention of over-analysing the selfies, videos and other apparently random pictures Britney Spears posted to her Instagram. They'd meant it as a light-hearted, fun sort of a podcast: its tagline was 'the happiest place on the internet'.

But by early 2019, there were signs that all was not well in Britneyworld. The previous October, at the launch event for her new Las Vegas residency, the singer rose out of a stage accompanied by fireworks, and then ... walked off and got into a car. In January, she announced an 'indefinite work hiatus' after her father Jamie was rushed to hospital with a near-fatal colon rupture. On her Instagram, all was silence.

---

* He would probably have let in the ones he fancied, let's be honest. John Robison would have had a fit about all the bare arms.

Which was probably quite annoying if you were trying to make a weekly podcast about it.

And then, on 4 April 2019, three months into the shut-down, there was contact. It wasn't a photograph, just magenta text on a pinkish background (in, it must be said, an upsetting range of fonts). 'FALL IN LOVE WITH TAKING CARE OF YOURSELF, MIND, BODY, SPIRIT,' it said. The accompanying caption read, 'We all need to take time for a little "me time." :)'

The community of people who hung out on Britney's Instagram page, listened to the podcast and otherwise dedi-cated a significant part of their brains to thinking about Britney Spears was thrown into chaos. People started franti-cally exchanging texts, as the surprise and excitement of a post was replaced almost instantly by an inescapable feeling that *something wasn't right*. As Gray said on the emergency podcast recorded that evening, 'It was one of those things where unless you're in as deep as we are, you're like, what the fuck?'[18]

What was wrong with the post? For one thing, there was the punctuation. 'Me time' was in quote marks; the sentence ended in a full stop. Britney's posts were usually more casual: she may have been a pop superstar of twenty years' standing, but the joy of her Instagram was that she posted like half the girls you went to school with. The language in this post, by contrast, was just a little too perfect.

Then there was what Barker referred to as 'the emoticon heard around the world'. Britney's posts were generally peppered with emojis, teeny tiny letter-sized cartoons. Instead, she'd used an emoticon, a smiley face made of punctuation marks, common in a much earlier phase of the internet. 'There's no conceivable reality to me in which Britney Jean

Spears, in the year of our Lord 2019, types "colon parenthesis" when she wants to put a happy face,' said Barker.

The result of all this was a post that looked exactly like the sort of thing that Britney Spears would post to her Instagram feed, unless you were the sort of person who obsessed over Britney Spears' Instagram feed, in which case everything about it felt very slightly wrong. It fell down the uncanny valley. It was so similar to her other posts, said Barker, 'but something's not quite right. It's more disturbing because it's closer to reality.'

Half an hour later, TMZ broke the news that Spears had checked herself into a mental health facility because of the stress of her father's illness. She was understood to have been there for about a week.[19] The Instagram post was clearly intended to explain this news before it broke, to reassure fans everything was fine – but since the post was littered with tell-tale signs that someone else had written it, it had inadvertently done the opposite.

There was another reason to suspect that someone else was impersonating Britney on the internet. The singer's 2007 breakdown – during which the star shaved her head and attacked a photographer's car with an umbrella – looks, in retrospect, like a fairly understandable reaction to both the collapse of her marriage and the fact she could not set foot in public without a small army of paparazzi taking photos of her from odd angles. But the result had been that a court had ruled Britney unfit to care for herself, and placed her into a legal structure called a conservatorship. By 2019, the singer had spent a dozen years unable to make decisions about her work, her finances, her PR, even her personal life, without the agreement of court-appointed conservators.

By definition, somebody else would have had to check Britney into a mental health facility. Now, somebody else was online, pretending to be Britney.

And so what had once been a light-hearted podcast obsessively dissecting a pop star's Instagram posts began to ask a far darker question: was Britney Spears essentially being held prisoner by the conservatorship?

The next day, the hashtag #FreeBritney began to trend.

Shortly after the emergency episode, the podcast received a voicemail from a man identifying himself as a former paralegal who had worked on the conservatorship. He claimed the podcasters had been spot on: that the singer had agreed to a legal mechanism designed primarily for elderly people and others whose decline was unlikely to go into reverse, without realising that it gave her no exit ramp. Now, he suggested, there was a mini-industry who had a financial interest in keeping Britney inside that mechanism. In other words, it was using conservatorship to control the finances and limit the personal autonomy of a perfectly functional adult woman.[20]

In the months that followed, the Free Britney movement attracted support from everyone from Cher to Paris Hilton to the American Civil Liberties Union, and fans began protesting court hearings about the conservatorship. Jamie Spears dismissed them as 'conspiracy theorists'. But the following September, the singer filed for release from the mechanism. In a matter of weeks, her father had been suspended from his role as conservator; on 12 November 2021, the arrangement was terminated altogether. Britney was freed.

Two things are worth noting about this story. One is that it follows the logic of so many other conspiracies: shadowy forces following their own sinister agenda; the truth revealed by secret symbols, invisible to most but obvious to the initiated; confirmations by anonymous sources.

The other is that those who claimed to be able to see those secret signals turned out to be bang on the money.

This shouldn't have been surprising: after all, just because the gossip swirling around a celebrity seems deranged, that doesn't mean it isn't true. Rumours had circulated that there was something creepy about the English DJ and television presenter Jimmy Savile for, quite literally, decades. As far back as the 1970s, he was making uncomfortable jokes of the 'She told me she was over sixteen' variety, and in 2000, the documentary-maker Louis Theroux asked him outright if he was a paedophile.[21] Everyone had heard the jokes: everyone knew that Savile, in the absolutely most generous of readings, had a taste for inappropriately young partners. But he was a prominent media figure, who had been knighted in 1990, so perhaps there was smoke without fire. No personal friend of Margaret Thatcher could have really been a child abuser, surely?

Savile died in October 2011. Just under a year later, ITV broadcast *Exposure: The Other Side of Jimmy Savile*, in which several women said he had abused them while they were still teenagers. By December, the number of alleged victims stood in the hundreds. Some had been as young as five.

The rumours had been accurate. They had, if anything, understated the scale of Savile's crimes. The thing that everybody 'knew' but nobody could prove had turned out to be true. The wiser-headed sensible sorts who'd implied that nothing so appalling could possibly have happened in plain sight had been wrong.

It's in the nature of things that most conspiracy theories

aren't true, and the more ridiculous the rumour, the more likely it is to be false. But that isn't an iron law of nature. People do bad things; unlikely things do sometimes happen. Paul wasn't really dead; but Britney really wasn't free.

5

Assassin Screed

G ermanicus was dying. This much he knew.

But he was dying gradually, in fits and starts, as a slow poison worked its pernicious way through his body. For a while, he would seem to be recovering; then he would decline again, and the inevitability of his demise would reassert itself. All in all, it took Germanicus – a commander in the Roman army, adopted son and presumptive heir of the Emperor Tiberius, one of the most famous people in the Empire, and a man with many equally famous enemies – almost a month to die. He finally passed away just outside Antioch in October of the year 19 CE. His skin was discoloured, and he would foam at the mouth, but he remained lucid to the end, able to talk to the distraught relatives and allies surrounding his deathbed.

Thanks to these very particular circumstances, Germanicus holds the questionable distinction of being one of the very few people in history who managed to start a conspiracy theory about their own death. In fact, he didn't just start one: he started two, because Germanicus was a messy bitch who lived for drama. To his comrades who'd gathered to hear his last words, he publicly blamed Piso – the governor of Syria, with whom he'd had a long-running and extremely petty feud ever since Tiberius had dispatched Germanicus to sort out the eastern part of his empire. But to his wife, in private, he suggested that he feared Tiberius himself was actually behind the poisoning: that this had all been a scheme to get rid of an heir whose popularity the emperor had grown to see as a threat.

These duelling conspiracy theories provoked uproar across much of the Empire, and news of his death was greeted by riots in Rome. Piso was eventually put on trial for conspiring against Germanicus; he died before the trial was over, found in a locked room with his throat slit and a sword by his side. Maybe he had taken his own life before justice could be done. Or maybe he was conveniently got rid of, before he could implicate someone more powerful.

Who actually killed Germanicus? Piso? Tiberius? Piso on the orders of Tiberius? Someone else entirely? We're sorry to say that without the invention of time travel, we'll never know.* The truth is lost in the messy narratives and counter-narratives of history. But the most likely answer is almost certainly 'none of the above' – living as he did in the time before modern medicine, the most plausible answer is that he simply died of some unknown disease. Also, much of this particular narrative is based on the histories written by Tacitus, whose track record when it comes to factual accuracy is occasionally a little patchy. It's certain that Germanicus

---

* Now we think about it, the invention of time travel would also introduce an almost infinite number of new potential suspects, so it's not clear that even that would be of much help.

died, that Piso was widely suspected of poisoning him by the Roman public, and that he was tried for crimes against Germanicus; the rest may be Tacitus going off on his own little train of speculation.

Whatever the truth, though, something this story shows beyond any doubt is that high-profile deaths have been attracting rampant conspiracy theories for at least 2,000 years. To see how pernicious these theories can be, how they come about and how they can spread, we'll need to look at a more recent political death than that of a Roman *praepositus* – one where we have a bit more historical evidence to play with. We need to look at the murder of an American president: an event that shocked a nation and spawned many decades' worth of conspiracy theories.

No, not that one.

The first point to make about the assassination of Abraham Lincoln is that it was, in fact, the result of a conspiracy. That much isn't in doubt: the conspirators were caught, many of them confessed, and an almost embarrassing amount of evidence corroborated their not-very-secret plan. The motivation, coming near the end of a nation-shattering war, was the most obvious imaginable. The man who both created the plan and pulled the trigger was the opposite of mysterious: one of the best-known actors of his day, who chose to carry out the killing in a crowded theatre where he'd performed just months earlier.

You *might* think – ha ha ha – that there would be very little space for rival conspiracy theories about the Lincoln murder, due to the extremely public and rapidly uncovered nature of the *actual conspiracy* that killed him.

Oh, you sweet, naive summer child.

In modern times, it may have been overshadowed by the tsunami of conspiracism that surrounds JFK, but Lincoln's assassination also gave rise to multiple long-lived and widely believed conspiracy theories. In his book *The Lincoln Murder Conspiracies*, historian William Hanchett distinguishes between the 'simple conspiracy' of the actual plot, and the 'grand conspiracy' theories of those for whom the simple version just didn't quite cut it. Some people, it seems, just weren't satisfied with the explanation that the real, verifiable conspiracy *fact* offered.

To recap the actual events behind Lincoln's assassination – the simple conspiracy – he was shot in the head by the actor John Wilkes Booth at Ford's Theatre in Washington, D.C. on 14 April 1865. The country was four years into a bloody civil war over slavery that Lincoln had pursued in the face of profound opposition, and which at the time seemed like it could prove fatal for the still-young country. The assassination came just a few months after Lincoln's inauguration for his second term as president, following an election notable for not including the states they were at war with.

Lincoln was widely despised – not just in the secessionist slave states of the American South, but also by a significant minority in his native North. Many in this minority were outright supporters of the Confederate cause; others opposed slavery, but still felt that his draconian actions had brought the American experiment to the brink of failure. Some of his fiercer opponents spoke openly of wanting Lincoln assassinated; one newspaper editor even wrote that he'd do it himself. Open threats and rumours of plots dogged Lincoln; a few ambiguous incidents in the years before his death may even have been unsuccessful attempts.

Booth, meanwhile, was by common acclaim one of the

greatest actors of his generation – the foremost among his famous acting brothers, sons of a famous acting father. He was a charming and well-loved man, with fine features and a captivating gaze, a rakish sweep of boyishly curled hair and a dangerous moustache. In a time when perceptions of male beauty and character were heavily influenced by the quality of a man's brow, John Wilkes Booth gave extremely good brow.

But he was, it's fair to say, a problematic fave. He was a long-term and vocal supporter of the Confederacy, whose zealotry in his support of slavery had caused a rift with his family, and he had been planning some form of dramatic, violent action against Lincoln for the best part of a year. The plot that Booth initially hatched with his co-conspirators was not to assassinate the President, however: it was to kidnap him, and deliver him to Confederate leaders so they could ransom him in exchange for a decisive advantage in the war.

The abduction plot can be charitably described as a shit-show. They kept missing Lincoln, because he wasn't where they thought he'd be (a problem they could have solved by simply reading the morning newspapers). They were so bad at keeping secrets that much of the neighbourhood knew about their plan. And Booth, for no clear reason, really wanted to kidnap Lincoln from his box at Ford's Theatre, in front of a crowd and with no easy exit route. Maybe he liked the dramatic symbolism – Booth had performed in front of Lincoln there just eighteen months earlier.

When exactly the abduction plot turned into an assassination is murky: Booth was by this point drinking heavily and becoming erratic. He may not have settled on his deadly course until the day before; his co-conspirators insisted that he only told them of the new plan on the morning of the attempt. The surrender of over 20,000

Confederate troops at Appomattox a few days previously had been a devastating blow for the South, effectively deciding the war – but it would be another month before it officially ended. While the Northern leadership breathed a sigh of relief and started to let their guard down, Booth may still have believed that a dramatic Hail Mary could swing things the South's way.

The assassination plot was, obviously, successful in its main aim. But it was still barely more competent than the failed abduction attempts. For starters, Lincoln was not the only intended target. While Booth attacked Lincoln, George Atzerodt was supposed to simultaneously kill Vice President Andrew Johnson, while Lewis Powell was meant to assassinate Secretary of State William Seward. In the event, Powell's gun misfired, and his frantic attempts to stab Seward in his bed failed to kill him; Atzerodt, meanwhile, never even tried to shoot Johnson, instead deciding to get drunk and go for a walk around the city.*

And while Booth did manage to shoot Lincoln, his sheer commitment to *drama* meant that things rapidly went wrong. He'd decided that, after killing the President, he should vault heroically from the box on to the stage twelve feet below, where he would shout a triumphant slogan to the audience before making his daring escape through the stage door. Things started to go awry when he caught his heel in a flag mid-leap, fell heavily on to the stage, and broke his leg. Before hobbling painfully away, he yelled something that might have been '*Sic semper tyrannis!*' ('Thus always to tyrants'), except that nobody could hear him clearly and witnesses

---

* Perhaps the most relatable thing anyone mentioned in this chapter does.

couldn't subsequently agree on what he'd said. From an acting perspective, Booth's greatest crime that night may have been a failure to project.

Most of Booth's co-conspirators were quickly arrested, their casual approach to secrecy coming back to haunt them. With his broken leg preventing him from making his planned escape, John Wilkes Booth spent twelve days hiding in a barn in Virginia before he was discovered and shot dead while resisting arrest. The fact he was killed when there had been orders to take him alive, of course, would come in later years to be a major plank of conspiracy theorising.

So. That's the simple conspiracy – the one that actually happened. It's a useful insight into what real-life conspiracies tend to look like: messy, desperate and completely lacking in genius masterminds who are always one step ahead. But what of the grand conspiracy theories, the ones that didn't accept the simple conspiracy as a full explanation for those traumatic events?

The most straightforward version of the grand conspiracy was also the first to become widely spread – indeed, it was already being aired in the hours between when Lincoln was shot and when he died. And, like many conspiracy theories, it didn't bubble up from the masses: it came straight from the top. Many senior figures in the US government were convinced that Booth and his ragtag band of collaborators couldn't possibly have been the brains behind the killing. There had to be a genius mastermind. They were certain that the Confederate leadership themselves must have ordered the operation, or at the very least been aware of it and allowed it to proceed.

This was an understandable suspicion, given the two sides were still technically at war and the Confederates were a) desperate and b) assholes. But it was also, the overwhelming weight of historical evidence suggests, not true. Despite Booth's possible connections to some parts of the Confederate war effort, no evidence has emerged – at the time or subsequently, despite plenty of intensive investigation – to suggest the South knew of either the original kidnapping plot or his impulsive decision to assassinate. The Confederacy seem to have been just as shocked by the assassination as the Union.

But whether out of genuine belief, political expediency or the simple emotional weight of grief and rage, the investigation into Lincoln's killing effectively came to the conclusion that the Confederate leadership was behind the murder as its starting point. It was less about finding out *whether* the suspicion was true than it was about finding evidence – any evidence – that it *was* true.

The result was an embarrassing mess. Andrew Johnson, the new president, was persuaded to issue a statement asserting as fact that the Confederate leadership were known to be behind the plot. Confederate leader Jefferson Davis was detained and imprisoned on suspicion of the assassination plot (also for the whole war thing). Joseph Holt, the Judge Advocate General of the United States Army, was put in charge of the investigation, and spent months assuring the cabinet that he was *this close* to assembling the case that would prove Davis's complicity. A trusted agent had identified eight witnesses who could testify that Booth had met Davis in Canada, he said. That trusted agent, a chap called Sandford Conover, turned out to be a fantasist, or a con man, or probably both. Under questioning, his 'witnesses' quickly admitted that he'd paid them to deliver testimony from a script he'd written himself.

When one of the abduction conspirators, John Surratt, managed to flee the country, the government arrested, tried, convicted and hung his mother Mary instead. Her actual degree of involvement remains uncertain; she may not have been aware of the assassination plan. At the trial of Powell, Atzerodt, Mrs Surratt and five other alleged conspirators, the government suppressed evidence that the abduction plot had ever existed, feeling it would weaken their case that assassination had always been the goal of the supposed grand conspiracy.

It turned out that executing an old woman on weak evidence was not a universally popular move – one that only looked worse once her son was located. John Surratt had been hiding out, as you do, by serving as a member of the Papal guard near Rome. When he was apprehended and returned to the US for trial, the extra time had only exposed the flimsiness of the government's case, and he ended up being freed following a hung jury. Which made his mother's execution, despite a plea for clemency from the commissioners who convicted her, rather hard to justify.

Jefferson Davis was eventually released from custody after two years, never having been brought to trial. History has, rightly, not been terribly forgiving of Jefferson Davis's choices in life – but it has made it pretty clear that he wasn't responsible for Lincoln's assassination. Many of the senior politicians involved in promoting the grand conspiracy theory spent much of the rest of their careers rather shamefacedly trying to avoid the subject, or to blame someone else. Holt, though, remained adamant his theory was true; he published a pamphlet in which he claimed that the criticisms of his case were proof of a conspiracy against him.

The Confederate grand conspiracy may have been the theory that received the heavyweight stamp of governmental approval, but it was hardly the only one. The second widespread conspiracy theory to emerge was just as simple in its basic shape, although it required a bit of a leap to get to the desired conclusion. This theory, which became most popular decades after the event – in the late 1800s and early 1900s – was this: the Catholics did it.

Readers may recognise this as being similar to other popular conspiracy theories throughout history (the Jews did this, the Jesuits did that, that one was the Muslims, and so on). The actual evidence behind the 'Catholics did it' theory amounts to little more than the general suspicion of Catholics that was common in America at the time. As William Hanchett puts it: 'Some Americans were in the habit of blaming whatever they did not like on the Catholics.'[1]

This kind of thing already had a long history in conspiratorial literature: in 1835, Samuel Morse (inventor of the eponymous code, and son of Illuminati-obsessed preacher Jedediah from a few chapters back) had published the influential *Foreign Conspiracy against the Liberties of the United States*, warning of a Catholic plot to seize power in America by flooding the country with immigrants. At the time of the assassination itself, one newspaper reported, wrongly, that every one of Booth's co-conspirators was Catholic, which would turn into something of a unkillable zombie fact. (The business with John Surratt going off to guard the Pope after the murder didn't help.)

But this general suspicion of Catholic conspiracy didn't grow into a fully fledged theory until two decades later when, in 1886, a chap called Charles Chiniquy published a book titled *Fifty Years in the Church of Rome*. Chiniquy was an ex-priest who'd had what can only be described as a spectacular falling out with his former colleagues. He'd left the Catholic Church decades earlier after he was sued for slander by a prominent member who was friends with his bishop. His counsel in that lawsuit had been one of the top lawyers in Illinois: one Abraham Lincoln.

Chiniquy's book was an outpouring of decades of resentment against his former co-religionists, a massive screed against the evils of Rome. The Lincoln conspiracy theory wasn't even the main focus of the book: he saved that for a kind of 'ta-da' moment more than 600 pages in. Nonetheless, he was clear that the assassination was undoubtedly 'the work of Popery'. Moreover, he claimed Lincoln himself had told him as much prior to his death – revealing that the true battle the president was fighting was not against the Confederacy, but against the Pope, and claiming that every one of the murderous plots against him was the work of the Jesuits.

Chiniquy's theory was no narrowly focused event conspiracy; it was far broader than that. The Roman Church, Chiniquy wrote, was 'nothing but a permanent political conspiracy', with the United States as its chief target. Not only had they killed Lincoln, they had engineered the Civil War, and (in echoes of Samuel Morse) they were plotting to take control of the US via mass Irish immigration. He wrote of implacable conspirators who said they were determined 'to take possession of the United States and rule them; but we cannot do that without acting secretly', and so 'silently and patiently, we must mass our Roman Catholics in the great cities of the United States'². Catholics had already seized power in most major cities from New York to San Francisco, he said, and were poised to take control of almost every institution in public life.

Chiniquy also included an early example of one of the most enduring conspiracy tropes: members of a group who let slip that they have advance knowledge of the plot. He claimed that a Protestant minister told him of how Catholics in a small Minnesota town were discussing the murder of Lincoln early in the evening of 14 April, several hours before the fatal shot was even fired. They had apparently heard this news from their local priests. The conclusion, obviously, was not that this witness had misremembered, or simply made it up. Clearly the Catholic hierarchy had done what any good conspiracy does – ensure that all details of the secret plot are distributed in advance to everybody in their organisation, including those in small towns over a thousand miles from where the thing is going to happen.

Chiniquy's claims have long been debunked – his supposed meetings with Lincoln in the White House, where the President told him of the Popish plots against him, never happened – but this didn't stop him from being the key source for a slew of further books advancing the Catholic grand conspiracy published in the decades that followed. It's a useful reminder of why it pays to be sceptical about 'insider' accounts, without which no good conspiracy theory is complete. There's a reason why investigative journalists generally insist on documents and other evidence to back up whistle-blowers' assertions: there are always people with long-nurtured grudges who will tell you their former colleagues are up to no good. 'My old boss was actually evil' is not an uncommon emotion, and some people will go to remarkable lengths to convince others of the literal truth of that sentiment.

The final major grand conspiracy theory about Lincoln came around eighty years after his death, but its influence would continue to be felt for decades afterwards. It kick-started a veritable cottage industry of books repeating or expanding on its premise, and the falsehoods it originated became accepted and amplified. It was the brainchild of one man: Otto Eisenschiml, a chemical engineer who had come to the USA from Austria as a child and eventually became a big deal in an oil company. He published his theory in a book, *Why was Lincoln Murdered?*, in 1937.

In its basic form, the theory amounted to a classic Agatha Christie twist: who ordered Lincoln's assassination? Why, it was none other than *his own Secretary of War, Edwin Stanton!* This curious conclusion was prompted by one part of the official Lincoln narrative that, for Eisenschiml, didn't add up: the fact that General Ulysses S. Grant had originally been supposed to accompany Lincoln to the theatre, but had pulled out before the performance. If Grant had been there, Eisenschiml reasoned, a military man with military guards would surely have stopped Booth from firing his deadly shot.

Now, this might strike you as a rather thin basis for throwing out the accepted narrative. 'Work colleague bails on a planned social engagement' doesn't seem like an event so improbable it requires an extraordinary explanation. But for Eisenschiml, it was the key to everything. He described how the answer to the conundrum came to him in a flash of inspiration – the only person who could have ordered Grant to ditch the President was his boss, the Secretary of War. Thus, Stanton must have been the mastermind behind the plot.

Once he had his conclusion, Eisenschiml took the same approach as conspiracists down the ages. He set about gathering evidence to prove his conclusion true, rather than to check if it might be false. He oddly insisted that this was following the scientific method, on the basis that chemists had gone looking for elements predicted by Mendeleyev's periodic table, and found them. But what he did was far from the equivalent of looking for gallium and finding gallium. It was more looking for gallium, finding a lump of coal, and going, 'Hey lads, I've discovered gallium!'

The majority of the 'evidence' he gathered came in the form of alleged anomalies in the official account of what happened that night. William Hanchett provides a concise list, which includes: 'Why did Secretary Stanton deny Lincoln the protection he requested at the theatre? ... Why was the telegraph service out of Washington interrupted for two hours at approximately the same time as the attack on Lincoln? ... After Booth's co-conspirators had been captured and imprisoned, why were they forced to wear canvas hoods over their heads, cutting them off from communication with the outside world?'[3]

It's classic conspiracy stuff, and as it turns out, the answers to these questions are 'it's not clear he did', 'it wasn't' and 'they weren't'. Eisenschiml was not a good historian. He'd cherry-pick evidence to suit his case, and twist evidence when it still didn't give him what he wanted. The claim that Stanton denied Lincoln a bodyguard came from one single witness, recalling events over four decades later. More importantly, while Eisenschiml picked out that one detail, he ignored the rest of the testimony saying it was because Stanton was trying to dissuade Lincoln from going to the theatre *at all*, which hardly supports the theory that he was luring him into a trap. It's not true that all the telegraph lines were cut, delaying the authorities from mounting a search for the culprits: a single commercial line between Washington and Baltimore went down, which did nothing to hinder the hunt. And the prisoners weren't prevented from talking (and, by implication, prevented from incriminating somebody powerful) – they all had ample opportunity to spill the beans.

Moreover, even if these claims – and the many others Eisenschiml made – had been completely true, they *still* wouldn't prove anything. Like many conspiracy theories before and since that rely on picking holes in the 'official narrative', they're based on a fundamentally flawed belief about how the world actually works: namely, that everything everybody does has to make complete logical sense, even when viewed in retrospect, with the advantage of knowing how things would turn out.

It's hindsight bias writ large. People caught up in dramatic events can never have simply made a mistake or been forced to make a decision based on imperfect information. They can't be stressed or confused or upset or petty, or looking for an excuse to avoid a theatre trip. Everybody involved has to be fully aware at all times of the historic significance of their actions, even when the thing that will make them significant hasn't happened yet. Nothing can happen due to coincidence, or chance, or the world simply being weird; everything must be meaningful.

At time of writing, forty-five men have served as US president. No fewer than eight of them died in office: four were assassinated, and the other four, as far as we know, died of natural causes. During one particularly unfortunate decade in the mid-nineteenth century, two different presidents died in office (William Henry Harrison in 1841 and Zachary Taylor in 1850), while a third, James K. Polk, survived barely a year after leaving it. This sounds unlikely, but there was probably nothing suspicious about it: historian Dr Philip Mackowiak has unearthed evidence suggesting that all three deaths may have been due to typhoid, a result of 1600 Pennsylvania Avenue's water supply being drawn from regrettably close to the local cesspits and thus, er, contaminated with sewage.[4]

Inevitably, though, this run of deaths was the subject of assassination conspiracy theories. In 1864, deep in the mutual paranoia of the Civil War and less than a year before Lincoln was shot, the Union-supporting writer John Smith Dye published a book blaming them on a cabal of slave owners led by the Southern politicians John C. Calhoun (who you may remember from the third chapter) and Jefferson Davis (who you may remember from a few pages ago). In a precursor to the Confederate grand conspiracy, Dye not only accused them of culpability for the deaths of Harrison and Taylor, but also a supposed attempted assassination of Lincoln in Baltimore, along with the attempted shooting of Andrew Jackson in 1835 by a mentally ill man believing himself to be Richard III, and an alleged effort to poison James Buchanan before his inauguration in 1857. This latter plot was said to have hinged on adding arsenic to the sugar cubes at the National Hotel in Washington, D.C., on the ingenious grounds that this would take out all the Northerners (who 'rarely drink anything' but tea, and thus would use cubed sugar) while leaving the Southerners unaffected (as they 'mostly prefer coffee', and hence used ground sugar).[5]

This last incident was probably an example of something we'll encounter again in a few chapters' time: people seeing conspiracy in the actions of infectious disease. There were several deadly outbreaks of dysentery at the hotel around the time of Buchanan's inauguration, which, like the White House deaths, were probably due to dodgy plumbing. Dye's conspiracy theory blaming slaveholders was just one of several rival theories that were circulating at the time attributing the bouts of sickness to foul play: others blamed radical abolitionists, or the Chinese.

Dye's book didn't make a huge impact when it was

originally published, but he had the good fortune – from a book publicity point of view, at least – to have printed it less than a year before Lincoln's assassination. A revised edition published a few years later folded those events into his grand conspiracy and boasted that his previous edition had warned of the in-progress conspiracy against Lincoln 'over six months before the plans were put into execution'. That, not surprisingly, made far more of a splash in a country still reeling from its loss.

But you don't need to buy into Dye's sugar-cube fantasies to see that the American presidency is a dangerous job. Those eight presidents who died in office amount to eighteen per cent of the total. Okay, US Presidents have tended to be a touch on the elderly side, but a close to one-in-five fatality rate from a gig is still pretty rough.

Even if you accept that all the in-office deaths from natural causes were perfectly above board and free of malarkey, then you're still left with four dead presidents who were shot. Four out of forty-five. If you were offered a job and were told that it involved a near one-in-ten chance of being murdered, it's a reasonable guess that you'd want to … you know, think about it a bit. You'd do a little cost-benefit analysis, even if the gig did come with free accommodation, a private plane and veto powers.

This is all before you count the failed presidential assassinations (such as Reagan), the assassinations of political figures below the presidential level (Martin Luther King, Bobby Kennedy), and the many attempted assassinations of other politicians over the years (for example, the near-fatal attacks on Democratic congresswoman Gabby Giffords and on a Republican congressional baseball practice session in recent years). That's to say nothing of the possible intentions of some of the more noose-loving Capitol insurgents on 6 January 2021. In short, if you're a politician in the USA, it's not wholly unreasonable to live in constant fear that someone's going to take a second amendment-based approach to resolving their disagreements with you.

The thing is, though, while it may have a reputation as a country that sees guns as the solution to virtually every problem, the United States is hardly alone in being a perilous place to be a big deal in politics.

As a general rule, in fact, being a national leader has historically been a profession with a terrifyingly high mortality rate. A study of European monarchs between the years 600 and 1800 showed that more than one in five met with a violent death. And intentional, non-battlefield, extrajudicial homicide – assassination, in other words – was by far the most common form of violent death, with certain or suspected hit jobs accounting for fifteen per cent of all monarch deaths across those 1,200 years of European history. The study concludes that 'European kingship before the Industrial Revolution was ... amongst the most dangerous occupations found anywhere in the world', with a murder rate that far outstrips even the most violent and crime-ridden contemporary cities, comparable only to the death rates of soldiers in the bloodiest of wars.[6]

What we're saying here is that *Game of Thrones* was a documentary.

As with many victims of other violent crimes, though, most kings were murdered by someone they knew. For the bulk of European history, regicide was very much an elite sport; in cases where the culprit was identifiable, the vast majority were other members of that country's nobility, killing either in the hope of securing succession (by far the most common reason) or simply to settle personal grudges. Stranger danger wasn't really a concern for European monarchs; the conspiracy was usually coming from inside the palace. In contrast to our modern image of the radicalised lone-wolf assassin, kingly murders by people from outside the court bubble were extremely rare – what you might call the 'Lee Harvey Oswald model' didn't come into vogue until more recent times.

It was in the nineteenth century that this changed, and political assassination became, in the words of historian Rachael Hoffman, 'no longer the preserve of an elite circle of the court and aristocracy; it was now committed by the popular political protestor – the common man'.[7] It's perhaps notable that the emergence of the modern form of conspiracy theories coincides with this change: you might argue that it represents a form of elite panic about *the wrong sort of people* suddenly getting in on the king-slaying game.

While the modern age may be marginally safer for national leaders than much of history – perhaps as a result of changing political systems, perhaps simply because of the professionalisation of security details – it's still, by any standards, a pretty risky job. In the few months between when we started writing this chapter and when we finished it, two national leaders met with violent deaths.*

There are many reasons why people are prone to believing

---

* Chad's authoritarian ruler Idriss Déby was shot in April 2021 while commanding his troops on the front line in a battle against rebel forces, on the very day he'd won a sixth term as president. There have been a lot of conspiracy theories about this. In July, Haiti's president Jovenel Moïse was assassinated by about thirty mostly Colombian mercenaries who shot him in the bedroom of his official residence. That this was a conspiracy isn't really in question, although who was behind it remains less clear.

conspiracy theories. They appeal to our cognitive biases; they allow us to put names and faces to otherwise invisible trends that shape our world; they offer the illusion of a non-random world where at least *someone* is in control. These are all true of assassination theories, too, but in this case there's also a much simpler explanation.

Why do we have a strong tendency to attribute the deaths of major figures to murderous conspiracy? Because at many times and in many places throughout an awful lot of history, it's been a perfectly reasonable guess.

Of course, the fact that, historically, lots of people really might have been conspiring to kill just about any high-profile political figure hasn't stopped people from coming up with a ton of false conspiracy theories as well.

Take, for example, the notorious claims of a vast conspiracy to murder King Charles II that swept England in 1678. Like Chiniquy's Lincoln theory, the supposed culprits in this case were Catholics – just about any Catholic would do. This led to three years of anti-Popish hysteria among the English political elite, with scores of arrests and over twenty Catholics being executed for a non-existent plot. This was all in spite of the fact the ostensible whistle-blower was a wildly implausible and disreputable figure named Titus Oates, who was once described as 'the most illiterate dunce', and whose story was full of extremely obvious holes. Perhaps the weirdest aspect of the whole affair is that Charles II – supposedly the intended victim – didn't believe a word of it, going as far as cross-examining Oates himself and catching him out in various falsehoods. The fact that the conspiracy theory dominated the country's political life for years in spite of the King himself desperately trying to fact-check it only goes to show the power that such theories can have – especially when they provide a convenient excuse for carrying out some of your favourite political aims, like oppressing Catholics.

Unfortunately for those of us who like a little certainty in life, very few assassination theories are quite this clear-cut. They lack some of the more convincing elements the Popish Plot had to disprove it, such as a very-much-alive victim repeatedly telling people that it wasn't true. Instead, we're forced to admit that we often can't know anything for certain, and that many of the most notorious cases are probably condemned to exist in a permanent state of ambiguity. For example, here's a quick rundown of a few of the more popular theories:

Dag Hammarskjöld

The Secretary-General of the UN, Hammarskjöld died in a plane crash in what is now Zambia while en route to mediate in the Congo Crisis of 1961. All told, this is probably one of the most plausible conspiracy theories out there. A Belgian mercenary pilot – who was named in a cable by the American ambassador to the Congo, sent just hours after the crash was confirmed, as having been a likely candidate for shooting the plane down – supposedly confessed to having been involved some years later. There were also some suspicious goings-on in the immediate aftermath of the incident, with odd delays in the crash site being secured and claims it had been interfered with. The fact that, shortly after the news broke, former US President Harry Truman reportedly said to the press that Hammarskjöld had been 'on the point of getting something done when they killed him.

Notice that I said "when they killed him"' is also something of an eyebrow-raiser.[8]

The one thing that gives you pause is that none of the subtly different flavours of this theory can quite agree on whether the plane was shot, bombed or sabotaged; whether Hammarskjöld was killed by the crash or subsequently shot on the ground; or exactly who it was giving the orders. The CIA, the KGB, MI6, South African racists, the breakaway state of Katanga and a shadowy collective of 'European business interests' have all been suggested as the ultimate culprits – so, honestly, take your pick.

Yasser Arafat

The President of the Palestinian National Authority and long-time bête noire of quite a few governments died from a mysterious illness in 2004. This, not unexpectedly, ignited a storm of conspiracy theories, ranging from allegations that he was poisoned, to the claim that his own people were covering up that he died of AIDS.

The thing is, it's hard to *entirely* rule out the possibility that he may have been bumped off, given that Israel's security cabinet had resolved in September 2003 to 'remove' Arafat.[9] In case anybody was in doubt about what that potentially meant, then-Deputy Prime Minister Ehud Olmert went on Israel Radio a few days later and clarified that 'killing is definitely one of the options'. (The foreign minister walked Olmert's comments back the following day, after an international outcry.) That, at the very least, would seem to take this one out of the 'completely unfounded paranoia' file.

But still. The specific Arafat theory that's gained the most credence is one that only emerged quite a few years later, after the Russian dissident Alexander Litvinenko was murdered with the radioactive poison polonium-210. The ripped-from-the-headlines theory is: so was Arafat. But forensic tests after Arafat's remains were exhumed proved inconclusive (some said maybe, others said maybe not), and, in any case, Arafat's reported symptoms don't really match up with polonium poisoning. Also, Arafat was an old man and, well, they do have a tendency to sometimes just die. By far the most likely explanations remain natural ones; that said, it's all but impossible to say definitively one way or the other.

Of course, it's doubtful this will stop anybody saying stuff definitively.

John F. Kennedy

Okay, okay, fine. Let's do this. The shocking truth.

If you're anything like the authors of this book, you've quite possibly always had some kind of baseline suspicion around the JFK assassination. You wouldn't be alone in that: while most Americans believed the Warren Commission report when it came out in 1964, in the years since, polling has consistently shown a growing scepticism. About sixty per cent now believe that there was a conspiracy of some kind; the figure has been over fifty per cent ever since the late sixties.[10]

You'd be in good company, too: one of the most prominent early promoters of the conspiracist position was no less a figure than Bertrand Russell, one of the twentieth century's greatest intellectuals. He started a group with (in his words) 'the unsatisfactory name of "The British Who Killed

Kennedy? Committee"', which brought together luminaries ranging from playwright J. B. Priestley to historian Hugh Trevor-Roper and future Labour leader Michael Foot. He also wrote a 1964 article titled '16 Questions on the Assassination' that's a classic example of creating a conspiracy by picking holes in 'the official version' – especially as it expands the definition of the official narrative to include off-the-cuff remarks from any authority figure, and just about anything published by any media outlet.[11]

So, yes, if you're anything like a large section of the population, you have your doubts: you might not subscribe to any specific theory of who was behind Kennedy's death, but it's quite likely you think that Lee Harvey Oswald couldn't have been the lone gunman.

Well: it turns out that the evidence strongly suggests that Lee Harvey Oswald was, in fact, the lone gunman. The sheer amount of Kennediana that's been produced in the years since makes it hard to address every possible theory. But let's take a few key claims normally held up as proving that there must have been multiple shooters, and that therefore (unless it was a *really* weird coincidence) it was a conspiracy.

Of these, the 'magic bullet' is probably the most important. It's certainly the one that Oliver Stone devotes an awful lot of time to in his compelling – but unfortunately, bullshit-ridden – movie JFK. It's also perhaps the aspect of the 'official narrative' that did the most to gradually discredit the findings of the Warren Commission in the eyes of the public, through its sheer apparent implausibility.

It's all based on the fact that Oswald fired only three shots. We know he couldn't have fired more in the time available, and he couldn't have fired them more rapidly than one every couple of seconds. One bullet went wide, hitting the kerb and causing a mild injury to a bystander. One struck Kennedy fatally in the head. That leaves just one more bullet to cause the remaining injuries to Kennedy's back and throat, and to Texas Governor John Connally's back, ribs, wrist and thigh. According to the single-bullet sceptics, this means the projectile needed to perform an inexplicable mid-air pirouette shortly after exiting the President's body, then take an unexpected right turn, before veering round again to slalom its way back and forth through various parts of the Governor. That's not a thing bullets can do.* The conclusion: there was at least one other bullet, which means at least one other shooter.

The thing is, though, that all this assumes the two men were sitting at the same level, one directly in front of the other. Which seems a reasonable assumption, because that's how cars normally work. But this was a presidential limousine. It was not like other cars. Kennedy's seat was actually significantly higher than Connally's, and photographs clearly show that the President was sitting much further to the right in his seat than the Governor. And once you take all that into account, looking at the men's actual body positions at the moment they were shot, the magic bullet's impossibly twisty trajectory simply vanishes. Instead, what you have is … a straight line. One that points back to the sixth floor of the Texas School Book Depository, as it happens.

Much of the other evidence crumbles in a similar fashion

---

* Except in that movie where James McAvoy can fire a gun round corners. Oh, and in the *X-Men* film where Magneto gets arrested for the Kennedy assassination, because he can alter the path of bullets with his superpowers. Come to think of it, James McAvoy's in that one, too. Does he … does he know something?

when looked at more closely. Analysis of audio from a police radio that supposedly proved there were four gunshots, one of which could be located on the grassy knoll, turned out to not be gunshots, not to have happened at the same time as the assassination, and not to have been anywhere near the grassy knoll. The claim that the route of the motorcade was changed at the last minute to take it past the Book Depository (a claim advanced by Bertrand Russell, among others) was false, based on no more than one slightly simplified map published in a single newspaper. The grand theory put forward by District Attorney Jim Garrison and promoted in Stone's film – that the Kennedy assassination was a conspiracy between the CIA, state and local government, a cabal of right-wing businessmen and the gay community – was based almost entirely on extremely dubious and partially recanted testimony from a few easily led witnesses. Much like Holt with Lincoln's assassination a century before, a prosecutor went looking for evidence to prove a pre-determined conclusion, and cheerfully ignored the very clear signals that it was all bunk.

And that Lee Harvey Oswald was an assassination-minded kinda guy is backed up by the fact that, a few months earlier, it's very likely that he tried to shoot Edwin Walker, a former general and dedicated racist who had resigned his commission because the US Army wouldn't let him distribute far-right literature from the John Birch Society to his troops. (We'll meet the John Birch Society again later in the book, by the way, when they'll be very much on the flip side of the conspiracy coin.)

In short: it might be less entertaining than Kevin Costner being melodramatic with diagrams, but the lone gunman theory is probably the right one.

Diana, Princess of Wales

Yeah, this one *really* doesn't make any sense. For starters, it would be just about the dumbest assassination strategy imaginable, with the possible exception of all the ones the CIA actually tried on Castro. It relies on the combination of a strobe light, which most eyewitnesses say they didn't see, a perfectly timed glancing collision with a much smaller vehicle forcing the car off the road, and the target of the assassination making things easier by helpfully not wearing her seatbelt. Oh, and the conspirators deciding to do all of this at a time when there are a huge number of press photographers just a few yards behind, which is obviously *exactly* the conditions you want for your secret murder plot.

The motive, which is usually said to be the sheer horror of the Royal Family at the idea a future king would have a Muslim half-brother, doesn't make any more sense, and is somewhat undermined by the fact that Diana wasn't pregnant – not to mention the fact the Royal Family had been entirely content with her having a much longer and far more serious relationship with a Muslim doctor for several years previously, none of which resulted in even a little bit of assassination. All of the supposed evidence offered in favour of the conspiracy has been shown to be flimsy at best and outright fabricated at worst, and the whole thing appears to be little more than the concerted efforts of a grieving man with a grudge against the British establishment, egged on by newspapers desperate for the thinnest excuse to stick a picture of Diana on their front page.

But yeah, other than that, it totally checks out.

*　　*　　*

All of these theories, and the many others like them around the world, exist on a spectrum of plausibility. Some may be more likely than others; few can be ruled out entirely. The reality of political assassination means that proving a negative is even harder than usual. Given the history of actual, verified assassination plots, it's often difficult to say that suspicions are entirely unjustified.

And yet, our suspicions can still lead us astray. In fact, we're so fond of suspicion that sometimes we'll manufacture it out of thin air. Nothing illustrates that better than the case of Harold Holt, the Prime Minister of Australia who, on a hot December day in 1967, walked into the sea and never came out again.

The fact that a major world leader simply vanished, at the height of the Cold War, just a few years after the Kennedy assassination, seems tailor-made for conspiracy theories. For decades, his disappearance from a beach near his family home on Australia's southern coast was officially an unsolved mystery. And, sure enough, the conspiracies arrived.

Some said he'd been assassinated by North Vietnam over his pro-Vietnam War stance; a newspaper wrote that he'd been assassinated by the CIA over his anti-Vietnam War stance. A letter from an American lawyer insisted that he'd been the victim of 'expert sabotage, probably foreign', perhaps as a result of some 'delayed-effect drug'[12]. The 'official narrative' got its traditional picking over, highlighting small inconsistencies from early announcements, when the government had been scrambling to work out who was actually in charge. The most extensive conspiracy theory didn't even involve assassination. A book titled *The Prime Minister Was a Spy* claimed that Holt had been in the pay of China for almost four decades, but fearing he was about to be exposed had chosen to defect, and was smuggled on to a Chinese submarine waiting just off the coast.

The thing about all this is that there was nothing remotely mysterious about what happened to Harold Holt. It was almost comically un-mysterious. Holt was a keen and confident swimmer – he would sometimes amuse himself by seeing how long he could hold his breath while listening to boring speeches in parliament – but the sea that day was incredibly rough. Two friends who'd been with him on the beach had initially tried to join him for a swim, but backed out. It was so bad that rescue efforts were severely hampered: one boat capsized, and a coastguard diver told the TV news that 'it was like being inside a washing machine'.[13]

Moreover, Holt's health wasn't great. He had a persistent shoulder injury, he'd collapsed in parliament a few months earlier, and he'd suffered two near-drowning incidents in the previous year. Friends, colleagues and his own doctor had all warned Holt about the risks of continuing to go in the water, which he dismissed, telling his press secretary, 'What are the odds of a prime minister being drowned or taken by a shark?'[14] On the day before his disappearance, *The Australian* had featured a front-page story headlined 'PM advised to swim less', which is the kind of heavy-handed foreshadowing that you get in movies but don't normally expect in real life.

Conspiracy theories grow in the gaps of more conventional explanations; they frequently claim to be able to explain the unexplained or implausible. But that means that, if you want to do conspiracy theories well, then there's a hurdle they need to clear: they can't be *less* plausible than the mainstream narrative they're replacing. What happened to Harold Holt was straightforward: he drowned. The thing that everybody had predicted would happen happened, not because they were in on some plot, but because it was extremely predictable.

So, why did the conspiracy theories flourish? It's proportionality bias in action: we find it hard to believe that dramatic events can have mundane or random causes. Losing the leader of a major country simply *can't* be down to mere bad luck or dumb choices. As the historian Ian Hancock put it, despite the plain truth that 'every summer, Australians of all ages do foolish things in the water, and drown', this didn't seem satisfactory. 'The obvious explanations,' he wrote, 'were not sufficiently momentous to match the gravity of the event.'[15]

Or, to put it another way, it's the exact same flawed logic that Holt himself displayed when he asked: 'What are the odds of a prime minister being drowned?' To which the answer is: no different to those of any other man in his sixtieth year, with a dodgy shoulder and a recent history of almost drowning, overconfidently plunging into waters that everybody else agreed were too dangerous to swim in. The sea doesn't care that you're the prime minister, mate. You get the same odds as everyone else.

6

Unidentified Lying Objects

One night in 1639, James Everell – 'a sober, discreet man', we're told – was aboard a boat on Muddy River near Boston when he and his two companions saw 'a great light' in the sky. 'When it stood still,' John Winthrop, the governor of the Massachusetts colony, records in his journals, 'it flamed up, and was about three yards square; when it ran, it was contracted into the figure of a swine.' This pig-shaped entity would spend several hours reportedly zooming back and forth between the river and Charlestown, 'as swift as an arrow'. When the incident was over, the gentlemen found that their boat had been carried a mile along the river against the tide.[1]

Everell's experience is generally accepted as the first recorded UFO sighting in colonial America. It wasn't the last.

For a long time, tales of alien abduction and government cover-ups of flying saucers were virtually synonymous with conspiracy theories. In the resurgence of conspiracy culture in the 1980s and 1990s, UFOs played a starring role, and the words 'Roswell' and 'Area 51' appeared in everything from the literature of right-wing militia movements to mainstream pop-culture hits like *The X-Files* and *Independence Day*.*

'It was aliens' has become a remarkably popular theory, with impressive staying power. In polls carried out since the 1960s, the percentage of the US population who believe that UFOs really do represent alien visits to Earth has consistently been over thirty per cent, and frequently much higher.[2] Not only that, but many of the people who aren't convinced that aliens are popping by for a visit still believe that there's some form of government cover-up: a large majority of Americans (sixty-eight per cent at the latest count) have consistently said they believe that their government knows more about UFOs than it publicly admits.[3]

And, as we'll see, they're basically right about that.

Despite the fact that, statistically, any gathering of Americans that isn't the AGM of the Skeptics Society has a decent chance of including at least one believer, the common image of the ufologist in popular culture has stayed firmly at the kookiest end of the weirdo scale – all manic, twitchy nerds or booze-hound hicks unsettlingly obsessed with the topic of anal probing. It was the conspiracy theory nobody quite wanted to admit they bought.

But then, in the last few years, something odd happened. Tentatively at first, but in steadily increasing numbers, relatively prominent people started to argue that maybe, just

---

* Will Smith became the world's biggest movie star in the late nineties on the basis of a run of three successive hit movies – *Independence Day*, *Men In Black* and *Enemy of the State* – all of which had as a central premise 'the conspiracy theorists were right all along'. Which raises the obvious question: what does he know?

maybe, we should be paying a bit more attention to this whole UFO business. Detailed stories were published in prestigious newspapers about the growing evidence for UFOs and government programmes that were grappling with them.[4] Academics and policymakers started to take note. The general tone of the shift is encapsulated neatly in the blunt headline of the 2019 *Washington Post* article by international relations professor Daniel Drezner: 'UFOs exist, and everyone needs to adjust to that fact.'[5]

None of these people were saying 'it's definitely aliens' (although they sometimes admitted we couldn't rule out the possibility that it is, in fact, aliens). Even if the acronym 'UFO' is now associated almost exclusively with little grey men, unidentified flying objects could be many other things. As the US Department of Defense's Unidentified Aerial Phenomena Task Force made clear in a report published in June 2021 – the moment that the US government came out as being officially into UFOs – the main concern isn't that UFOs are aliens, it's that they're 'foreign adversary systems'. In other words, some kind of fancy new Russian or Chinese spy plane.[6]

This isn't a new fear: in fact, it's exactly this kind of concern that gave rise to a lot of the shady behaviour that fuelled UFO conspiracy theories in the first place.

James Everell's 1639 UFO sighting was joined by others the following decade. In 1644, John Winthrop's journals record, three other men in a boat outside Boston saw 'two lights arise out of the water near the north point of the town cove, in form like a man ... [It] went at a small distance to the town, and so to the south point, and there vanished away'. This became the talk of the town, and over the following weeks there were numerous other sightings of the lights, accompanied by a ghostly voice 'calling out in a most dreadful manner, "Boy! Boy! Come away! Come away!"'.[7] In 1647, the Reverend Cotton Mather tells us in his history of New England, there was a sighting of a ship sailing through the air near New Haven, Connecticut, moving against the wind for a mile before it 'vanished into a smoaky cloud'.[8]

The fact that the New England colonists were resident in a new continent with unfamiliar weather conditions might explain all this, except that people had seen plenty of weird stuff in the skies over Europe, too. A broadsheet from April 1561 reports the mass sighting one dawn of blood-red or black globes, crosses and rods in the sky above Nuremberg. These apparently proceeded to fight, before seeming to tire, falling to earth and burning away. The article was accompanied by a woodcut engraving based on witness reports, a sort of early modern artist's impression.[9]

Five years later and 200 miles away, a suspiciously similar-sounding phenomenon was reported in the sky over Basel, Switzerland. Again, it happened at the times of day when the sun was lowest in the sky; again, it involved black and red spheres that seemed to do battle before crumpling to the ground.[10]

In September 1609, a UFO the shape of a 'large gourd' was reported in the skies above Korea.[11] In 1668, a silver lizard was seen above Slovakia.[12] The work of the historian Livy, who was writing in the late first century BCE, is absolutely packed with weird stuff spotted in the sky above Rome, including a ball of fire, 'phantom ships ... gleaming in the sky' and some men in white standing before an altar.[13] From one perspective, indeed, the entire history of Western civilisation is the result of a UFO sighting: before the battle of the

Milvian Bridge, the Emperor Constantine saw a cross of light in the sky above the sun with words, in Greek, reading 'In this sign, conquer'. Imagine how embarrassed he'd be to discover that it wasn't a sign from God, merely some passing aliens, and he'd converted the entire Empire to Christianity for nothing.

Many ufologists have taken these tales as evidence of historic close encounters on the grounds that, to modern ears, they sound a lot like UFO sightings. Except, crucially, they also kind of don't. UFOs don't normally take the form of a pig or a lizard, a sailing boat or a giant black spear. They don't normally call out in spooky voices, or have Greek writing, either.

Instead, what these stories suggest is that humans have always been prone to seeing weird stuff in the sky, and our brains have interpreted it in accordance with the beliefs, anxieties and technologies of the time. In seventeenth-century New England, it might be the ghosts of dead sailors; in ancient Rome, they were messages from pagan or Christian gods. It's only once it's suggested to people that it's aliens that it starts being interpreted as such. It's striking that, whatever it was above Nuremberg, nobody seems to have considered extra-terrestrial explanations until the ufologists got involved.

In fact, most historical sightings have pretty plausible explanations.[14] That's because there's a range of extremely non-alien weird things that can happen in the sky. For example:

Sun dogs

An optical illusion, present in certain colder weather conditions, in which a low sun appears to be accompanied by two, smaller suns. The phrase may come from 'dag', meaning dew or mist; but the possibility we're choosing to believe, because it's better, is that it's because it makes the sun look a bit like a man walking his dogs.

Will-o-the-wisp

Mysterious lights prevalent in damper landscapes. Historically attributed to ghosts, fairies, etc. that like to lure travellers into dangerous bogs; now known to be caused by spontaneously combusting marsh gas. Either way: manifests as weird flying lights in a way perfectly designed to scare the bejesus out of you.

Ball lightning

A widely reported but barely studied phenomenon that is exactly what it sounds like. May not even exist, physically, and instead just be a trick electrical storms play with our perceptions, but has been reported in many different times and places.

Fata Morgana

A mirage in which a mass of cold air beneath a layer of warm air causes light to bend in strange ways, meaning images stretch, warp or appear multiple times stacked on top of each other. Although these have been recorded on land, they're more common at sea, where they've been known to make far-off ships appear to be floating in the sky, sometimes even upside down – as if flying ships weren't enough to mess you up already. Named for the Italian translation of the name of the Arthurian witch Morgan le Fay, because of their habit of making land in the straits of Messina appear like castles in the air. Which is apparently the sort of thing she'd do.

Actual space stuff

Sometimes, objects really do come to Earth from outer space and emit weird light on the way down. Mostly, though, these aren't spaceships so much as 'rocks', and the light is less a sign of internal power sources than of 'literally being on fire'. We used to call those shooting stars; now we call them meteors.[*]

There are a whole bunch of other boringly rational phenomena that one could, if in the right frame of mind, interpret as evidence the gods were angry or aliens were on their way. Leslie Kean, the American journalist who has done so much to get the US government to fess up to its longstanding interest in aliens, has noted that the vast majority of UFO sightings can be explained by the above, along with human aircraft, ice crystals, birds reflecting the sun, spinning eddies, the planets Mars or Venus, and so on – all reframed as something more mystical or sinister by good old mass hysteria.[†] [15]

*   *   *

---

[*] Those that don't vaporise completely, so that something actually hits the ground, we call meteorites; asteroids are rather bigger, and if we hit one we're in trouble.

[†] You're probably familiar with the witch trials that spread across Europe and America after the Reformation, which ended with tens of thousands of people – the vast majority women – being burned at the stake. But have you heard of the numerous documented cases of 'dancing plagues', in which entire towns would just start dancing and keep at it for months? Or the outbreak of nuns biting other nuns in fifteenth-century convents? Or the entire French convent that started meowing like cats, who only stopped once the (inevitably male) authorities threatened to whip them? Little wonder people could convince themselves and each other they'd seen an alien, really.

If people have been seeing weird stuff in the sky for most of human history, though, the tendency for people to attribute that weird stuff to aliens is more recent.

The late nineteenth century saw wave after wave of reports about mysterious lights in the skies that were attributed to some kind of newfangled 'airship'. In November 1896, for example, newspapers in northern California reported seeing a slow-moving light some 1,000 feet up. One witness reported that he had seen two men pedalling it; another, that he had come across it on the ground and met some Martians, who had promptly attempted to kidnap him. (The strapping fella in question had, luckily, proved too strong for them.)

In part, stories like this seem to have been the result of both witnesses and newspapers being willing, not to put too fine a point on it, to completely make stuff up.* But it is striking that the things they made up began to take the form of 'Look, a flying machine!' at almost exactly the point when such things were, for the first time, plausible. One popular explanation for the sightings was that someone *had* invented a flying machine, but – presumably afraid of all the praise and wealth that would follow – didn't want to tell anyone. By 1897, Thomas Edison had grown so sick of getting the blame for whatever nonsense people imagined in the sky that he issued a strongly worded statement denying having invented any such thing.[16]

---

* Another story from around this time: in 1897, Alexander Hamilton (not that one) claimed to have seen an airship steal his cows, and then, rather ungratefully, leave their mutilated bodies back on the ground. Decades later, it emerged that he was attempting to win a competition held by something called the 'Liar's Club'. We had trolls long before we had the internet.

Six years later, the Wright Brothers really did manage to get a flying machine off the ground; but still people kept reporting feats of aviation that technology didn't allow. In 1909, a man named Wallace Tillinghast told the Boston Herald he had flown his amazing new plane 300 miles from Worcester, Massachusetts, to New York City and back – nearly three times further than anyone else had yet managed, and with a loop around the Statue of Liberty for added flair. Nobody noticed this amazing feat, but in the days that followed, more than 2,000 people claimed to have seen him on further flights. No evidence has ever emerged that Tillinghast actually had a plane.*

Then, in the years before the First World War, hysteria reigned in the United Kingdom, as people reported seeing airships in the skies everywhere from Kent to Galway to Orkney. The Germans did, as it happens, have an airship; but there's no evidence it ever visited the UK. What certainly was abroad in the winter of 1912–13, however, was the fear of an increasingly confident industrial and military rival that now had the technology to rain death from the sky.†

This fear was not entirely misplaced. The Zeppelin raids that accompanied the First World War killed around 550 in Britain; the more sustained Blitz that accompanied the Second World War killed more than 40,000. That was followed by

---

* One mass sighting of Tillinghast's 'airship' took place on Christmas Eve in Providence, Rhode Island. It was left to H. P. Lovecraft, of all people, to point out that what they were actually looking at was the planet Venus (and not, say, some kind of indescribable Eldritch Horror).

† These stories were relayed in Tom's previous book, *Truth: A Brief History of Total Bullsh*t*.

flying bombs, *silent* flying bombs, and then, after August 1945, the threat of nuclear annihilation. In what may or may not have been a coincidence, it was roughly then – as mere flight became more commonplace, the space race got going, and everyone got comfortable with the fact that one foot wrong by the superpowers could mean Armageddon – that the belief in visitors from another world went into overdrive.

Perhaps imagining the skies to be a source of terror was, at this point, a rational response to reality. But to the psychologist Dr Carl Jung – he of the archetypes – there was something else going on, reminiscent of the ancient belief in interventionist gods. The sudden interest in UFOs, he told an interviewer in 1954, was a subconscious, spontaneous response to looming threat of catastrophe, in which 'eyes turn heavenward in search of help, and miraculous forebodings of a threatening or consoling nature appear from on high'.[17]

The belief in alien visitors, in other words, was not just a symptom of a terrifying and unstable world. It was, on some level, an attempt to escape it.

In the US, in the summer of 1947, two of the founding myths of modern ufology happened in quick succession. Firstly, an amateur pilot named Kenneth Arnold claimed to have seen nine shiny disc-shaped objects flying at around 1,200 miles per hour past Mount Rainier, not far from Seattle. Arnold came across as sober and respectable, and not prone to exaggeration, so the reporters who interviewed him decided he probably wasn't a crank and wrote up his story pretty straight.

The resulting coverage led to:

a) the popularisation of the phrase 'flying saucer' as a description for UFOs, and

b) Kenneth Arnold, who thought he'd seen some secret

military technology rather than an alien craft, seemingly
wishing he'd kept his mouth shut. 'This whole thing has
gotten out of hand,' runs one widely reproduced quote. 'I
want to talk to the FBI or someone ... I wonder what my
wife back in Idaho thinks.'[18]

Two weeks later, a public information officer at Roswell
Army Air Field in New Mexico did exactly the kind of thing
you're not supposed to do when involved in a conspiracy to
cover up the existence of alien life, and issued a press release,
announcing that the military had recovered the debris of a
'flying disc'. The next day, over in Texas, someone rather higher
up the chain of command clarified that the object was actually
just 'the remnant of a weather balloon and a radar reflector'.

This could well have been the truth: the wreckage weighed
only a few pounds, and the rancher who'd found it described
it as 'rubber strips, tin foil, a rather tough paper and sticks',
which doesn't sound massively alien. But the US Army had
announced they had a flying saucer, and then tried to walk it
back. Whoops.[19]

In some ways, it was a miracle it took as long for the
conspiracists to find this one as they did. But in 1947,
Americans still largely trusted their government. Thirty years
later – after the assassination of a president, Vietnam and
Watergate – they did not.[20]

And in 1978, conspiracy theorists got a very good reason
not to trust the official account of the Roswell incident:
someone who had been there told them not to. Jesse Marcel,
a lieutenant colonel who had been one of the first to handle
the debris, told the ufologist Stan Friedman that it was not of
this world. Result: a string of books claiming both that the
Roswell debris had been alien in origin, and that the military
had covered it up.[21]

In 1997, another lieutenant colonel, Philip J. Corso, published a tell-all memoir called *The Day After Roswell*. In it, he claimed to have examined alien bodies recovered from the crash site (four feet tall, four-fingered hands, light bulb-shaped head, you know the sort of thing), and to have worked for a secret government programme charged with reverse engineering alien tech for corporate use. This had produced all sorts of technologies (fibre optics, integrated circuits, lasers) without which the modern world is unimaginable, as well as others that, depending on what job you do, you probably *can* imagine the world without (night-vision goggles, Kevlar). The book was not taken entirely seriously – in 2001, the *Guardian* included it in its all-time top-ten literary hoaxes – but it spent weeks at the top of the best-seller lists all the same.*[22]

The 1990s also saw a growing number of conspiracy theories attach to another site in the deserts of the American west. Area 51, a classified Air Force test site not far from Rachel, Nevada, has been linked to everything from the development of secret energy weapons and teleport or time-travel technology, to the autopsy of the alien corpses recovered from the crash at Roswell.† The site was, the conspiracy theorists agreed, a sort of underground skyscraper, descending dozens of storeys beneath the Nevada desert.

The thing is, the US military really *was* doing top-secret things at both Area 51 and Roswell. The former had been used in the development of things like the U-2 spy plane: consequently, the US government spent decades pretending that the site didn't exist, even though it was extremely

---

* Corso died in 1998. Hmmm.

† The two sites are often bracketed together, but are actually almost 700 miles apart, with the whole of Arizona between them.

obvious to anyone standing on a nearby mountainside that it did.

In 1994, the Air Force admitted that it had covered up the truth about Roswell: the debris was no ordinary weather balloon, but a *spy* weather balloon, which had been loaded up with microphones and radio transmitters and sent to the upper atmosphere to monitor Soviet nuclear tests, as a part of the top-secret Project Mogul. (The same report suggested that rumours of alien bodies that had crept into news of the incident were probably anthropomorphic crash dummies, or maybe actual human bodies from a real crash that happened near Roswell in 1956.) In 2013, the US government rather grumpily admitted that Area 51 existed, too.[23]

And gradually, over the last few years, the US government has admitted to two things: that it has long been interested in UFOs, and that it has historically tried extremely hard to hide this interest from the public. Its logic had been, basically, that it had wanted to prevent real and valuable intelligence about threats to the United States being lost in a flood of hysterical reports about flying saucers. In 1966, it went as far as to hire CBS news anchor Walter Cronkite to helm a documentary entitled *UFO: Friend, Foe or Fantasy?*. When ufologists claimed the government was out to discredit them, they weren't actually wrong.

But this strategy had two unhelpful side effects. One was to make real secret projects seem a lot more exciting than they actually were. The other was to deter military officers and other credible witnesses from reporting genuine intelligence, for fear of looking stupid.[24]

And so, the government changed its stance. In December 2017, on the front page of the *New York Times*, Leslie Kean and two other journalists reported that the Pentagon had been monitoring the skies for UFOs for years.[25] And the Pentagon confirmed it.*

Again: 'Unidentified' is not the same as 'alien'. But also, for the first time, the US government is not entirely ruling out aliens. It is admitting that there's stuff out there we don't yet understand.

There are a number of other conspiracy theories that are, at the very least, UFO-adjacent, such as:

The black helicopter

In the paranoid years that followed the Watergate scandal, the black helicopter became a symbol of faceless government authority. In rural communities where people genuinely loved their guns, formed militias, and unironically believed Hillary Clinton to be not so much a politician they don't rate as literally Satan, the unmarked helicopters became associated with the sort of 'men in black' that would later inspire films like *The Matrix* and another whose name escapes us right now.

In the more extreme versions of the myth, the helicopters' occupants were representatives of the New World Order/ Zionist World Government/the federal government's alien allies, intent on conducting horrific experiments that involved

---

* In April 2020, the Pentagon declassified a number of videos of supposed UFOs. These videos had previously been released to the public by Tom DeLonge, a noted UFO conspiracy theorist and the former lead singer of skate punk band Blink-182. This is mentioned here largely to reiterate the point made in a previous chapter's footnotes: *skate punk absolutely was a thing.*

mutilating cattle or worse. In the tamer versions, they were merely UN-sponsored stormtroopers, there to impose international law on Montana.

Then again, perhaps they merely represented the federal government, but to some people that was bad enough. In 1995, the Idaho congresswoman Helen Chenoweth told the *New York Times* that the US Fish and Wildlife Service was landing the helicopters on ranchers' land in order to enforce the Endangered Species Act at gunpoint.[26] She held hearings on the helicopters and everything.[27]

Complicating things further is the fact that many federal agencies really do use black helicopters for surveillance or transportation. For all their paranoia, the militiamen were not wrong that the federal government expected a level of involvement in what happened inside the US.

Chemtrails

Chemtrails are another conspiracy theory resulting from a generalised distrust in authority, married, in this case, to a poor grasp of science and a psychological tic called the Baader-Meinhof phenomenon: the tendency to spot something more often once you're aware of it.*

Planes have always left 'contrails' in certain weather conditions: they're a normal result of the water vapour produced by

---

* The frequency illusion, as it's also sometimes known, did not drive the West German far-left group also known as the Red Army Faction to a campaign of terrorism: it's just that one of the earliest documented cases of it involved someone learning about them and then seeing their name a lot.

the combustion of fuel in the engines condensing around the particles left by the exhaust. But in 1996 – just as the internet was taking its first baby steps towards being a hive of conspiracy thinking that might one day kill us all – the US Air Force published a report about the potential for using nanotechnology, seeded by planes, to create 'artificial weather'. First the internet, then talk radio, got hold of the idea, with predictable results.

A few years later a whole bunch of US government bodies, including the Environmental Protection Agency and NASA, got together to explain that contrails were perfectly natural results of aviation, and not a sign that the government or corporations were pouring chemicals into the sky for the purposes of weather modification/psychological manipulation/population control/biological or chemical warfare [delete according to preference]. This, inevitably, made things worse.

There are several reasons the chemtrails theory has proved so insidious. One is that weather modification – cloud seeding to produce rainfall – is a real thing that has existed for decades. Another is that the formation and dissipation of real contrails varies depending on weather conditions, making them seem like they might be different things. Yet another is that the internet is awash with videos and photographs of 'chemtrail planes' filled with sinister-looking barrels: the planes are real, but the barrels are either water, to help fight fires or to act as ballast by simulating the presence of passengers in test planes.

The chemtrails conspiracy theory also seems to be an especially good way of getting someone into the rabbit hole, thanks to the aforementioned Baader-Meinhof phenomenon. Before they watch your YouTube video, they may never have spotted the confusing behaviour of contrails; after you've pointed it out, they won't be able to stop seeing it. Then, you can hit them with another theory, which leads us to:

The moon landing

The United States, after all, was very obviously losing the early stages of the Space Race. In 1957, the Soviet Union launched Sputnik 1, the first satellite, into space, then in quick succession managed the first animal in space, the first man in space, the first woman in space, and the first spacewalk. In May 1961, NASA successfully turned Alan Shephard into the first American in space. Because launch was delayed by several hours, he simultaneously became the first person to go to space in a suit full of his own wee.[28]

So when, two weeks later, President Kennedy stood before Congress and announced that the United States would put a man on the moon before the decade was out, it sounded pretty unlikely. And yet, one day shy of eight years and two months later, Neil Armstrong and Buzz Aldrin stepped on to the lunar surface.

Does that sound particularly plausible to you?

One man who didn't think so was Bill Kaysing,* who in 1976 published a pamphlet with the spoiler-heavy title of *We Never Went to the Moon: America's Thirty Billion Dollar Swindle*. In

---

* He wasn't alone: in 2021, the British satirist and broadcaster Ian Hislop told the *New Conspiracist* podcast that he remembered queuing for hours to visit some moon rock in a museum, only for some of his school fellows to laugh at his credulity for believing in the moon landings in the first place. Kids, like sinister globe-spanning conspiracies, can be very cruel.

it, he pointed out that no stars were visible in the pictures taken from the moon; that there was no blast crater under the landing module; and that shadows seemed to fall the wrong way. It would probably have stayed a fringe conspiracy, except that in 2001 Fox News broadcast a documentary under the title *Did We Land On The Moon?*, hosted by *X-Files* regular Mitch Pileggi, which concluded that, no, we did not.

The following year, the French director William Karel released the 'documentary' *Dark Side of the Moon*, which alleged that footage of the landing had been cooked up between the CIA and Stanley Kubrick. The director had narrowly escaped a clean-up operation that had seen most of those involved in the project assassinated on the orders of Richard Nixon, and spent the next twenty years as a recluse to protect his own life.[29]

Not only was all this fiction, it didn't even try to hide it: the film included a blooperreel, which runs over the credits. But those who came across isolated clips on YouTube didn't see that part. And the anomalies Kaysing identifies do, at first, sound deeply suspicious. There are rational explanations for all of them – camera exposure times make the stars invisible; blast doesn't work the same in a vacuum; the reflective properties of moondust affect the way shadows fall – but these are a lot harder to grasp.[30] So many conspiracists never get that far.*

Something else that's hard to grasp is why a government that couldn't fix the economy or win the war in Vietnam could achieve something as momentous as putting a man on

---

* One 'problem' with the moon footage that isn't hard to dismiss: the idea that the stars and stripes flag should be hanging limp but isn't. The reason it isn't is that it is very obviously being supported by a pole along its upper edge.

the moon. In the decades since, the space programme has receded into history, but making films has become the sort of thing any kid could do on their laptop. Perhaps it's no wonder that some people find it easier to believe that thousands of people could conspire to pretend the US went to the moon just to win a PR victory, than to accept that it actually did go there.

The lost cosmonauts

There is a sort of Soviet equivalent of the moon-landing hoax theory. The lost cosmonauts theory states that Yuri Gagarin was not, in fact, the first man in space: earlier cosmonauts either died in flight or, in the case of Vladimir Ilyushin, crash-landed, critically injured, in China.

The Soviet authorities did hush up the death of one would-be cosmonaut, Valentin Bondarenko, during a training exercise in 1961 – but this has been openly discussed since the 1980s. And when the archives in former Soviet countries opened up, no evidence emerged of any other lost cosmonauts.

What's more, while this theory does seem to have originated somewhere in the east, it's been most widely propagated in the West, where, aside from the places you'd expect to find conspiracy theories, it's also popped up in novels, comics, films and deliberate hoaxes. The Ilyushin story first appeared in the *Daily Worker*, the British communist newspaper today known as the *Morning Star*.[31]

Perhaps the capitalist West is unable to cope with a genuine communist achievement. Perhaps Soviet pride in their space programme meant there simply wasn't a market for stories that undermined it. Or perhaps there's no need for conspiracy theories, if you don't have any faith in your government to begin with.

In 1678, a farmer in Hertfordshire laughed in the face of a labourer who had just told him how much he wanted to be paid to mow his field, and swore he'd rather the devil did it instead. That night, the field appeared to be in flames; the next morning, he discovered it had been perfectly mowed. Alas, according to a woodcut pamphlet with the magnificent name of *The Mowing-Devil: Or, Strange NEWS out of Hartfordshire*, the farmer had 'not Power to fetch [his oats] away'.[32]

Crop circle enthusiasts have sometimes cited this as the first depiction of a crop circle, despite the fact that

a) the stalks in this story were cut, rather than, as in most crop circles, bent; and

b) there is a very obvious alternative explanation involving a vengeful farm labourer and a two-word phrase ending in 'you'.

But this incident did rather set the tone for the crop circle phenomenon: strange patterns in a field that are impossible to explain (as long as you ignore the possibility of 'some blokes mucking about'). Where once the otherworldly cause was assumed to be a devil, in the modern age, those seeking explanations for crop circles have instead tended to go with 'flying saucer woz ere'.

Those who think the true cause is the latter have yet to explain not only why nobody has ever seen a flying saucer making a crop circle, but also why they are most likely to appear near roads and towns. In 2003, nearly half of all the UK's crop circles were located within ten miles of the Avebury stone circles.[33] This may suggest some kind of mystical connection between alien visitors and the Neolithic people who built that monument; then again, it may be because someone in the Wiltshire area was just really into making crop circles.

Support for the 'blokes mucking about' hypothesis can also be found in the fact we know the identity of a couple of the blokes in question. Doug Bower and Dave Chorley came forward in 1991 and admitted to having been at it since the late 1970s, since when they had made around 200 crop circles. To prove their point, they made a new one in front of reporters, who then had it examined by prominent 'cerealogist' – that is, a believer in a supernatural explanation – Pat Delgado, who declared it to be authentic. On discovering he'd been had, Delgado promptly announced his retirement from the field.*

So no, crop circles are extremely unlikely to have been evidence of aliens. They are, however, evidence of a conspiracy: it's just that the conspiracy in question was cooked up not by a government trying to keep secret knowledge out of public hands, but by a couple of guys in a pub.[34]

Despite all this, the idea that we've been visited by aliens may be one of the less outlandish in this book. Indeed, everything we know about science suggests that it would be extremely weird if aliens *didn't* exist. The really weird thing is the absence of evidence for them.[35]

Consider the Fermi paradox, the problem, named after the Italian physicist Enrico Fermi, which stems from a contrast between two sets of observations. The first of these is that, as far as we can tell, alien life should be *everywhere*. In 1961, the

---

* Sorry about that joke. Also: Delgado's 1990 book on the subject was called *Circular Evidence*, which is just asking for trouble.

American astronomer Frank Drake came up with an equation[*] that attempted to calculate how many advanced civilisations there should be in the galaxy. It starts with physical constraints, like the rate of star formation, or the number of habitable planets; then moves into speculative biology, like the odds of intelligence evolving. Plugging the best numbers we have into Drake's equation suggests the galaxy should be absolutely teeming with life.

The second observation is that we've been scanning the heavens for any sign of intelligent life for decades now, and we haven't seen shit. Hence, the Fermi paradox, which can be pithily summed up by the phrase, 'Where is everybody?'

Now, there are various solutions to this problem. Maybe we just suck at spotting the signs of intelligent life; maybe, even if life is common, the evolution of intelligence is rare; or maybe – and this is where it gets bleak – there's *something else* that keeps the skies empty.

What might that something else be? One possibility concerns the last variable in the Drake equation, the mean length of time civilisations last. Perhaps the Darwinian drive to triumph in the battle for finite resources – necessary for intelligent life to evolve in the first place – also embeds within us a catastrophic impulse for competition to the death. Perhaps civilisation is, inherently, very short-lived.

The other, equally depressing, possibility is that the universe is an incredibly dangerous place, one that operates on a xeno-cidal 'shoot first, don't ask questions later' basis. Perhaps the difficulty of communicating over interstellar distances traps every civilisation in a logically inescapable example of the

---

[*] The equation goes as follows: $N = R_* \times f_p \times n_e \times f_l \times f_i \times f_c \times L$

prisoner's dilemma where cooperation isn't an option, and the only viable strategy is to ensure that any up-and-coming planetary intelligences are wiped out before they can do the same to you. Meanwhile, we've been cheerfully broadcasting our, 'Hey guys! Is there anybody out there?' messages into the cosmos for several decades. Perhaps, somewhere out in the darkness, there's already a bullet the size of the Burj Khalifa hurtling towards us at ninety-nine per cent of the speed of light.

In comparison, the possibility that aliens have already visited us and didn't destroy us on sight actually seems quite heartening. It would prove it's possible to be an active high-tech planetary civilisation without either killing yourselves or being annihilated by a paranoid space god. Even if the aliens are prone to acting like creepy weirdos – not saying hello, just occasionally kidnapping farmers to do experiments on them – it's *familiar enough* creepy weirdo behaviour to suggest that, on some level, they're like us.

There are some pretty compelling reasons why it's unlikely aliens have visited us – notably, the fact the universe has a hard speed limit. Still: we know a lot about how complex human societies are, and we know a lot about how rigid the laws of physics are. And given both of those, the idea that aliens might have discovered a workaround for the speed of light seems *much* more plausible than the idea that a small group of humans have discovered a fool-proof technique for invisibly controlling the direction of global society.

The reason so many people believe aliens have visited us, however, has a lot less to do with the likelihood or otherwise that they exist than it does with the human brain's almost infinite capacity to spot patterns, then assume someone must have made them. But, as we'll see in the next chapter, while some are looking at the stars, others are just looking at the gutter.

7

Viral Misinformation

I f you sit yourself down to watch *Les Misérables*, a number of thoughts might occur to you. You might be swept up in the epic story of nemeses and lovers set against the backdrop of revolution. You might be slightly less swept up, and be wondering how long it is before you can go to the loo. If you're watching the recent film version, you *might* be thinking that Russell Crowe was, perhaps, not an intuitive choice for a lead role that involves singing all of the dialogue.

What you're probably not thinking is that you're watching a musical about pandemic conspiracy theories.

And yet! At its heart, that's kind of what it is. The failed June Uprising of 1832, which serves as the setting for the bulk of the story, took place as a catastrophic cholera outbreak swept through Paris, a local flare-up of a devastating rolling pandemic that would cover three continents over the course of a decade. This was the first wave of a disease new to much of the world, only recently arrived from Asia – a terrifying new killer that would cause havoc for decades to come. And duelling conspiracy theories about the cause of the disease were one thing that helped light the spark of rebellion in the already febrile atmosphere of early nineteenth-century France.

In this, it was hardly unique. Throughout history, pandemics have acted as a magnet for conspiracy theories – false beliefs that have seen cities burn and innocents killed, all the while frustrating efforts to actually control the sickness.

Now, it has to be said that France in 1832 did not need much of an excuse for political upheaval: it had just had at least two revolutions, multiple *coups d'état*, two restorations of the monarchy and, temporarily, a massive great empire over the course of four extremely busy decades. But you'll be unsurprised to learn that all this rather bloody shuffling of the chessboard still hadn't *quite* fixed the underlying problems: a wealthy elite whose power struggles were detached from society, as the Industrial Revolution upended the traditional economy and brought people streaming into increasingly crowded cities, where a growing underclass lived in poverty and squalor. It was the kind of situation that would make a tinderbox think, 'Uh-oh, you're in danger of catching fire there.'

So it's important to be clear that cholera, and its associated conspiracy theories, didn't *cause* the June Uprising. It was way too complicated to have any single cause, and the long-term trends would most likely have eventually spilled over into revolt anyway. They had before, and would do so again before everything eventually settled down a bit. But both the epidemic and the conspiratorial beliefs about it certainly poured fuel on the fire. And then stood there, holding a match, waggling their eyebrows suggestively.

Ultimately, it was one man's death from the cholera outbreak that provided the catalyst for the uprising – that of the popular war hero General Lamarque, during whose funeral the rebellion began. (He gets a brief namecheck in the musical: 'Lamarque is ill and fading fast / Won't last the week out so they say.') Lamarque wasn't even the only member of the great and the good to succumb to the disease that year – the great naturalist, Georges Cuvier, and the Prime Minister himself, Casimir Pierre Périer, were also counted among the victims. But while the disease took some people from every station in life, it was far from being a great leveller – and that's where the conspiracy theories began.

The 1832 outbreak, like most cholera epidemics of the nineteenth century, was vicious in its inequality, tearing through the poor and the disadvantaged like some kind of microscopic Tory chancellor. Sailors and dock workers, domestic servants and cleaners, labourers and paupers were among those hardest hit by cholera; in one part of Paris, where artisans and workers made up around thirty per cent of the total population, they accounted for seventy per cent of the deaths in 1832.[1] This was decades before the true cause of the disease – a bacterium spreading through sewage-contaminated water – was established, and so people tried to make sense of these patterns as best they could. For the wealthy, it simply confirmed all their prejudices about the working class: that they were unclean, slovenly, prone to bad habits and deserving of their poverty. But for the poor themselves, it looked an awful lot like evidence that the elites were deliberately trying to kill them.

And so rumours of a plot to murder the masses began to spread like ... well, like the disease that was actually poisoning the masses. In his *French Affairs: Letters from Paris*, the visiting German poet Heinrich Heine wrote of the conspiracy theories that began to take hold: 'There rose all at once a rumour that many of those who had been so promptly buried had died not from disease but by poison. It was said that certain persons had found out how to introduce a poison into all kinds of food ... The more extraordinary these reports were, the more eagerly were they received by the multitude ...'[2] In his memoirs, the author Alexandre Dumas described how the public turned to these theories when confronted by an 'invisible enemy', writing that it 'irritated the people by its invisibility ... A material, visible, palpable cause would do its business much more effectually – at all events, revenge could be taken on a tangible cause.'[3]

The theories multiplied. Some said it was an attempt by the government to reduce the population to conceal imminent food shortages; others that the disease was a phantom, 'planted in people's minds by the government in order to distract attention from public affairs'.[4] Almost every political faction would be blamed at some point. The accusations turned to violence, as suspected poisoners were beaten and murdered. 'A man would be pointed at with a finger – pursued, attacked and killed!' Dumas wrote; Heine recalled seeing an innocent man attacked by a mob, as 'old women plucked the shoes from their feet and beat him on the head till he was dead'.[5]

Suspicion turned towards the medical establishment, who were seen as agents of the government and the instigators of the poisoning; doctors were among the main targets for attacks, and were 'forced to disguise themselves while making calls so as not to be recognised by the mobs'.[6] (Some medics and hygienists gave the public good reason for their suspicions, writing that the epidemic might be beneficial, as it would reduce the ranks of the impoverished and leave a healthier population behind. 'Great epidemics are followed by periods of great health,' one wrote, noting that 'the disease has claimed mainly sickly individuals of delicate constitution.')[7]

So fervent was the belief in the conspiracy theories that the authorities, calamitously, decided that the best approach was to try and blame someone else using a conspiracy theory of their own. The police – 'who in every country seem to be less inclined to prevent crime than to appear to know all about it', Heine wrote[8] – promptly put out statements claiming that the poisoning scares were being deliberately faked by anti-government activists going around pretending to poison things, in order to stir up discontent. This did not have the intended effect of placating the masses; instead it simply confirmed their suspicions that something dodgy was going on. It's hardly surprising that it led to an attempted rebellion – if you were convinced you were being poisoned by the elite, we suspect you'd be tempted to rebel, too.

Paris was far from the only place where cholera sparked violence: in fact, cholera riots were remarkably frequent throughout most of the nineteenth century, in countries right across Europe and beyond. Not only were they common, but they had an awful lot *in* common. As with Paris, they were often driven by a belief that the 'disease' was in fact a deliberate act, a campaign of poisoning targeted at the poor. And, as with Paris, the anger over this was directed not just at the wealthy, but at the medical establishment. As the historian Samuel Cohn put it: 'Without any evident communication among rioters from New York City to Asiatic Russia, or evidence that protestors were aware of similar riots taking place often simultaneously across these long distances, the cholera conspiracies repeated themselves in stories of elites masterminding a cull of the poor to lessen population pressures, with doctors, pharmacists, nurses, and government officials as the agents of this planned class mass murder.'[9]

These conspiracy-fuelled riots sometimes had major consequences. For example, the modern city of Donetsk was originally a settlement named Hughesovka: its curious linguistic hybrid of a name stemmed from the fact that it was built by Welsh metal workers and was named after its founder, a chap from Merthyr Tydfil called John Hughes. Not much of the original Hughesovka remained in modern Donetsk, even before recent conflicts, however: an awful lot of it was burned to the ground in 1892 in a cholera riot that reportedly drew a 10,000-strong mob.*

Perhaps confusion about the true cause of the disease was understandable in the early nineteenth century, when the prevailing medical explanations, such as miasma or 'bad air', weren't significantly more accurate. But it's worth noting that – as in Hughesovka – cholera conspiracies were still leading to violence many decades after John Snow demonstrated in 1854 that the disease was a water-borne one. Indeed, some persisted into the twentieth century, with at least twenty-six cholera riots taking place in Italy during the outbreak of 1910–11.[10] Conspiracies are not necessarily born of simple ignorance; they reflect deeper anxieties.

The UK didn't escape cholera riots – far from it. During the first, continent-wide outbreak that coincided with the

---

* The destruction of Hughesovka was also an oddity among cholera riots, in that it was anti-Semitic – targeting the city's Jewish population – as much as it was anti-medic. On the whole, cholera riots were notable in the history of European conspiratorial violence for their unusual *lack* of anti-Semitism, or indeed any ethnic or sectarian dimension.

Paris uprising, a series of riots occurred in cities across the country. Many of them targeted the medical establishment. In Aberdeen in December 1831, a large crowd destroyed the city's new anatomical theatre; in Leeds in 1832, a temporary treatment centre for victims was stoned by a mob, smashing windows; in Manchester the same year, soldiers were called in to disperse a crowd violently trashing a hospital.[11] Ambulances (or rather their nineteenth-century equivalents: litters and palanquins) were frequent targets, as crowds tried to prevent patients being removed to supposedly deadly hospitals.

Riots came also to Glasgow, London, Dublin, Sunderland, Bristol, Londonderry and Sligo, and a host of other towns and cities; across the British and Irish Isles, there were over seventy cholera riots in a fourteen-month period.[12] The British city worst affected by the 1832 violence was Liverpool, where at least eight individual riots broke out over the course of an intense couple of weeks in late May and early June.

While mistrust of the medical establishment as elitist, ineffectual and possibly malign was common across virtually all cholera riots, in Britain there was an extra reason for widespread scepticism of medical men. The cholera epidemic came just a few years after the Burke and Hare scandal had gripped the public imagination in Britain. The rise of professionalised medicine had led to a major surge in demand for cadavers to dissect; corpse-smuggling, grave-robbing and (in the case of Burke and Hare) murder had all moved in to fill the shortage of supply. As a major port city, Liverpool was a hub of the illicit corpse trade, which resulted in a number of grave-robbing scandals and trials in the city in the late 1820s. Mistrust of doctors may have been heightened by the fact that in at least one of these trials – of a 'middle man' named William Gill – at least some in the medical establishment rallied around him, starting a fund to pay for his defence.

All this had left the people of Britain in general, and Liverpool in particular, with a very clear notion that anatomists had an almost insatiable hunger for dead bodies, and would stop at nothing to ensure a regular supply of them. When cholera came along, it was extremely easy for people to put two and two together.

The first riot in Liverpool, on 29 May 1832, saw a crowd descend on a hospital in Toxteth, smashing windows as they attempted to stop someone being hospitalised. The anger was directed at medical staff, with a cry of 'Bring out the Burkers!' going up and one doctor being labelled a 'murderer'. This epithet would be repeated across the rest of the riots in Liverpool, and in many other cities around the UK, with medical professionals – and, in at least one case, a woman who was simply unlucky enough to be spotted leaving the hospital at the wrong time – being chased through the streets and accused of 'Burking'.[13]

Some in the UK's medical profession didn't help themselves. The riot in Manchester, which resulted in Hussars from the local barracks being called in, was sparked when a trainee doctor at a hospital in one of the city's poorest slums decided to cut off the head of a three-year-old boy who'd died of cholera, and take it home with him to experiment on. He replaced the child's head in the coffin with a brick. When this was discovered during the infant's funeral, a crowd decided to go and smash the hospital to bits. Which, honestly, seems understandable.[14]

The entwined history of cholera and conspiracism is far from the only example of how disease and misinformation go together, although it's certainly one of the longest-running and most consequential. It also illustrates well several of the repeating themes that emerge from this history.

In general, conspiracy theories about epidemics tend to spring from two areas of suspicion: on the one hand, theories that focus on the origins and causes of the disease, and on the other, theories about the medical and governmental *response* to the epidemic. The cholera conspiracies embodied both of these – and as often happens, the two merged in the attitude towards the medical profession, who were accused of both being the cause and of providing an even more malign cure.

Epidemic conspiracy theories can also vary in the extent to which they accept the reality of the disease itself. Some seek to lay blame for the sickness, as the poisoning theories did; others may suggest that the real danger actually isn't the sickness itself, and that it's simply a pretext for whatever nefarious schemes the authorities have in mind.

Still others may choose to deny the existence of the disease at all. That also happened in the UK during the first cholera outbreak – in a reaction that may seem rather familiar today, some people decided it was simply all a scam, referring to it as the 'cholera humbug'. One correspondent in the *Lancet* wrote in 1831 that cholera was merely a 'government hoax, got up for the purpose of … distracting the attention of the people away from the reform bill' – adding that they feared this trick had been pulled by the government before, with the assistance of 'the faculty' and the 'Liespapers'.[15]

The existence of the first type of theory – the kind that seeks to blame something or someone other than a disease for the sickness – has a long history. One of the most notorious examples started in 1348: as the Black Death swept Europe, a conspiracy theory about who was responsible for the disease went with it, leading to violent purges and massacres that lasted for several years. The true cause of the plague, it was said, was the Jews, who had been poisoning wells. This unleashed an orgy of violence and destruction on communities across much of Europe. Jewish people were driven from their homes, Jewish neighbourhoods were razed to the ground, and, in many cases, Jews were massacred in large numbers.

The most horrific case was probably in Strasbourg on Valentine's Day 1349, when hundreds of Jews were burned alive and thousands more expelled from the city. This massacre was notable not just for its savagery, but also for the inconvenient fact that the Black Death wasn't even present in Strasbourg at the time. Instead, the conspiracy theory became self-perpetuating: the fact that the master tradesmen who controlled the city authorities were taking steps to protect the Jewish community from unwarranted violence became, itself, evidence that they must have been bribed by the Jews. In an example of how powerful people can weaponise conspiracy theories to advance their own interests, one of the other outcomes of the Strasbourg massacre was that the tradesmen lost much of their political authority, and several noble families – who had participated in the expulsion of the Jews – saw their power restored.

The notion of wells being poisoned wasn't itself a new idea: in 1321, decades before the plague arrived, a similar conspiracy mania for claiming that wells were being poisoned *en masse* had swept much of France and the neighbouring regions. In that case, there wasn't even an epidemic going round to prompt the scare: it was a classic of pure rumour-driven panic, with nothing to support it. But even that had still been driven by primal fears of disease, contamination and outsiders: the panic initially blamed lepers for the supposed poisoning, with the result that hundreds of leprosy sufferers were imprisoned or executed. It was only as the panic spread and entered the political realm – where elites could impose their own agendas and anxieties on it – that the focus switched from lepers to Jews, or sometimes Muslims.

While the anti-Semitic purges of the mid-fourteenth century were probably the most destructive acts caused by such poisoning panics, they were by no means the last. Poisoning conspiracy theories would continue to be a common part of life in Europe for several centuries, often acting as an explanation for the continued threat posed by the Black Death, and occasionally bursting through into smaller acts of local violence.

One particularly notorious example took place in Milan in 1630, as the city attempted to hold another wave of the plague at bay. As in previous cases, it was an example of the conspiracy theory both bubbling up from widespread public fears and flowing down from the top of society.

The stage had been set by King Philip IV of Spain, who in 1629 sent out a warning that four Frenchmen had escaped from prison in Madrid, and were suspected of travelling the realm seeking to spread 'poisonous and pestilential ointments'.[16]

No malefic Frenchmen were discovered in Milan that year, but the theory was revived the following May as plague paranoia reigned – and turned into a full-blown panic after reports circulated that suspicious individuals had been seen placing 'poison' in the city's cathedral. This resulted in a wave of show trials, and a general air of paranoia that divided families and friends. Oh, and it also resulted in mobs beating up and nearly killing random people who attracted suspicion, including one old man, who was simply wiping down a church pew before sitting, and three young Frenchmen, who turned out to just be tourists who wanted to admire the cathedral.*

Outsiders weren't the only ones getting blamed for causing disease; sometimes there would be other targets, like new technology. In 1890, while an influenza pandemic raged – the 'Russian' or 'Asiatic' flu, which originated somewhere near Bukhara in the Russian Empire and would kill about a million people worldwide – the European edition of the *New York Herald* reported on what it described as the 'latest influenza theory'. 'Instead of being the work of the usual influenza microbe,' the paper wrote, admittedly somewhat sceptically, 'the Russian influenza is produced by an entirely new microbe that has been developed by the electric light.' Evidence for this theory included the fact that the disease 'has raged chiefly in towns where the electric light is in common use', and that it 'has everywhere attacked telegraph employés'.[17] This particular theory doesn't seem to have widely caught on, fortunately, sparing the nascent lightbulb industry from a PR crisis.

The next great influenza pandemic, the inaccurately named 'Spanish Flu' of 1918 that killed tens of millions worldwide, also saw its fair share of conspiracy theories. The fact that it began spreading in the last days of the First World War was a major factor here: it's hardly surprising that, coming during a conflict that had already seen a variety of horrible and terrifying new battlefield techniques unleashed, many suspected it was a weapon, and, in the United States especially, it was widely believed that it had been deliberately spread by German agents. Accusations and rumours

---

* In the history of suspected foreign poisoners claiming they were merely innocent cathedral enthusiasts on holiday, this probably ranks as one of the more convincing examples.

abounded – for example, the influenza was actually transmitted by aspirin tablets manufactured by the German firm Bayer. (Bayer's US operation were forced to take out press adverts across the nation insisting that their company was 'completely under American control' and that every 'officer and director of the Company manufacturing [the tablets] is a native American'.)[18]

As we've seen elsewhere, a fair amount of this conspiracising seems to have come from official sources getting carried away, rather than the ill-informed masses. 'It is quite possible that the epidemic was started by Huns sent ashore by Boche submarine commanders,' opined the head of Health and Sanitation for the USA's wartime merchant shipping fleet in September 1918. 'The Germans have started epidemics in Europe, and there is no reason they should be particularly gentle with America.'[19] (They hadn't actually done that in Europe – and a month later, an official US government investigation would conclude that, no, they hadn't done it in America either, after which the anti-German conspiracies seemed to subside.)

In more recent times, the HIV pandemic has also been the subject of a huge amount of conspiracist theorising about its origins. In the West, this was often turned against its victims – gays were spreading the infection to decent society, it was suggested, perhaps deliberately. Elsewhere, it was malign outside forces who were to blame. In the Democratic Republic of Congo, the virus was said to originate in imported canned food. In South Africa, some claimed that it was spread by teargas, and was the final genocidal act of the departing apartheid regime. In Haiti, the story went that HIV had been manufactured in a US government lab.[20]

This last is probably the most enduring HIV conspiracy,

and again it's one that has been repeatedly advanced by elites with political agendas. It may well have originated in the last years of the Cold War as Soviet propaganda, and was widely adopted around the world in places primed by history to believe in acts of American malevolence. Notably, it was echoed by South Africa's President Thabo Mbeki, as part of his widespread campaign of AIDS denialism in the early 2000s. This wasn't limited to conspiracy theories about the origins of the virus – Mbeki also indulged in the second strand of epidemic conspiracism, attacking the medical response to the disease. The therapeutic drug AZT, he claimed, was toxic and dangerous, and part of a plot by Western pharma companies to both profit from and kill Africans.

Mbeki would go on to appoint a health minister who promoted natural remedies including beetroot and lemon juice for AIDS, and diverted funding from HIV prevention programmes – actions that probably resulted in hundreds of thousands of deaths. In this, he was aided by a small coterie of contrarian Western scientists, who continued to insist that HIV was not the cause of AIDS, and sometimes questioned whether there was even a pandemic happening at all.

That second kind of conspiracy theory – which focuses on the medical responses – also has a long history. It's visible in responses to the Ebola epidemics of the twenty-first century, which – like the cholera riots of the nineteenth century – have regularly seen outbreaks of violence directed at medical workers based on conspiracy theories about the disease. Some of these theories deny the existence of the disease; many focus on the perception that people are taken to hospital to be killed, or that the disease is spread by Western organisations for profit or population control or both. The Red Cross has been a particular target of attacks; some rumours even suggested that Red Cross workers were spraying Ebola into schools.[21]

This kind of distrust in medical responses goes back a long way. But it's frequently been exacerbated when the forces of inequality, colonialism and culture clash have combined to make people suspicious of outside authorities.

When a catastrophic outbreak of bubonic plague arrived in Hong Kong in 1894, for example, the British authorities acted swiftly, decisively, and with all the tact and grace that you would expect of the British Empire circa 1894. Soldiers carried out house-to-house inspections in the Tai Ping Shan district, where the Chinese workers lived in terribly overcrowded conditions, and which was by far the worst affected by the epidemic. ('I am glad to say that the Europeans here are unaffected,' the British Medical Journal's correspondent noted cheerily at the time.)[22] A suspected case in a household would result in mandatory evacuations and often the complete destruction of the property; before the year was out, 7,000 people had been forced from their homes and 350 houses destroyed. Traditional Chinese burial practices were also blithely ignored. All this added up to produce a profound sense of anger and distrust among the local population – so it's hardly surprising that conspiracy theories began to circu-late, accompanied by an anonymous poster campaign assailing the government. British doctors, it was claimed, were 'cutting open pregnant women and scooping out the eyes of children to make medicines for the treatment of plague-stricken patients'.[23]

The British response to this opposition was a campaign of community outreach, listening to grievances, and working to address misconceptions through increased openness and transparency. Ha ha, no – only joking. Their response was actually to park a gunship just off the coast of Tai Ping Shan. Which is one way of building trust, I suppose.

A similar story played out a few years later, when the same wave of plague reached India. In many cities, the colonial administration's, uh, energetic response of mandatory quarantine, segregation camps and forced hospitalisation also prompted a fierce backlash, in the form of a wave of riots from Mumbai to Kanpur and the Punjab, that saw hospitals attacked and plague camps burned. Again, high-handed actions and a casual disregard for local customs – sidelining local medics, forcibly entering houses, military-style search parties and surprise raids, separating families, manhandling women, preventing proper funerals, *and* destroying possessions and homes – were the root of it, although it didn't help that, in at least some locations, Europeans were exempt from the rules. The resulting conspiracy theories trod plenty of familiar ground: people were being taken to hospital so they could be poisoned; the epidemic was a means of exterminating the poor and thinning out overcrowded cities; the disease was not real, and was just an excuse to impose stringent regulations and to extort bribes from people by threatening to report them as symptomatic.[24]

As we've seen, when it comes to building public trust, the medical establishment has often been its own worst enemy. And you don't need to go all the way to the more drastic end of the scale – decapitating children's corpses, say – to see why. Too often, throughout medical history, you find the same things cropping up: blaming the lifestyle of sufferers for their illness, even when there was no blame to be assigned; dismissing patients' descriptions of their own symptoms or situations; dismissing knowledge that comes from outside their carefully gatekept profession; treating their patients more like experimental subjects than people; generally being kind of arrogant.

But there are other issues, for which you can't really blame the medical profession, but which help explain why they so often attract conspiracy theories. For one thing, doctors are closely associated with ... well, death. As in the cholera outbreaks, the fact that more people died in hospital than at home was taken as evidence that hospitals themselves were deadly, rather than as evidence of a broadly accurate system of diagnosis and triage. (And, fair play, before the modern understanding of germ theory and medical hygiene, hospitals were kind of death traps. Even today, hospital-acquired infections remain a major issue.)

For another thing, what doctors actually do – even though it may be medically necessary – is often unpleasant, and triggers a whole range of primal fears around things like blood, pain and bodily violation. You may know intellectually that your doctor is wise and well-intentioned. But still, it's hard to not instinctively believe that somebody's up to no good when they're planning to literally put their hands inside you. (Not in a fun way.)

Nowhere is that instinctive worry more obvious than when doctors say, 'You know that disease you're very worried about? We've got a plan. We're going to basically give you the disease, to stop you getting the disease. Does that sound good?'

Anti-vaccination sentiment is as old as ... well, vaccination. In fact, in some ways it's older. Edward Jenner's pioneering development of the first smallpox vaccine in the late eighteenth century was really just a development of the pre-existing concept of 'variolation', which had been practised in many parts of the world for thousands of years. (Vaccination and variolation are both types of inoculation, which is the general term for artificially building up immunity.) Variolation is a fairly blunt tool: it involves directly exposing people to the actual pathogen in order to build up an immune response. Vaccination, meanwhile, uses a milder, inactive or harmless version to achieve the same result with less risk – Jenner's breakthrough used the less-deadly cowpox as a safer proxy for smallpox. The key to variolation was achieving the exposure in a controlled way (for example, via a small incision to the skin rather than through the respiratory system, which lessened the chance of the resulting illness being severe).

It was this practice that led, in the small hours of the morning on 14 November 1721, to someone throwing a bomb through the window of a Puritan minister's home in Boston.

The minister in question was the Reverend Cotton Mather, who fans of the previous chapter may remember as the guy who wrote about a ship sailing through the air in Connecticut. Fans of the Salem Witch Trials, meanwhile, may also know him as one of the key instigators of that particular outbreak of hysteria. But three decades after those trials, a very different kind of trial would see Mather on the other end of conspiratorial accusations, when a smallpox epidemic swept through Boston. Influenced by both medical texts and his slave Onesimus – who had been variolated in Africa, where the technique was common – he began advocating for local doctors to start inoculating people in the American colonies, where the practice was virtually unknown at the time.[25]

The Boston medical community was mostly set against the idea: it was untested, and quite probably also against God's will. But Mather found one doctor willing to go along with his plans, and together they began their experiment. This set off a wave of furious opposition from both the general populace and the medical establishment, who accused them of deliberately spreading the disease. The battle was conducted in a series of vicious back-and-forths in pamphlets, early newspapers and public meetings – plus, of course, one instance of a bomb being chucked into Mather's house, with a note reading 'I'll inoculate you with this' attached.[26] (The device did not go off.) Many of Mather's opponents drew a link between his belief in inoculation and his earlier fondness for killing witches; the *New-England Courant*, a newspaper published by Benjamin Franklin's older brother James, decried those who had been 'Instruments of Mischief and Trouble ... from the Witchcraft to Inoculation'. Mather, for his part, suggested that those who opposed him had probably been possessed by the devil.[27]

But still, Mather had succeeded in getting several hundred people inoculated. And, in a notable post-Salem improvement in his attitude towards quality of evidence, he made sure to gather data on the outcomes, which showed very clearly that death rates in the inoculated were far lower than in the rest of the population. The technique grew in popularity in the colonies over the following century, with the great and the good from Benjamin Franklin to Thomas Jefferson signing up to it, and George Washington famously mandating that all of his troops in the Revolutionary War should be inoculated.

Naturally, that wasn't the end of vaccine scepticism – not least because the word 'vaccine' didn't even exist yet. But in the nineteenth century, even after Jenner's work had been widely accepted, resistance to vaccination measures was common. In 1853, anti-vaccine riots were seen in several English towns. In the early 1870s, Stockholm saw a majority of its population refuse vaccines, a situation that only changed after a major smallpox epidemic in 1874. In the latter half of the century, a multitude of organisations with names like the Anti-Compulsory Vaccination League and the Anti-Vaccination Society of America sprang up on both sides of the Atlantic.[28]

In Leicester, towards the end of the century, there was a stand-off lasting many years in which the vaccine-sceptical local health authorities flatly refused to carry out the government's policy of mandatory vaccination. (That draconian regime, which included steep fines for vaccine refusal, was rightly seen as victimising those who couldn't afford to pay; the opposition succeeded in getting the principle of consent encoded in British law.) Ironically, the alternative approach advocated by the city's anti-vaccination activists mirrored exactly the kind of techniques that fuelled backlash in other circumstances – tracking and tracing the infected, imposing strict quarantine and isolation, and burning their possessions.[29]

A key thing about much of this early opposition to vaccination is that it wasn't especially conspiratorial in nature. As with many of the topics we've looked at, vaccine scepticism isn't inherently a conspiracy theory. You *could* think that vaccinations, on balance, do more harm than good without believing that there's anything conspiratorial behind them. Early vaccination techniques were frequently so unpleasant ('cut open a child's arm and rub in pus from another child's blisters') that resistance to them doesn't require a complicated explanation – simple disgust was enough. And, in the nineteenth century, the evidence for vaccination's safety and efficacy was far patchier than it is now, and those on both sides of the debate would trade statistics of questionable veracity in a way that seems very familiar today.

But these fights laid much of the groundwork for modern anti-vaccination movements – and in the modern age, as we'll see, the implicit conspiracism that lies in vaccine scepticism came to the fore. The sheer weight of evidence and medical consensus in favour of vaccines means it's quite hard to sustain the position that they're harmful – unless, that is, you believe that something malicious, rather than misguided, is going on.

It's worth pausing here for a moment to ask why, exactly, do pandemics attract conspiracy theories in this way?

Partly it's because the fear of disease – more broadly, the fear of contamination and contagion – is among the most deeply rooted and primal of our fears. And conspiracy theories that draw on primal fears are well set to spread like wildfire. Our instinct to avoid things that might harm us is incredibly powerful – it's why we find the sight or smell of rotting food repellent, and why we may feel a strong aversion to people who appear sickly.

This isn't just limited to disease, of course. As with the well-poisoning manias of the Middle Ages, panics about contaminated food or drink have been common throughout history – for example, in Belgium in June 1999, when the government banned Coca-Cola for two weeks amid a nation-wide scare that it was making people ill. (Investigations later concluded that these fears were baseless.) These panics can sometimes rise to the level of conspiracy theory; a few years before the Belgian Coke panic, a series of scares about deliber-ately contaminated chewing gum sprang up in the Middle East, first in Egypt, in 1996, then again a year later in the Palestinian territories. This gum was supposedly tainted with hormones that would drive the youth into sexual frenzy;

perhaps unsurprisingly, Israel was blamed. (There's no evidence to suggest that this supposed psychoactive sex gum was ever actually a thing.)[30]

Such contamination fears lie behind some of our more enduring conspiracy theories. The fear of chemtrails rests on a fear that our very air is being surreptitiously poisoned for some nefarious purpose. Likewise, while the long-running arguments about adding fluoride to water supplies isn't necessarily conspiratorial in nature – there's a legitimate debate to be had about basically any public health measure, even if the medical consensus is largely in favour of fluorida-tion – it can definitely tip over into conspiracism: for example, when it's suggested that fluoridation is a tool of population control, or that, as one right-wing periodical put it in 1960, 'fluoridation is known to Communists as a method of Red warfare'.[31]

But this fear of contamination and contagion, powerful as it is, isn't the only explanation of why disease outbreaks tend to spark conspiracy theories. It's also because disease outbreaks are almost perfectly set up to trigger our instinctive disbelief that massive events can have small or random causes.

For a long time, of course, we didn't even know what the causes of many diseases were. But even now we do know – about parasites and bacteria and viruses and what-have-you – they still don't *feel* like a satisfying explanation for a pandemic, especially when you're stuck in the middle of one of the bloody things. How can these huge, world-changing events – which upend lives, kill on a vast scale and reshape the very fabric of society – possibly be caused by something that's literally invisible to the naked eye? A molecule gets copied slightly wrong inside a bat inside a cave somewhere in Yunnan province, and that sets off a chain of events that, a little while later, means it's now a crime for me to leave my house? Come on.

And there's something else at work in the nature of epidemics themselves that leads us to see hidden hands at work behind them. Infectious diseases are perhaps the world's most tangible examples of rapid-fire, real-time evolution in action – and, just like any of the other outcomes of evolution that we see all around us, we often struggle to see how they could be the result of a purely natural process. Instead, they seem to have all the characteristics of ... well, intelligent design.

In short, diseases often *look* an awful lot like somebody planned them.

That's not what's going on, of course; it's just the brutally effective process of natural selection playing out. Every pathogen is, fundamentally, just a set of instructions for producing more copies of those instructions. If the instructions aren't very good at making more copies of themselves, then, over time, you'll get fewer of them; if they turn out to be very good instructions that are extremely effective at getting themselves reproduced, before long you'll be flooded with copies. Sometimes the instructions get copied a bit wrong. Most of the time, those copying errors make them worse, or basically useless. But every now and then, by pure random chance, those errors will make the instructions even *more* effective at getting copies of themselves made – at which point, our disease is off to the metaphorical races.

Imagine a large office filled with very dutiful – but unfortunately also extremely gullible – staff. Now imagine that, one day, you sneak into this office and leave a piece of paper on someone's desk. That paper says, simply, 'Retype the words on this paper, print out 2 copies, and place those copies around the office.' The first office worker to encounter it will do as they're told, and after a short while, we'll have 3 copies of the paper in the office. The next two staff to come across the newly distributed sheets of paper will do the same, then the next four, and so on. This would be bad enough on its own, from an office productivity point of view. But somewhere along the line, someone makes a typo as they're copying out the text. Their version of the paper now says 'print out 3 copies'. Oops.

Before too long, the number of pieces of paper that say '3 copies' will outstrip those that say the original '2 copies'. And as the number of pieces of paper increase, and more staff set themselves to the task of retyping the message, so the opportunities for further errors grow. Some of these will make our paper virus less effective – they'll reduce the number of copies, back to two or one. Some typos will be disastrous – 'print out 3 capes' results in three pictures of Superman with no instructions on them at all, and that line of the paper virus ends there. But some, by sheer chance, will be dramatically more successful at getting themselves copied. Shortly after lunch, during which all the staff were congratulating themselves on what a good job they'd done that morning, and how pleased their CEO would be with their diligent work, someone mistakenly types 'print out 30 copies' instead of '3'. By the time everyone clocks off that day, that thirty-copy variant has come to dominate all others in the office, almost all staff are now hard at work typing and printing pieces of paper, and the company is on the verge of collapse.

That's roughly what happens with viruses, except the office is your body.

If 'pure dumb luck' still doesn't seem like a good

explanation for how new diseases emerge, then it's perhaps worth considering the scale of what we're talking about here. It's literally unimaginable – the human mind can't really conceive of things of this scope. There are (deep breath) an estimated 10,000,000,000,000,000,000,000,000,000,000,000 individual viruses on our planet – that's ten nonillion, a one followed by thirty-one zeros, a ridiculous number you will basically never need to use in your life.[32] It works out at more than a sextillion viruses for every living person right now (another ridiculous number, one followed by twenty-one zeros). If you divided Earth's viral load equally among every star in the universe, each star could house at least ten million viruses before you ran out. And that's just viruses! We haven't even talked about bacteria or parasites or protozoa! What we're saying is: diseases have an awful lot of chances to get lucky.

Next, consider that what works best for diseases in making more copies of themselves will change with their circumstances. A disease strategy that involves, say, jumping from cows to humans will work pretty well in an agrarian society where people interact with cattle a lot. It will be notably less effective at infecting commuters on the London Underground.* But a disease that makes infected people cough, on the other hand …

This means that, as our living conditions change over time, so too do the diseases that thrive in them. As such, infectious

---

* Cows are not, as far as we can tell, explicitly banned under Transport for London's conditions of carriage, but station staff have the discretion to prevent people bringing animals on board trains if they cannot be carried by that person. Yes we actually researched this. Shut up.

diseases have an almost uncanny ability to reflect our societies back at us, and to starkly expose their flaws and vulnerabilities: that simple process of natural selection automatically amplifies all of the things that we hoped we could ignore. Diseases are like weeds growing through a pavement. They force cracks open wide – but really, they're just showing us where the cracks were in the first place.

And so, the history of our pandemics closely matches that of the societies they occurred in. They become a darkly satirical running commentary on stories of human progress, a cruel funhouse mirror reflecting back at us all our anxieties about change.

So, in medieval times, the plague moves along new continent-spanning trade routes, hitching a ride on fleas who hitched a ride on rats who hitched a ride on wagons and boats; an early eruption of modernity intruding on a largely pre-modern world. The colonial age is accompanied by a deadly, asymmetrical two-way exchange of pathogens, with 'tropical' diseases helping to convince settlers that these new lands are hostile and must be tamed, while the sicknesses they bring with them wipe out entire populations. Cholera, spread through dirty water, is the disease of the industrial nineteenth century – a thing of overcrowded, unsanitary cities and widening inequality. Respiratory diseases like influenza come to the fore in the twentieth century, finding a happy hunting ground in our dense, hyper-networked world of rapid international travel – where a person can cough on one side of the world and, within a day, someone on the other side has been infected. And then there's HIV, a ruthless exploiter of inequalities, whether it's devastating marginalised groups in wealthier nations or running riot in poorer countries, exposing the vast gaps between the global haves and have-nots.

They seem like they know what they're doing. They seem like they're making a point. No wonder people end up believing that some sinister force is behind them.

Part III
All Systems Go

In which the conspiracies expand in space and time, every aspect of life eventually becomes folded into increasingly systemic theories, and everybody involved gradually loses their grip on reality.

8

2020 Hindsight

Okay, so. We don't know if you noticed, but ... well, we've had a little bit of a pandemic recently.* And as you'd expect, just about every aspect of the conspiracy theories that accompanied historical outbreaks was replicated once more – only, this time, with many years of additional conspiracy lore to draw on. Where most previous epidemics produced event theories, limited to trying to explain what was happening in front of them, Covid-19 theories were able to pull pre-existing and far more wide-ranging theories from the hive mind, and apply them to what was happening. These theories were *systemic*.

---

* Current events are one of those areas where a book's readers have an advantage over the book's authors, because you're reading from the future. What's it like there? Is it ... over? Over-ish? Please believe us when we say that we have no more profound hope for the book than this: we hope you're reading this in a pub. Or beside a pool on holiday. We really hope you have to put it down and stop reading *right now*, because all your friends have arrived.

That the pandemic provoked conspiracy theories, just like all those previous outbreaks of something new and scary, was not surprising. Neither was the fact that we talked an awful lot of *other* types of nonsense too. Conspiracy theories are only one of the myriad inventive ways humans have of looking at the world and getting it totally wrong. As the novel coronavirus spread around the world, so too did a thousand strains of falsehood. Like the virus itself, misinformation passed easily from country to country, with no respect for international borders.

Spurious rumours, mass panics and fake cures were everywhere, and they had serious consequences. In Arizona, a man died after ingesting chloroquine phosphate – in the form of fish-tank cleaner – after President Trump touted chloroquine as a possible cure for Covid. In Iran, hundreds died from drinking industrial alcohol, thanks to a belief that it could ward off the sickness. The President of Tanzania denied Covid, and then reportedly died of Covid (although this was officially denied).[1] Those are just some of the more dramatic examples. We'll probably never know how many lives the spread of misinformation truly cost, whether it was ineffective folk remedies that bred false reassurance, ideologically motivated arguments against public health measures, or even the misguided certainties of health authorities confronted with an imperfectly understood disease.

The SARS-CoV-2 pandemic provided probably the most fertile ground ever for misinformation to flourish on a worldwide scale. As we've seen, conspiracy theories tend to attach themselves, limpet-like, to big and dramatic news stories. So do other types of misinformation. And there was no story bigger, more dramatic or more all-encompassing than the coronavirus. In the space of just weeks, as outbreaks blossomed across the planet and it became apparent that this thing was not going to stay a local concern, other news stories fell away from the front pages. Suddenly there was one single topic that crowded every other out of the global conversation – and that conversation was genuinely worldwide, in ways that very few truly are.

It's hard to imagine a scenario that could be better suited to the spread of untruths: a single global news story, one that directly impacted people's lives with the terrifying but intangible threat of contamination, dropped into a world more connected than it had ever been before. More than that, it was also a threat about which there was genuine scientific uncertainty. For the first few months of the pandemic, at least, there was a true information vacuum. You could reasonably judge the credibility of any expert by how often they said, 'We don't know.' Anybody who claimed certainty where none existed deserved to be greeted with scepticism. It's not clear that anybody came through the pandemic with a 100 per cent track record of getting everything right, and plenty of experts got some things very badly wrong.

Quite how rapidly misinformation spread around the world in those early weeks can be illustrated with one story: that of the imaginary helicopters. It's far from the most serious case study: it's unlikely anybody died because of it, and the harm it caused probably doesn't extend much beyond a little extra anxiety, at a time when there was no shortage of genuine reasons for worry.

As far as anyone can tell, the rumour began in Italy, some time around 10 March 2020, when the country was deep in the nightmarish reality of the first major European outbreak. It was a short message, which was passed from person to person over social networks, both private and public, via tweets and Facebook posts and texts and WhatsApps. The message said (to use an English version): 'Tonight from 11.40pm, nobody should be on the street. Doors and windows should remain closed as five helicopters spray disinfectants into the air to eradicate the coronavirus.' It then exhorted readers to pass the message on to all of their contacts.

The message almost immediately went global. As Dr Peter Burger – a Dutch academic who studies misinformation and who tracked the spread of the helicopter rumour around the world – told UK fact-checking organisation Full Fact at the time, the helicopter message 'reached citizens all over the world in a mere two weeks. From Colombia to Egypt, Kuwait, India, Pakistan, Indonesia, the Philippines, Belgium, Switzerland, Spain, Italy and the Netherlands: everywhere the story was adapted to local circumstances, and fitted with fake credentials'.[2] What's fascinating is that, while the international spread was occurring, with the warning being translated between languages, and local details like the logos of police forces or armies being added, some aspects almost always remained the same: there were five helicopters, and they'd arrive at the oddly precise time of 11.40pm.

It's not quite a conspiracy theory, although it's packed with conspiracy-adjacent tropes: mysterious helicopters are a recurring theme in conspiratorial tales, as is the secretive airborne dispersal of dangerous chemicals. It's chemtrails and the men in black all rolled into one, except here they're presented as the good guys.

But this sort of stuff was *everywhere*. The army was on the streets of Clapham, preparing to impose martial law; thieves were robbing houses by handing out chloroform-soaked masks; hand sanitiser would explode in hot cars. None of this should have been unexpected, given the history of pandemic misinformation. And, if we're honest, it's also totally under-standable, given how suddenly and profoundly everybody's lives were upended. It's worth remembering just how deeply *weird* those first few months of the crisis were. In a world turned suddenly on its head, it's not surprising that people struggled to tell the real from the fake. When everything is strange, nothing seems implausible.

Which is where the conspiracy theories come in.

One thing that's worth remembering about the major Covid conspiracy theories is: by and large, they didn't spring from nowhere. They weren't created afresh in response to the pandemic. They were pre-existing beliefs, often with an extensive history, that were adapted to incorporate the pandemic – and suddenly found themselves with a much larger and more receptive audience than before.

Not only that, but the centrality of a single news story led to cross-pollination between previously siloed conspiracist subcultures: people who'd been into one theory suddenly found a sympathetic ear for their views in other communities, and in turn folded the new theories they'd encountered on their travels into their own narratives. Previously niche views (did you know there's a subset of the alternative medicine community that believes viruses don't exist?) could be picked up and integrated into larger theories if they bolstered the underlying worldview, or filled in a plot hole. Covid created a sort of conspiracy Voltron, with disparate parts coming together to form a much larger beast. The superconspiracy was growing.

Consider 5G. The fear that the relatively new 5G mobile technology was somehow causing the pandemic ended up spreading around much of the world; in the UK, where it was particularly prominent, the theory had real-world consequences. Mobile phone masts and other infrastructure were the subject of arson attacks, while telecoms engineers were publicly abused and threatened as they went about their jobs.[3] There was a particularly grim irony that this all happened just as the country was relying on its phone and internet connections for the essentials of life in a way it never had before. (An additional irony: many of the vandalised masts and abused engineers had nothing to do with 5G.)

The Covid/5G theories began early on in the outbreak. The first social media posts linking 5G and the new coronavirus appeared in January 2020, not long after the rapid spread of the novel virus in China began getting significant coverage in the international press, and before it had even been declared a pandemic. Initially, the link was drawn somewhat tentatively: for example, one (now deleted) Facebook post said: 'Wuhan was where 5G was first rolled out ... What if 5G wrecked immune systems and thereby boosted the virulency of the common cold?'[4]

Now, a lot of conspiracy theorising is based on exactly this kind of coincidence – or rather, on the insistence that coincidences simply can't be coincidences. And just as in this case, those coincidences have a tendency to melt away once you actually look a bit deeper.

It's absolutely true that Wuhan did have 5G, and it was one of the first cities to get it in China. But the key phrase there is 'one of'. China's 5G roll-out was launched in fifty cities all at the same time. Beijing, Shanghai, Shenzhen, Nanjing, Chengdu, Gaozhou, Tianjin, and many more all got invites to the 5G party as well. And China's cities were nowhere near the first around the world to have commercially available 5G – it was already up and running in numerous countries, including the USA, the UK and South Korea. By the time Covid came along, far from being a lone pioneer, Wuhan was one of hundreds of cities worldwide to have 5G.

When you put it like that, the coincidence seems a bit less spooky. This did not stop people taking the 5G theory and running with it.

You might think that the fact the first major Covid outbreak outside China happened in Iran should have stopped the 5G theory in its tracks, on the seemingly conclusive grounds that Iran didn't have 5G at all. Sadly not. Throughout the pandemic, the fact that Covid outbreaks kept occurring in cities or countries where 5G had yet to be introduced didn't deter those determined to believe; nor did the fact that South Korea, the undisputed world leader in 5G coverage, was also one of the world's few Covid success stories. Because the virus was particularly good at spreading in large, dense, hyperconnected cities – exactly the kind of place that telecoms companies tend to launch their shiny new tech – there were always enough of these coincidences to keep it going, as long as you didn't mind some heavy-duty cherry-picking.

It's probably worth making clear at this point that, for the avoidance of doubt, 5G did not cause Covid – or any other health problem, for that matter. 5G isn't some radical new technology; it's just good old-fashioned radio waves, at a slightly different frequency to the ones we were already using. Importantly, it's what's known as 'non-ionising' radiation – which means it's at a lower frequency than visible light, and doesn't have enough energy to cause molecular damage (such as to your DNA). It's only when you get beyond visible light on the electromagnetic spectrum – ultraviolet, X-rays and gamma rays – that radiation causes the problems we're familiar with, like sunburn, cancer or Hulks. Everything below that either passes through your body harmlessly, or doesn't pass through it at all (5G actually penetrates your body less deeply than previous mobile phone frequencies; the higher the frequency, the more energy gets dissipated at the surface). The worst it could do is maybe heat you up a bit as the energy is absorbed, but no mobile phone technology comes anywhere close to the power needed for that to have a noticeable effect.

We know all this because, well, electromagnetic radiation is literally one of the most studied and best understood natural phenomena in the entire universe. We've tested it a *lot* to see what it does to humans. A nice bunch of nerds called the International Commission on Non-Ionizing Radiation Protection are in charge of setting the standards for these things, and they're happy to tell you that 5G base stations only put out about a hundredth of the power you'd need to reach their (already cautious) limits.

We're now several decades into the widespread global use of mobile phones, and also several decades into the accompanying health scares. And we've yet to see any increase in the base rate of illnesses that the cell-phone sceptics warned about, such as brain tumours.[5] Those who believe that such electromagnetic radiation is harmful have compiled very extensive lists of symptoms that exposure supposedly causes – migraines, dizziness and so forth – which are also notable for not being major symptoms of Covid-19.

So why did the Covid/5G conspiracy theory persist? Well, for one thing, the theory wasn't one theory at all, but several mutually contradictory ones. If you ventured into any of the big anti-5G Facebook groups in March or April 2020, you could find them all coexisting, relatively peacefully, side by side. Some agreed that the virus was real, but said that 5G was making a mild illness more severe, either by suppressing the immune system or supercharging the virus itself. Others said that there was no virus, that the sickness was caused directly by 5G, and the symptoms were actually those of exposure to electromagnetic radiation. A third camp insisted that not only was there no virus, but nobody was getting ill at all: the hospitals were empty and the whole pandemic was a giant hoax to allow the government to secretly install 5G under cover of lockdown. The fact that these couldn't all be true at the same time was not a major problem; these communities were brought together by a conviction that there was *something* bad about 5G, and it was probably something to do with the pandemic. The conclusion was fixed; the arguments flexible.

Which brings us to the second key point: this all happened because 5G scepticism had been brewing for a long time before the pandemic arrived. The community already existed; it had its influencers and evangelists, with the backstory and supporting material already compiled. Online misinformation about 5G had been ticking up for at least a year before Covid came along, as many countries' roll-out of 5G began in earnest.[6] For a while, it seemed like a flock of birds couldn't fall dead from the sky anywhere in the world without 5G being blamed.*

Not only that, but it didn't begin with 5G: conspiracies and health scares about mobile phones have a history that goes back

---

* So this is actually a surprisingly common event, one that's been recorded for centuries. Dead birds just fall from the sky en masse, and people – quite naturally – freak out and look for something to blame. But it's just a thing birds do, it seems. Although it does make an excellent bit of ominous iconography in sci-fi shows.

more than two decades. In the UK, the roll-out of 3G in the early 2000s saw almost identical arguments, and almost identical incidents of phone masts being vandalised.[7] (A similar panic about Wi-Fi was also happening in the US at around the same time.) Crucially, these panics aren't limited to online cultures. Because opposition often takes place at the neighbourhood level, objecting to specific bits of infrastructure, it can be genuinely community-building: neighbour talks to neighbour, creating networks of in-person connections and shared activities that can sustain and incubate the underlying beliefs. People who think phone masts are a health hazard can find allies – and potential converts – in those who just think they're ugly.[8] After all, there's little that rouses a community to action, or engenders long-lasting resentments, better than getting involved in implausibly rancorous local planning disputes.

As time passed, the wireless health apocalypse failed to materialise, and the public embraced their unlimited data future with wild abandon, it's not surprising that what may have begun as largely non-conspiratorial health anxieties around new technology became more conspiracy-minded. The implicit conspiracism of trying to explain how everybody else could be getting this *so wrong* made it hard to sustain anything else. All of which meant that, when the coronavirus came along, there was a ready-made set of beliefs that could be easily tweaked to explain what was going on.

And that believers would try to connect Covid to their beliefs about phone radiation is unsurprising. Because of course, systemic conspiracy theories need to explain *everything*. They don't tend to look at major news stories and go, 'Hmmm, not one for us.'

All of which is also true, to an even greater extent, with vaccines.

The vaccine-sceptical movement has come a long way since the Anti-Vaccination Leagues of the 1800s. Most notably, it had a rocket shoved under it by Andrew Wakefield's fraudulent 1998 study that falsely claimed a link between vaccines and autism, and the media and political frenzy this sparked.*
Again, what may have begun as perfectly reasonable – if inaccurate – health fears had gradually morphed into outright conspiracism as the evidence stubbornly continued to show no such links. (There are few issues in modern medicine that have been quite as intensively studied and conclusively disproven as the vaccine–autism link.[9]) Narratives linked to things like the New World Order and population control grew up, to provide the all-important motive – an explanation for exactly *why* the medical profession was so keen to inject people with vaccines and cover up the truth.

And so, as with 5G, when the novel coronavirus started hitting international headlines, there was already a community there happy to explain that the reason Bill Gates supposedly wanted mandatory vaccination was so that he could implant microchips into everybody on the planet in order to track them.

The first thing to say here is: no, the vaccines do not have microchips in them. We can say this with some certainty

---

* Also not helping: the fact that, in their efforts to find Osama bin Laden, the CIA created a fake hepatitis B vaccination program in Pakistan to steal people's DNA. They literally did the thing the conspiracy theories accuse real vaccine programmes of doing. The result was a surge in vaccine scepticism, with local leaders in several areas banning vaccination teams, setting back the efforts to eradicate both hepatitis and polio. Hepatitis kills over 100,000 people in Pakistan every year.

because we've seen the vaccines and ... well, they don't have microchips in them. Microchips are pretty small these days, but they're not yet *invisible*. A vial of microchip-laden vaccine, even with the tiniest possible chips, would still prompt some rather inevitable questions, such as, 'Hey, why is there a cloud of grit in that otherwise clear vaccine?' If you want to keep up the 'vaccines have microchips in them' narrative, you'll need to assume that there's been some kind of secret break-through in microscopic microchip development.

That's before we get to some of the other practical prob-lems with the whole tracking-people-with-microchips plan. You can see these in the way that there are in fact people in the world right now who – entirely voluntarily – have had microchips implanted in their hands. There are even compa-nies that sell it as a service; it's weirdly popular in Sweden. ('Popular', in this context, still only means a few thousand people.)[10] These chips can be used to pay for services, or to replace building-entry swipe cards, although according to one news report, the most popular use is still enabling people 'to launch their LinkedIn accounts to share their profile more quickly'.[11] Which, even in a chapter about mass death, might be the most horrifying sentence we've had to type.

But the key point here is that these furiously networking wannabe cyborgs still have to hold their hand *right up to a scanner* in order for their chips to actually do anything, just as you do with a contactless payment card. The chips – which aren't even microscopic, but about the size of a grain of rice – don't broadcast any kind of signal. They merely respond to incoming radio waves from a separate device.

This would seem to somewhat limit the whole 'secretly track people' aspect of the vaccine-microchip scheme. If, in order for you to get any information out of the people you've covertly microchipped, you have to press a scanner against their face, then it's possible that your plan is no longer terribly covert. If you wanted your chips to surreptitiously *broadcast* their info, then you'd need to include a power source as well, which makes the whole thing even trickier.

And that's before you hit a final snag. The chips that our friendly Swedish cyborgs have in their hands are implanted subcutaneously, just under the skin. Why? Well, see, the thing about radio waves is that they travel better through some substances than others. And one substance that they travel particularly poorly through is … water. Which is what our bodies are made out of. (Do you have a pair of Bluetooth earphones? Ever noticed the way that the earbud in one ear sometimes cuts out if your phone is on the other side of your body? Your huge wet body is basically a massive radio jamming device.) As such, if you're trying to answer the question 'where should we put our covert tracking micro-chips?', then 'in people's bloodstreams' comes quite far down the list of answers.

So if you actually did want to secretly track people, then from just about every angle, the plan outlined in this theory would seem to be almost the worst possible way to do it. Just for fun, let's ask the question: if you were in fact an evil supervillain, hypothetically, how could you improve this plan to track people?

Well, a much better approach would be a chip that was outside the body. Ideally one that came with its own power source, and had the ability to broadcast a signal rather than just respond to incoming signals. Maybe you could house it in … some sort of device? Something that people would … carry with them everywhere?

This is the great unspoken hole in the middle of the 'kill

millions of people by starting a pandemic in order to force people to get your microchip vaccine so that you can then track them' theory. The problem is simple: WE ALREADY HAVE PHONES.

Everything that this vaccine plan is supposed to accomplish has already been achieved – and it wasn't imposed on an unwilling populace, it was adopted by the public with wild enthusiasm, through little more than a few decades of advancing consumer technology and a bit of decent marketing. Close to ninety per cent of adults in the UK have a smartphone, a figure near the upper end of even the most hopeful vaccine roll-out plan.[12] Vast tranches of tracking data on millions and millions of individuals are bought and sold on the open market entirely legally; while you're fretting about vaccines, some dumb game you downloaded and played for two weeks last year is still sitting on your phone, quietly sending your details to god knows who.

If Bill Gates was really super-keen on the idea of tracking people, why would he leave one of the world's largest technology companies to pursue the rather more speculative vaccine approach? Is the idea here that this is all a reaction to the failure of the Windows Phone to gain market share in the wake of Microsoft's ill-fated purchase of Nokia's mobile hardware division in 2013? If so, that raises another question: if Bill Gates has in fact made the kind of radical breakthrough in low-power nanoscale microchip technology that the vaccine conspiracy theory insists he must have, then *why did Microsoft's phones suck?*

The magical microscopic microchip issue is illustrative of a common problem with many conspiracy theories: in order to fix a plot hole in your theory, you give your conspirators capabilities that render the original conspiracy completely redundant. If they can do the things you need them to do for your theory to make sense, then they could also achieve the same ends by a ton of other means that would be a lot easier, much more reliable and significantly less criminal.

The popularity of this theory also shows once again that it really helps if your theory has a celebrity supervillain who can be its face. Bill Gates, a technology oligarch who pivoted to global health and vaccine advocacy, is almost perfect for it.

Most of the conspiracy theories about Covid were complete nonsense, but there is one we can't definitively say is untrue: the 'lab-leak hypothesis' of the virus's origins. This comes in a variety of different flavours, which, once again, are not all inherently conspiracy theories. There's no conspiracy in the idea that the virus might have accidentally escaped from a laboratory studying bat coronaviruses (a fairly sensible field of study, given how close the world came to a really bad pandemic with the original SARS in 2003). The same goes for the slightly more accusatory version – that the qualities that made SARS-CoV-2 so potent might have been added artificially during so-called 'gain of function' research (which is basically trying to prepare your defences for a virological worst-case scenario by engineering a pet worst-case scenario in a lab).

These theories are both more in the 'cock-up' than 'conspiracy' file, and nobody writes books about 'cock-up theories'.* In these versions, nobody *meant* to set the virus loose. Any conspiratorial element only really comes into play with the (assumed) cover up of the error, given that the Chinese authorities haven't come out publicly and gone, 'Oh yeah, that was us guys – really sorry, our bad.'

---

* Okay, one of Tom's previous works – *Humans: A Brief History of How We F*cked It All Up* – is in fact a book about cock-up theories.

There is, of course, a more extreme version of these theories: the idea that SARS-CoV-2 was deliberately developed by China as a bioweapon, which it then released in order to crash the world economy. That one definitely counts as a conspiracy theory.

It also ... doesn't make a whole ton of sense, if we're honest. A highly transmissible respiratory virus that gives most victims little more than moderate symptoms – and that only about a week after infection – seems a pretty poor candidate for a bioweapon. After all, if you're designing a bioweapon, presumably you'd want it to cause your enemy significant and immediate damage. If it was going to affect any one age group more than others, you'd probably want that to be people in the prime of life – the soldiers and workers – rather than the very old. And, ideally, you'd want it to be targeted with enough precision that it doesn't, you know, infect your side as well. Beyond that, exactly why China – a country whose finances are closely linked to the health of the global economy – would want to crash that economy remains ... unclear.

We're not saying it didn't happen, just that it would extremely stupid if it did.

But still: at time of writing, it's not possible to say with certainty that any version of the lab-leak hypothesis is false. There's no particularly convincing case in favour of it, beyond very uncertain circumstantial evidence, while the evidence suggesting a natural origin is far more compelling. (The earliest cases cluster around the Huanan market, where animals known to be susceptible to the virus were sold; they notably don't cluster around the Wuhan Institute of Virology, which is seven miles away on the other side of the Yangtze River.)[13] But still, we simply don't know enough about the outbreak's origins to conclusively rule a lab leak out – and given the microscopic-needle-in-the-world's-biggest-haystack nature of virological detective work, it's entirely possible that we never will.

What we can say, however, is that it's *unnecessary*. There's no hole in the 'natural origins' explanation of Covid that needs to be filled. There is nothing strange or inexplicable about SARS-CoV-2 that suggests human intervention was needed to start an outbreak; everything about it is consistent with a virus behaving perfectly naturally, just doing virus-y things.

The virus itself gives every indication of being something that evolved. The kind of mutations that made it a more effective replicator have been observed in the wild in other varieties of coronavirus.[14] Its genome contains none of the tell-tale signs that would suggest genetic manipulation.[15] Moreover, while its molecular toolkit certainly has a couple of nifty tricks up its sleeve, they're not the most effective or efficient approach to achieving its ends. If you were trying to design an epidemic-ready coronavirus, you wouldn't do it this way. Instead, Covid-19 has all the hallmarks of the unplanned, haphazard, trial-and-error jury-rigging that natural selection produces. The fact that the original virus wasn't perfectly engineered is obvious when you consider that, out in the wild, the process of natural selection very rapidly produced a string of variants that were dramatically better at spreading them-selves – something we've become all too familiar with as we work our way through the Greek alphabet.

Just as importantly, the virus would need no helping hand from us to make the leap between bats and humans, because this is something that viruses are really good at. Terrifyingly, nightmare-inducingly good. Zoonotic events – infections jumping from animals to humans – are alarmingly common-place, and are probably becoming more common as humans encroach ever further into animal habitats. More than half of all emerging infectious diseases are zoonotic in origin, and millions of people die from zoonotic diseases every year.[16] In the last century or so, zoonoses have given us our most feared and destructive epidemics – the 1918 'Spanish flu', HIV and Ebola – as well as a host of more obscure but still fairly terrifying killers with names like Marburg, Nipah, and Sin Nombre. Two deadly new zoonotic coronaviruses (SARS and MERS) made the jump to humans in just the past two decades. It's not clear why the third to do so – one that's very similar to the original SARS – requires some kind of special explanation.

To put it another way, if you keep getting attacked by lions, it's a bit weird to point at the fiftieth lion and say, 'Okay, but I bet *this* one escaped from a passing circus.' Like, sure, maybe it did, but at some point you're going to have to confront the fact that you just live in a place that's absolutely stuffed with lions.

It's perfectly natural, when confronted with events as strange and traumatic as the Covid pandemic, to believe that their cause must be equally out of the ordinary: proportion-ality bias is a thing, and the proportions of this crisis were huge. But such beliefs ignore the fact that, from a virological standpoint at least, the whole thing just wasn't especially weird. For all the use that word 'unprecedented' got in 2020, and for all that our lives got turned upside down in baffling ways, a lot of what happened that year was actually ... fairly precedented.

And that's where our final – and, to our mind, most infuriating – set of Covid conspiracy theories come in.

These are the theories that say there's evidence that global public health bodies knew about the coronavirus in advance. These will point to things like the World Health Organization talking about preparing for a mysterious 'Disease X' in 2018. They'll highlight the fact that, in October 2019, just months before Covid-19 was first identified, the Johns Hopkins Center for Health Security ran a simulation called 'Event 201', in which participants gamed out how they would respond to a SARS-like coronavirus outbreak. They'll dig up study proposals and patent applications for coronavirus research that predate the current outbreak. *You see,* they'll say: *they were in on it. This whole thing was planned.*

No.

Some of this initially sprang from a simple misunderstanding. While lots of people may have heard of SARS, the term 'coronavirus' wasn't widely used in Western media coverage during the 2003 outbreak; by the time it became clear that this disease was going to be a bit of a problem, the name SARS had already been coined. So for a lot of people, media reports of a 'novel coronavirus' in early 2020 might well have been the first time they'd heard the word. That coronaviruses are a large family of well-known viruses, and that we've all probably caught at least one of them in the past, wasn't always clear. So it's not entirely surprising that, when some people found references to 'coronaviruses' from the Before Times, they thought they'd found a smoking gun.

Many of these theories were more comical than sinister. Some pointed to the prior existence of a coronavirus vaccine as evidence of a grand plot – not realising that they were talking about vaccines *for cows* (bovine coronaviruses give cattle diarrhoea). Thousands of people on Facebook started freaking out that bottles of disinfectant spray purchased before the epidemic began had promised that they were effective against 'human coronaviruses', with the result that the makers of Dettol suddenly found themselves suspected of being part of a global conspiracy.[17]

But there's another strand to these theories that is less amusing, and both more frustrating and more dangerous. This is the one that treats expertise as inherently suspicious, which says that accurate warnings should make us distrust those who gave the warnings. Because Covid-19 wasn't just predictable – it was predicted.

Not in detail. Nobody said, 'Okay, so in December 2019 there'll be this thing called SARS-CoV-2, you might want to stockpile loo roll and buy a decent webcam.' But the key points – that there was a high risk of exactly this kind of novel disease pandemic; that it could very well be a coronavirus; and that there was a good chance all this would happen sooner rather than later – were all well understood. The fact that coronaviruses had a high pandemic-causing potential, based on their proven ability to cause epidemics in animal populations and their innate propensity for rapid evolution, was flagged as early as 1997 by the epidemiologist Donald Burke, who warned that they should be 'considered as serious threats to human health'.[18] This was six years before SARS; at that point, as far as we know, there had never been a deadly coronavirus epidemic in humans. Yet the warning signs were already there.

In the years since, as the exact threat that Burke had identified materialised, the drumbeat of warnings from infectious disease experts became more and more urgent – but they often fell on deaf ears. The same cycle would repeat: a possible threat would emerge; policymakers and the media would temporarily freak out; then they'd rapidly lose interest as soon as the threat receded. Large budgets would be pledged, and then just as quickly be cut again. The world dodged a bullet with the original SARS, and again with swine flu in 2009; too many people acted like this meant the enemy had run out of bullets.

So when the World Health Organization talked about 'Disease X', that wasn't a secret pre-launch codename for SARS-CoV-2. It was just a placeholder reflecting the fact that experts knew that some kind of unknown infectious disease was likely to emerge that could pose a serious global health risk. And guess what? They were right! When Johns Hopkins used a fictional coronavirus for a pandemic-preparedness planning exercise, that's because it knew perfectly well that coronaviruses were one of the top candidates for the next 'big one'. Again: bang on, lads, can't fault you for your working there. Public health experts have spent decades practically *begging* politicians and the public to take the threat of zoonotic pandemics more seriously, and to properly fund research and early warning systems and preparedness plans. To then turn around and say that those warnings are evidence of sinister intent isn't just wrong, it's wildly unfair. People who've dedicated their lives to trying to protect humanity from a host of deadly unseen enemies went straight from being accused of crying wolf to getting blamed for the arrival of the exact wolf they'd been trying to warn us about.

We've mostly tried to avoid suggesting that conspiracy theories are stupid. A lot of the time, they're not, even if they're wrong. But this? Yeah, this one is maddeningly stupid. It's like believing the Met Office created a rainstorm, because the weatherman told you to bring an umbrella. That's not evidence of a conspiracy. It's evidence that *they knew what they were talking about*, and you should have listened to them.

9

Plots of Land

By 1870, Alfred Russel Wallace's career was going well. The geographer and naturalist had spent much of his youth in the Amazon or South East Asia, collecting samples and pondering where species came from. In 1858, he'd written an essay on the topic, and sent it to Charles Darwin – Wallace was a fan – asking his thoughts. Darwin, realising how closely the younger man's theories aligned with those he'd been sitting on for twenty years, rushed out a joint paper, followed by *On the Origin of Species*.

Suddenly, Wallace – a man who had spent years toiling away in obscurity – was the co-discoverer of evolution by natural selection, and one of the leading scientific thinkers of his age. In 1862, he returned to England and swiftly became friends with his heroes. Six years after that, he won the Royal Society's prestigious Royal Medal. Things were looking up.

There was one way in which things weren't going so well, however: not coming from wealth, Wallace was frequently short of cash. So in January 1870, when he spotted the following ad in *Scientific Opinion*, you can forgive him for being tempted:

> *What is to be said of the pretended philosophy of the 19th century, when not one educated man in ten thousand knows the shape of the earth on which he dwells? ... The undersigned is willing to deposit from £50 to £500, on reciprocal terms, and defies all the philosophers, divines and scientific professors in the United Kingdom to prove the rotundity and revolution of the world from Scripture, from reason, or from fact ...*

The advert was signed 'John Hampden'.

In 1870, that £500 was the equivalent of over £30,000 today. And all Wallace had to do to get it was to demonstrate the obvious and established fact that the Earth was round. And so, he decided to take the bet.

It almost ruined him.[1]

The conspiracy theories we've examined up until now have mostly concerned discrete events: even their believers generally accepted the standard view on such fundamental matters as when and where they were living. Some theories, though, bring into doubt even that level of consensus reality.

The nineteenth century was an age filled with scientific discoveries. The shape of the Earth was not among them: by Wallace's time, the fact we are all clinging to the surface of a big, round rock had been known for millennia. From ancient Greece, the idea spread to Rome, India, the Islamic world and medieval Europe. In 1492, Christopher Columbus misunderstood some Persian calculations, under-estimated the size of the Earth by around a third and sailed to the Bahamas, which he believed to be somewhere off the east coast of Asia and confidently christened 'the Indies'. This was a cock-up, but at no point in this process did he imagine the Earth to be anything but a globe.[2]

How did anyone know the Earth was round before anyone could get up in the sky to check? In the fourth century BCE, Aristotle noted that the shadow of the Earth on the moon during a lunar eclipse was round; that there were stars visible in Egypt that weren't visible further north; and that, the further south you went, the higher these were in the sky. Other thinkers observed that, when ships disappeared over the horizon, the mast remained visible longer than the hull: they weren't simply moving beyond the range of the human eye, but were gradually being hidden by the curve of the intervening ocean.

By Wallace's time, then, there was nothing new in either the idea that the Earth was round, or the belief among scientists that they could demonstrate the fact. What *was* new was that there was an increasingly noisy group of people convinced that somebody, somewhere, had made the whole thing up. Many of these were biblical literalists, concerned that the new scientific discoveries (evolution by natural selection; an Earth that was millions of years old) were undermining Christian teachings (man was created by God; the Earth could be dated to one Thursday in October 4004 BCE). 'Proving' the Earth flat was a way of showing the Bible was right, and the newfangled science wrong.

So it was that, one day in 1838, a twenty-two-year-old named Samuel Birley Rowbotham waded out into the middle of a drainage ditch in the Norfolk Fens armed with a tele-scope and a sense of his own Christian righteousness.

The Old Bedford River is, despite its name, an artificial canal that runs for six miles in a straight line through an entirely flat English landscape. Rowbotham reasoned that, if the Earth really was a sphere with a circumference of 25,000 miles, then a boat moving away from him would gradually fall from view, dropping eight inches over one mile, thirty-two inches over two miles and so on, until, after six miles, the top of its mast would be several feet below his line of sight.

So he held his telescope eight inches above the surface of the water, and watched. After six miles, the boat was still clearly visible. Rowbotham was triumphant. The Earth was flat.

Nobody paid much attention to the Bedford Level Experiment at the time, which was lucky for Rowbotham, because he'd mucked it up: by holding the telescope so close to the water, atmospheric refraction had come into play, making things visible that otherwise wouldn't have been. But the mistake worked out rather well for Parallax, as he called himself when he published a book under the helpfully literal title *Zetetic Astronomy: Earth Not a Globe*. In his telling, the Earth was (stop us if you've already worked this out) not a globe: instead, it was a flat plane, with the North Pole at the centre. The South Pole, by contrast, wasn't a single point at all, but a massive circle: where maps showed the frozen continent of Antarctica, there was instead a wall of ice, preventing humanity from seeing what lay beyond.

Rowbotham was well incentivised to keep pushing this theory. As well as his publications, he took up a profitable, if not always convincing, sideline in lecturing on the topic. In 1849, he did a runner from a lecture in Burnley after failing to explain why it was that ships disappeared over the horizon. In 1864, an astronomy writer challenged him to prove his theories by appearing at a particular time on a beach in Plymouth and demonstrating that the Eddystone lighthouse, fourteen miles away, was entirely visible. Only the very top of it was; the rest was hidden behind the horizon. Rowbotham simply claimed this proved the Earth was flat and went on with his day.*

Asides from money, all this brought him followers. One was a printer named William Carpenter, who adopted the pseudonym Common Sense and took to publishing his own books and pamphlets with titles like *A Hundred Proofs the Earth is Not a Globe*. Another was a Christian polemicist who had dropped out of Oxford to dedicate more time to shouting about the corruption of the modern Church, and who had been converted to flat-Earther-ism after reading Carpenter's book. His name was John Hampden.

On 15 January 1870, Wallace wrote to Hampden offering 'to stake that sum on the undertaking to show visibly, and to measure in feet and inches, the convexity of a canal or lake'. He proposed Bala Lake in North Wales as a good site for the experiment, but professed himself open to other suggestions, which was lucky, because Hampden already had his heart set on repeating the Bedford Levels Experiment that Rowbotham had screwed up some thirty-two years earlier.

The experiment went well for Wallace. Despite being unaware of Rowbotham's original attempt, he corrected the mistakes his predecessor had made, and used bridges and poles to place three objects at a consistent level above the waterline several miles apart. On a flat Earth, these would appear to be in a straight line; because the Earth is round, they didn't.

The judging, however, did not go well for Wallace. He'd wanted an independent, expert referee. Hampden initially

---

* 'Surely this proves the exact opposite?' we hear you ask. Yes. Yes it does.

agreed, but then – once the stakes were already in the adjudicator's hands – seemed to change his mind, and despite the fact the chosen man knew neither of the competitors personally, demanded a referee of his own. Wallace, wanting all to seem fair and above board, agreed.

Hampden proposed William Carpenter. Yep, the man whose publications, such as the eight-part masterwork *Theoretical Astronomy Examined and Exposed – Proving the Earth Not a Globe*, had convinced Hampden the Earth was flat in the first place. It was at least possible Carpenter already had a dog in this particular fight. He declined to accept the results, claiming that Wallace's instruments had not been properly calibrated.

Wallace, with a touching faith in human rationality, agreed to repeat the experiment, recalibrated his instruments, and even toddled off to King's Lynn to borrow equipment from a disinterested third party before trying again. This time, Hampden refused to even look through the telescope, deferring instead to Carpenter. Then, in a turn of phrase familiar to anyone who has ever wasted an afternoon arguing on social media, he 'declared positively that they had won, and that we knew it'.[3]

Finally, a third umpire was called in, who reviewed both side's accounts of the experiment, concluded that Wallace was correct, and published an account in his journal, the *Field*, for good measure. Wallace initially took the winnings – but since a gentleman's wager had about as much force in English law as a duel, was eventually forced to give them back. Hampden spent the next fifteen years writing letters calling Wallace names to everyone he could think of, up to and including his wife ('Madam, if your infernal thief of a husband is brought home some day on a hurdle, with every bone in his head

smashed to pulp, you will know the reason ...'). Both the
death threats and the libel landed him in court and even jail
on multiple occasions, but he wriggled out of payment by
declaring bankruptcy.

Wallace was denied his winnings – indeed, the vast sums
he spent on legal action left him massively out of pocket.
Worse, many of his peers thought him an idiot for having
taken the bet in the first place, criticising 'his "injudicious"
involvement in a bet to "decide" the most fundamental and
established of scientific facts'.[4]

Or to put it another way: why was he wasting time trying
to be rational with these lunatics?

Simply believing that the Earth is flat, or a giant lemon, or
any other shape you care to choose, doesn't automatically
make you a conspiracy theorist, of course: Hampden,
Carpenter and Co. might simply have been wrong. What
raises the flat Earth claim to the level of conspiracy theory is
the need to explain why everybody else disagrees. This implicit
conspiracism has gone into overdrive in modern times –
because now we don't only have *theoretical* proofs of the shape
of the Earth.

Seventy-six years after Wallace's big mistake, a modified
German V-2 rocket took off from White Sands, New
Mexico, flew to an altitude of around 100km, and took a
photograph. The resolution isn't great, and cloud cover
makes it hard to tell which part of the planet it actually
features. Nonetheless, it clearly shows the Earth to be
curved, not flat.[5]

Other images followed, and each showed the same thing,
which wasn't a surprise to the vast majority of the people on
the planet. The big one came in December 1972, when one of

the crew of Apollo 17* took a photograph that would go on to become one of the most famous images of all time. *The Blue Marble*, as it is known, shows Africa, the Arabian Peninsula and, disappearing beneath the clouds at the bottom, Antarctica. First published as the environmental movement got going, it became one of the most widely distributed photographs ever taken – a symbol of the fragility of the planet we share. It also, as it happens, shows that the Earth is a globe.[6]

You might think that would be the end of the matter. But that's without reckoning with three things.

One is simple pig-headedness. A widely repeated story has a reporter triumphantly hand Samuel Shenton, founder and president of the International Flat Earth Research Society, a picture of the Earth from space and asking him, in not so many words, to explain *that*. He glanced at it and then replied, 'It's easy to see how a photograph like that could fool the untrained eye.'[7] No further explanation was forthcoming.

Another reason for the persistence of the flat Earth theory is that – in recent years, at least – many of the better images of the Earth have been, for want of a better word, faked. There aren't many whole-Earth images like *The Blue Marble*, because there haven't been many occasions on which a camera has been far enough away to take one: Apollo 17 was the last mission to travel that far. Most images of the Earth from space are taken from orbit, which is a bit like trying to photograph someone's face when you're holding the camera four inches from their nose.

So most modern images of the Earth from space are

---

* All three of the crew have said they were the one who took the famous photograph. Well, you would, wouldn't you?

actually composites. The one that used to be the default lock screen on the iPhone, for example, was created in 2002 by a NASA employee called Robert Simmons, using four months' worth of data. If you are the sort of person who is minded to believe that NASA has been involved in a conspiracy to fake the shape of the planet, then all this is very suspicious.[8]

There was one more thing that allowed the flat Earth movement to thrive even after we *literally had photographs showing that the Earth was a globe*: the internet. In a world in which you met people through school or work or down the pub, it was hard to even express your doubts about the shape of the world, let alone to find others who agreed with you, for fear of getting laughed at. But in a world with social media, suddenly it was easy: the four people in a town who thought there was something iffy about that *Blue Marble* photograph could find each other and organise. And the rise of YouTube and its algorithm made it possible for believers to find possible converts.

And so, having lain dormant for several years, the Flat Earth Society officially reopened to new members in 2009.

Except ... why, in the twenty-first century, would anyone believe all this?

The first exposure Mark Sargent had to conspiracy theories came when he watched Oliver Stone's *JFK*. Growing up on an island in the Pacific Northwest of the United States, he says: 'I didn't believe in any conspiracies, to be honest. [But] I walked out of the theatre thinking, wow, people actually do lie about big things.' He still watches it every couple of years.[9]

Over the next few years, he researched almost every conspiracy theory going, and developed an opinion on all of them. 'But I didn't look at flat Earth. Why would I? It's stupid. But then I made the mistake of thinking, eh, I'm not getting any younger, I might as well look at this thing.'

For nine months, he stared at the arguments, trying to convince himself the Flat Earthers were wrong and the Earth was a globe. He couldn't do it. So he put his arguments on to the internet, and waited for someone to explain what he was missing. 'And nobody did. I had subject matter experts calling me up – military people and pilots and air-traffic controllers, all these people that have dealt with transportation, saying, "You know what? It's not that crazy."'

And so, he became a Flat Earther. A few years on, in fact, he's one of the globe's most famous Flat Earthers.* His YouTube video series, *Flat Earth Clues*, brought the theory to the attention of many new people, and gave him a measure of celebrity, too. When the first Flat Earth International Conference was held in Raleigh, North Carolina, in 2017, Mark was one of the star attractions. When *Behind the Curve*, a 2018 documentary about the conference and the wider movement appeared, Mark was the protagonist.†

---

* Incidentally, you can buy a T-shirt that features the slogan 'The Flat Earth Society has members all around the globe'. These are words that, best we can tell, the actual Flat Earth Society has never used, because they are just as capable of spotting the joke there as anybody else.
† Sargent's growing fame seems to have been helped both by the fact he's incredibly affable, and by the fact there are others in the movement who really, really aren't. At one point in the documentary, a notice pops up noting that a rival conspiracist said he would only appear if the filmmakers gave him creative control and a share of the profits, and promised to 'support his unverified claim that Mark Sargent was secretly a Warner Bros. executive using an alias. We were unable to meet his demands,' it concludes. Well, no.

Since then, Mark has travelled all over the world, whatever shape it may be, doing interviews, attending meet-ups, appearing as himself in an ad campaign for the Australian gambling firm SportsBet's Foolproof app. (You can probably guess how that plays out, to be honest.) There's even a clip of ITV's *This Morning* in which he tries to convince Phil and Holly that the Earth is flat in less than a minute. His argument, from these various interviews, runs, roughly, thus.

1. The atmosphere
In a battle between gravity and the vacuum of space, the latter wins every time, right? So how come there's anything to breathe?

2. Long-distance photography
Cameras have improved at an astonishing rate, and now you can find photographs of mountains taken from many dozens, even hundreds, of miles away. If the Earth is really a globe, these things should be well below the line of sight. So how come the camera can see them, unless the Earth is flat?

3. The Van Allen belt
The Earth is surrounded by a thick layer of radioactive particles. So if astronauts really did travel into space, why didn't they all die of radiation poisoning? Is it possible they *never left the planet at all?*

4. Flights
There aren't that many of them in the Southern Hemisphere, and those that do exist often seem to involve layovers in places to the north. If the south is

really the same as the north, why aren't they flying directly? Is it because places in the Southern Hemisphere are actually a lot further away from each other than they would be on a globe-shaped Earth?

5. Antarctica

An area of the planet larger than any sovereign state except Russia has been locked down to all but a few scientists for sixty years. Who knows what resources are hidden there under the ice – yet corporations aren't allowed to go looking for them. Does that sound remotely likely to you?

Unless there's something there no one wants us to find – like a *massive wall of ice*.

All of this raises two obvious questions. One is why anyone would want to hush up something as basic as the shape of the Earth – and want it enough to fake several entire space programmes over a period of decades.

Sargent's answer is that the ruling class have only known since the mid-twentieth century – and that they've been too scared about the consequences of telling the rest of us. 'Academically, every university in the world has to rebuild their science programme. Economically, you'd have to suspend world markets for months just to figure out what the ramifications are.' But the big one would be the spiritual effects: news that the Earth was flat would give every major religion 'leverage over science simultaneously. And you're telling them to show restraint! So it's not going to happen.'

The other question raised by all this is, if the Earth isn't a globe, then what is it? There's keen debate on this topic inside the movement ('Unlike the mainstream, Flat Earth theory does not follow the leader, it encourages free thought and open-mindedness,' claims the Society's website). But Sargent's view is this: 'You're talking about basically a snow globe. You're basically in a giant building with walls and a floor and a ceiling.'

Beyond that lies a realm that sounds a lot like, well, heaven: a place from which we've been cast out – or perhaps we chose to leave – so that when we depart this world of pain and conflict and return to paradise, we'll appreciate it properly once again. 'I don't think it's a prison planet, I don't think it's pure entertainment. I think it's a school: you're here to learn something.'

The universe familiar from the science books is aggravatingly poorly designed for human exploration: there are plenty of other planets out there, maybe even inhabited ones, but physics doesn't allow us to travel fast enough to reach them in the time we're going to be around for. The idea that something else isn't light years away, but merely a few thousand miles, is a seductive one. Perhaps you find the idea that everything you think you know is wrong kind of thrilling.

So it seems worth noting at this point that not everyone in the flat Earth movement is enjoying it as much as Mark Sargent. 'I don't want to be a Flat Earther,' a renewable energy specialist called David Weiss told CNN in 2019. 'Would you wake up in the morning and want everyone to think you're an idiot?'[10] The same year, another attendee at the conference in Raleigh told the *Guardian* that he'd dearly love to be convinced the world was a globe after all: 'It'd be a relief.'[11] The idea that everything you think you know is wrong can, from one perspective, be exhilarating. From another, it can be utterly terrifying.

If you find it so, you would perhaps take some comfort from the fact there is a rational explanation for every one of the issues Sargent raises. They are:

1. The atmosphere
Vacuums don't suck: air pressure pushes. In the upper atmosphere, the air is so thin that there's very little air pressure, so there's no force pushing the atmosphere to dissipate into space.[12]

2. Long-distance photography
Such photographs are almost always taken from high elevations, increasing the distance of the horizon. The photographers who take them also make deliberate use of refraction – the tendency for light to bend around the Earth – and deliberately go for their record-breaking shots shortly after sunrise, when refraction is at its greatest.[13] This is basically Rowbotham's original error in the Old Bedford River, only bigger.

3. The Van Allen belt
Traversing it generally takes just over an hour, during which astronauts are exposed to around sixteen rads of radiation. The lethal dose is 300 rads per hour. You wouldn't want to do it every day, but it's safe.[14]

4. Flights
There aren't many commercially viable south-to-south routes. Even those that exist are generally not going to take a shortcut across Antarctica, because there's nowhere to stop in an emergency.

5. Antarctica

Whatever resources may or may not be down there, it's
going to be a hellish job to get them out, so it's not
been worth anyone's while to breach the treaty.
Whether that will hold if the ice begins to melt is a
different question, but it hasn't happened yet.

In other words, science can explain all of the modern Flat
Earther's arguments – it's just that the science required is
sometimes a bit more complicated than is immediately accessible to the layman. To put it another way: their arguments
are, 'Well, it looks flat from here,' for the digital age.*

The shape of the Earth isn't the only geographical matter to
have attracted conspiracy theories, of course. Consider the
question – because it turns out that there *is* a question – of
Finland.

If you know anything at all about Finland, you probably
believe that it's a large but sparsely populated country in
northern Europe, which lies between Sweden and Russia, and
is famous for its lakes, forests, saunas, and winning Eurovision
by fielding a heavy-metal band dressed as monsters. But you
would be wrong about all of those things, because, according
to some corners of the internet, Finland has never existed.
That large but sparsely populated stretch of northern Europe?
Just another bit of the Baltic Sea. Its capital, Helsinki?
Actually eastern Sweden. All those people, who confidently

---

* Just so you know, this section of the book was originally much,
much longer, because one of the authors couldn't immediately see the
problems in Sargent's thesis and wrote several thousand words on the
shape of the Earth to stop himself freaking out.

believe themselves to be Finns? Also from eastern Sweden, or western Russia, or northern Estonia. Because *there is no such thing as Finland.*[15]

All this started, as so many of the worst things do, on Reddit. In 2015, a thread on the AskReddit subforum posed the question, 'What did your parents show you to do that you assumed was completely normal, only to discover later that it was not normal at all?' A user named u/Raregan gave the example of the Finland conspiracy theory.[16]

The roots of the plot, he explained, related to fishing rights. Japan, you see, has an almost insatiable appetite for sushi, consuming far more fish than it'd be allowed to take from the seas by international law. To get around this problem, so the theory goes, it conspired with the USSR to invent a country lying off Russia's Baltic Coast, in a place where it could fish undisturbed. 'After all,' explains an account of the theory on the r/FinlandConspiracy subreddit, 'nobody's going to expect fishing regulations to be broken in a place where everyone thinks there's a landmass, will they?'[17] Indeed.

The resulting catch was then transported via the suspiciously useful Trans-Siberian Railway, under the guise of Nokia products. This apparently explains both why Nokia was so successful in Japan despite hardly anyone there owning a Nokia phone, and how Nokia managed to become the largest Finnish company when, as everybody knows, Finland doesn't exist.

As to the world's other 191 or so countries – at least some of which, one assumes, might have noticed that the Baltic Sea is roughly twice as big as it was supposed to be – the reason they've gone along with all this is simple: the Finland myth gives the rest of us something to aspire to. Imagine a country with great education, good healthcare, gender equality and brilliant literacy rates. Finland is, in more than one sense, a dream.

Oh, and a clue to the truth can be found in the name. Finland is secretly just a place for the Japanese to fish. What do fish have? Think about it.

The notion that a huge geographical region, containing people who you might have literally met, is nothing but a lie is so outlandish that you could be forgiven for thinking that this would be a one-off. You would be wrong. The online world has been declaring bits of its offline counterpart to be Narnia without the talking animals for about as long as there has been an internet to do it on.

Bielefeld is, at least according to the official narrative, the eighteenth-largest city in Germany. It is home to no significant corporations or public institutions; no tourist attractions; no major river. It has no significant features whatsoever.

So in 1994, after passing an *autobahn* sign on which all the signs to Bielefeld had been taped over, a student named Achim Held came up with a theory to explain how a city of 340,000 people could be quite so unknown: it didn't exist. This would explain why he had never met anybody from the city, nor anyone who had even visited it. Who could be propagating such a diabolical conspiracy, he asked in a Usenet post? A group known only as 'SIE': 'they'.[18]

A generation later, and there's one thing everybody does know about Bielefeld: that it's really funny to pretend it doesn't exist. In 2010, film students at Bielefeld University made a film about the conspiracy, and exactly what SIE wanted. By 2012, Chancellor Angela Merkel was cracking jokes about the non-existence of a fair-sized German city.

By 2014, the city itself was in on the joke, promoting its 800th anniversary under the slogan *'Das gibt's doch gar nicht'*:

'That cannot be real'. Five years after that, it was offering €1 million to anyone who could offer 'incontrovertible evidence' that it did not exist.[19] When the prize went unclaimed, the city announced that it definitely did exist after all, and declared the joke over. Whether that'll be enough remains to be seen.[20]

Other places that the internet has declared to be unreal in much the same manner have included the US state of Wyoming, the Brazilian state of Acre or the Italian region of Molise. All these places fit a particular profile. They are peripheral, sparsely populated, off the tourist track – and famous for nothing other than their own questionable ontological status. The 'proofs' they don't exist can thus follow the same logic as that which Held applied to Bielefeld. Have you ever been to X? Do you know anyone who's from X? Do you know anyone who has ever been to X? If the answer to all three questions is 'no', then, well, it stands to reason that X probably doesn't exist, doesn't it?*

The biggest geographical conspiracy theory of all, however, doesn't fit this pattern. It involves a place that you are all but certain to know someone who has visited, or even someone who calls it home.

In 2018, a Swedish Facebook user named Shelley Floryd racked up nearly 20,000 shares with a post outlining 'one of the greatest genocides in history'. Over eighty years, she claimed, the British Empire had loaded 162,000 criminals on to ships, ostensibly with the intention of deporting them to

---

* The Mexican state of Tlaxcala is another that fits this profile. It's not just the smallest state in the union: it's also still seen as a nest of traitors because the Tlaxcalans allied with the Spanish against the Aztecs over 500 years ago. Way to hold a grudge, guys.

its new prison on the other side of the world. 'In reality,' she wrote, 'all these criminals were loaded off the ships into the waters, drowning before they could ever see land again ... They never reached that promised land.' They couldn't have: Australia, it turns out, is a hoax.[21]

But what, you may be wondering at this point, of all the flights to Australia, some of which you might have even flown on? Actually, they're to islands, or perhaps parts of South America. (The entire aviation industry is in on the scheme.) Your Australian friends? 'They're all actors and computer-generated personas, part of the plot to trick the world.' In other words, as a sort of subplot of the 'Australia is not real' conspiracy, truth-seekers are free to indulge in additional theories such as 'Hugh Jackman never existed', 'Kylie Minogue is a computer avatar', or any other claim that involves the non-existence of any Australian they happen to have taken against.

All this, Floryd wrote in her post, constituted 'one of the biggest hoaxes ever created'. This, notes an article on Culture Trip, is 'an extraordinary statement in itself – if the fabrication of the sixth-largest nation on Earth isn't the biggest hoax ever created, the No.1 ruse must be an absolute whopper'.[22]

The original post is long gone (although, the same article notes, whether it was the intervention of nefarious governments or the abuse from angry Australians that did it remains unclear). But its footprint remains in the form of memes and write-ups by media organisations from countries, real or imagined, all around the world.

And it was, in any case, not the first time that the idea that an entire continental landmass was a fiction has found its way on to the internet. A 2006 post on the Flat Earth Society forum also claimed that Australia didn't exist, though it made no attempt to give a motivation for the fabrication. The message was preceded by the disclaimer, 'Although I believe that the Earth is flat, this is not actually part of the Flat Earth Theory'. Many of the Flat Earthers replying either mocked the post, or replied, simply, 'Evidence?'[23]

That does not mean there's a hard line between trolling and 'real' conspiracy theories such as the flat Earth theory, however. Ideas intended as jokes may not be received that way, and those who go looking for evidence will soon encounter other theories. If the YouTube algorithm means that those researching the existence of Bielefeld soon find themselves watching 'Flat Earth Clues', how does it really matter that the original post was a joke?

These big, geographical conspiracy theories highlight another problem: how can you actually *prove* that Australia exists? Maps can be fabricated; satellite photographs altered. You may believe you've been there, but you travelled by plane: all you really know is that you've been *somewhere*. At some point, the evidence of our own eyes and ears ceases to be enough: we believe in Australia because the media and the authorities tell us it exists. But if you cease to trust that media and those authorities, what would be enough to convince you?

Incidentally, Raregan, whose real name was Jack, has said he doesn't believe a word of the Finland theory he shared. Neither do his parents, who apparently had forgotten ever telling their kid this ridiculous lie and now find the whole thing hilarious. Nor, come to that, do many of the internet users enthusiastically asking how to break the news of Finland's non-existence to their Finnish friends in the r/FinlandConspiracy subreddit.

But that doesn't mean nobody does. As Jack told *Vice* in

2016: 'It's honestly impossible to tell who's joking and who's serious sometimes.'[24]

If people are driven to doubt the reality of the very ground beneath our feet, there may be a reason for that. As strange as it may seem to view landmasses as inherently dubious, for quite a bit of history, scepticism was a sensible response to someone telling you about this brilliant new country they'd found. At the opposite ontological extreme from people denying the existence of places that definitely exist, you'll find those who were passionately engaged in promoting the existence of lands that almost certainly do not.

These are – mostly – not conspiracies, not least because 'conspiring to pretend a non-existent place exists' is frequently both difficult and somewhat pointless. But some of them do begin to edge in that direction.

First, there are those that would perhaps best be labelled as 'speculative cartography': imaginary places early map-makers placed on maps to sex them up a bit. Geradus Mercator – not content with coming up with a map projection that was misleadingly generous to land around the Poles, thus sparking several centuries of opportunity for people to surprise their mates with how small Greenland actually was – decided that the reason why compasses all point north must be because of a massive magnetic rock sited at the North Pole. He began including this on maps with the label 'Rupes Nigra' ('Black Rock'). His description of a mountain in the sea, surrounded by four countries inhabited by giants and pygmies, and bounded by a whirlpool ('the water rushes round and descends into the Earth just as if one were pouring it through a filter funnel') is very evocative, though, alas, not very accurate.[25]

Other non-existent places have similarly stemmed from

straightforward mistakes, but have had rather more real-world consequences. The widespread belief in Davis Land, a sandy island in the South Pacific spotted by the pirate Edward Davis in 1687, which supposedly sat on a line of latitude associated with gold mines, led to several expeditions seeking riches and finding, instead, rather a lot of sea and not a lot of island.[26] In the same way, Jacquet Island, a landmass somewhere in the North Atlantic, was considered as a possible stopping point for the new transatlantic telegraph cables in the mid-nineteenth century.[27] These discussions didn't get very far, because it turned out, again, not to exist.

We edge closer to the territory of actual conspiracy when people start outright lying about land. In 1913, an expedition set out to find 'Crocker Land', an island discovered by the polar explorer Robert Peary (and named after a wealthy investor he hoped to impress). The expedition didn't – couldn't – succeed, because Peary appears to have invented it wholesale, much as he also invented having reached the North Pole. But the attempt to find Crocker Land would result in the explorers getting trapped in the frozen north for months, a rescue ship becoming trapped in the ice for years, and at least one Inuit being shot in the back by an angry American.

Even closer to conspiracies are the deliberate hoaxes. In the early 1820s, an imaginative Scottish businessman by the unlikely name of Gregor MacGregor managed to persuade several hundred Scots to invest their life savings to acquire land in Poyais: a hyper-fertile and gold-strewn Central American land that he just happened to be the ruler of. A couple of hundred of them discovered the hard way – that is, by emigrating – that there was no such place as Poyais, and all that awaited them where the capital city supposedly stood were jungle and disease. Only a few of them returned alive.

The only reason it's ambiguous whether Poyais was a conspiracy is that it's unclear whether anybody was in on it with MacGregor, or if he'd personally managed to hoodwink literally everyone involved.*

But if you want a story of a fictional landmass with even bigger potential real-world consequences – and one that takes us fully back into the land of conspiracy theories – consider the story of Bermeja. In 2009, a National Autonomous University of Mexico study came to the conclusion that the 80km² island off the north coast of the Yucatán peninsula, which had been appearing on maps since as early as the sixteenth century, did not exist. This was unfortunate, from the Mexican point of view, since it reduced the country's zone of maritime sovereignty in an area that offered lots of lovely oil.

So what happened to the island? The obvious explanation is that it never really existed – those early map-makers made a mistake, or perhaps were trying to mislead rivals for long-forgotten reasons. But some would have it that the island disappeared beneath the waves, an early victim of climate change. Or, just perhaps, Mexican Senator José Angel Conchello was on to something when he suggested it had been deliberately destroyed by the CIA in order to improve US territorial oil rights in the region.

The idea that even the US government would be able to eliminate an entire island unnoticed seems ludicrous, but the theory was given an uncomfortable boost by the fact that Conchello mysteriously died in a car crash in 1998, right

---

* The stories of both MacGregor's fictional country and Peary's inaccurate polar expedition are explored in more depth in Tom's previous book *Truth: A Brief History of Total Bullsh*t*.

around the time the US and Mexico were first seriously debating their maritime boundaries.

The Bermeja story[28] highlights the uncomfortable fact that it doesn't always matter whether the people spreading geographical conspiracy theories really believe them: even if they don't, they can still have an effect on things that actually do exist, like politics or international relations here in the real world. In the same way, the version of geography that Rowbotham, Hampden and their followers promoted may not have been real, but the battle they launched between science and religion clearly was.

So at some point, the sincerity with which a conspiracy theory is promoted comes to matter a lot less than the number of people who actually hear it. The old-in-internet-terms adage Poe's Law states that it is not possible to create a parody of extreme views so ridiculous that somebody, some-where, won't mistake it for the real thing. By the same token, it is not possible to create a conspiracy theory so ridiculous that somebody, somewhere won't believe it.

'We are opening minds,' says Mark Sargent. 'What happens is, when you get into flat Earth, you revisit all the other conspiracies. People are reopening books that they had closed for a long, long time.' After all, he says, 'If you can keep this a secret, then you can do just about anything.'

10

In Search of Lost Time

In the fifth century, the Western Roman Empire 'fell'. Exactly what that means is beyond the scope of this book: while plenty of eminent historians have argued that power simply transferred from a central emperor to locally administered kingdoms, or from civil authorities to the Church, no conspiracy theory has yet emerged arguing that the Empire never really fell at all, and that everywhere from Carlisle to Cairo is still secretly being run by an emperor hidden somewhere under Rome. Which is a pity, because that would be brilliant.

Anyway, what isn't contested is that in the year 400, much of western Europe was under Roman control, and by the year 500 it wasn't, and that for quite a while after that, things got a bit hairy. For the next couple of centuries, population declined, agricultural output fell, trade collapsed, and life generally became less about having urbane philosophical discussions in city tavernas, and more about subsistence farming and hoping that the tribe massing on the horizon wouldn't slaughter your entire family when they showed up to take your land.

Or rather, that's probably what it was like. Roughly. We don't know for sure, because one side effect of the decline of central administration is that there were far fewer people writing stuff down. As a result, in sizeable chunks of Europe, we know less about these centuries than we do about either the Roman period that preceded them or the later Middle Ages that followed. This lack of records led some later scholars to give the years after the Roman collapse the now deeply unfashionable label 'the Dark Ages'*, to reflect the fact they literally couldn't see what was going on. At any rate, one of the hallmarks of urban civilisations is that they leave a paper trail, and when they collapse, that paper trail tends to stop, because everyone has more important things to worry about. So one school of thought would have it that there's nothing remotely surprising or suspicious about these gaps in the record.

There is another school of thought, however, that has a rival explanation for the lack of written records from the centuries after Rome fell. It's this:

They never took place.

Okay, sure, Rome fell, and there was a bit of a gap before medieval Europe got going, with its knights and its chivalry and its long, infuriating poems about how the most romantic thing to do here would actually be *not* to have sex. But, according to this theory, the year 1000 took place not a thousand years after the standard date for the birth of Christ,† but only 703 years

---

* Seriously do not use this term if you're talking to a medieval historian, they will fight you.

† This is almost certainly not when the historical figure Jesus of Nazareth was actually born – his birth was probably somewhere in the window between 6 BCE and 4 BCE – but that's a whole different debate.

later. Roughly 300 years of European history simply never happened.[1]

The Phantom Time Hypothesis, as it's known, was first published in 1694, according to its own calendar – or, as we generally know it, 1991. It was the work of Heribert Illig, a German writer and publisher who has spent much of his career producing or promoting works of revisionist history. But it does have other supporters, such as technologist Hans-Ulrich Niemitz, who in 1995 published a paper under the heading 'Did the Early Middle Ages Really Exist?' – a classic example of what one might term the 'Hey, I'm just asking questions' approach to scholarship.[2]

By way of evidence for their hypothesis, these guys cite the scarcity of archaeological evidence that can be reliably dated to this period, and the limits of other techniques involving radiometric dating or dendrochronology (that is, looking at the rings in wood).* They note the strange gap in the history of Jewish communities, which seem to vanish from the record for several centuries in the Early Middle Ages before reappearing around the year 1000, and the way the development of everything from agricultural or military techniques to mosaic art and Christian doctrine seems to have ground to a halt for several centuries. They point to

---

* This is worth spelling out in some detail, because it is mind-blowing. Tree trunks include a new ring for each year, whose exact width depends on climatic conditions at the time that the tree grew. It is thus possible to look at a piece of timber that was cut down centuries ago and, by comparing it to a database of samples of the same type of wood, determine exactly what year the tree it came from was cut down. Why would you need conspiracy theories when real science is that amazing?

the fact that, over the same period, Constantinople stopped putting up great buildings, but that the Chapel at Aachen, which was built around the year 800 and involves all sorts of clever things like arches and vaulting, seems to have come around 200 years too early.

And they note that much of what we do know about the history of this period comes from what was written about it later. This means that somebody, somewhere, might have fabricated it. Such as, for example, a coalition of rulers around the turn of the second millennium – Pope Sylvester II, Holy Roman Emperor Otto III and Byzantine Emperor Constantine V, say – who conspired to fix the calendar because it would be much cooler and sexier to be ruling in the 1000th year since Christ rather than the 703rd, and who invented a load of history, including the first Holy Roman Emperor Charlemagne, in the process.

The Phantom Time fans' killer point, though, relates to how we measure time itself. The Julian calendar, proposed by Julius Caesar in 46 BCE and in use for the next 1,600 years or so, proposes a simple cycle of three regular years followed by one leap year, making the average year 365.25 days long. That, though, is slightly more than the 365.24219 days it actually takes the Earth to go around the sun – which means that the Julian calendar gains a day every 128 years. And so, by the late sixteenth century, it should have been out by thirteen days. But when astronomers working for Pope Gregory XIII came to reform that calendar, they found it was only out by ten days. A papal decree that Thursday 4 October 1582 was to be followed by Friday 15 October 1582 was enough to get the calendar back on track.

You know what could explain this discrepancy? If it hadn't been 1,582 years since the birth of Christ, but merely 1,285 years. In other words: if roughly three centuries of history had *never happened*.

At first glance, then, the Phantom Time Hypothesis does seem to fit, both with that circumstantial evidence, and with the vague sense that it's a bit *weird* that there are several centuries of history we just don't know very much about. And can we really be sure that the time of the Caesars and Jesus Christ was really 2,000 years ago, and not 1,700? After all, the calendar we know today wasn't even in use until around the year 800, roughly when those arches were going up in Aachen. All we have to go on is the word of long-dead authorities.

What if those authorities were wrong? What if they were lying, even? Can we be sure? Can we ever truly know?

Well: yes, we can. The Phantom Time Hypothesis is nonsense. It only works if you focus solely on western Europe, where the decline of Rome left a nasty gap in the records. Elsewhere – in Tang China, Abbasid Persia and in the rest of the Islamic world, which only developed in the seventh century – history continued apace. The same is true of the Byzantine Empire, the successor to the Eastern Roman Empire, which continued right down to 1453, even if it wasn't always building quite as many grand monuments in Constantinople as today's more cynical observers believe it should have been. The hypothesis requires you to ignore astronomical evidence, too, such as the solar eclipse reported by Pliny the Elder in 59 CE, which shows that events in antiquity are exactly as far into the past as you'd expect them to be.[3]

As for the shift from the Julian to the Gregorian calendar, that was never intended to reset the calendar to how it stood when Julius Caesar came up with it in 45 BCE, but to the *status quo* at the time of the Council of Nicea, when the

Catholic Church officially adopted it, in 325. Gregory's astronomers adjusted the calendar by ten days, not thirteen, because they were only trying to deal with twelve centuries of drift, not sixteen. There's no problem that needs solving.

It would be wrong to say that vast numbers of people subscribe to this conspiracy theory: few of the YouTubers poring over the JFK assassination or the latest pronouncements from Q seem concerned we've all had the wool pulled over our eyes by Emperor Otto III. But the Phantom Time Hypothesis tells us something about how conspiracy theories work, nonetheless. It takes a bunch of 'facts' – some of which are accurate but entirely explicable, some of which are just plain wrong – and knits them together into an ostensibly compelling narrative. If you're an American or Western European, with a basic layman's grasp of history, it feels true. The only problem is, it isn't.

There's another flaw in the Phantom Time Hypothesis, from one perspective: its lack of ambition. Human history has been going on, in some form or another, for millennia; but in most of the world, for the vast majority of that time, events have been documented at least as poorly as they were in western Europe during the Dark Ages. If you're going to start questioning whether such periods happened at all, why would you limit yourselves to eliminating a mere three centuries from the record? Why wouldn't you cast doubt on all of it?

Helpfully, a rival history-never-happened theory thinks bigger. The key assumption of the 'New Chronology', proposed by the Russian mathematician Anatoly Fomenko, is that there is no such thing as ancient history. Ancient Rome? Actually happened in the Middle Ages. Ancient Greece? Ditto. Ancient Egypt? You get the picture.

According to Fomenko, in fact, almost everything that we

believe to have happened before around the twelfth century –
and literally everything before the ninth century – actually
happened later, and probably somewhere else. We have no
record of what went on before somewhere around the year
800: what we think we know about antiquity is actually a
warped reflection of more recent events, and the reason
history sometimes seems to repeat itself is because the events
being written about are literally the same ones.[4]

Specific examples of people or events that are, in
Fomenko's telling, actually completely different people or
events, include:

The Peloponnesian War

This took place in the fifth century BCE, and saw the Delian
League (led by Athens) defeated by the Peloponnesian League
(led by Sparta). It was one of the most pivotal events in the
early history of Europe; Greek historian Thucydides' history
of the war remains a foundational text of international
relations. But according to Fomenko, it was actually a poor
photocopy of a fourteenth-century conflict between the
Duchy of Athens and a bunch of mercenaries called the
Navarrese Company. Which wasn't quite so pivotal.

King Solomon

The biblical King Solomon – he of the wisdom, who, if he
existed, probably ruled in the tenth century BCE – was actually, according to Fomenko, the sixteenth-century Ottoman
Emperor Suleiman the Magnificent.

The Babylon Captivity

Described in the Bible, this covers the seventy-ish years in the
fifth and sixth centuries BCE in which people from the Jewish

kingdom of Judah were held captive in Babylon. Fomenko says this was actually the seventy-ish years of the fourteenth century in which the papacy resided in Avignon. To be fair to Fomenko, this period *is* sometimes referred to as the Babylonian Captivity, but most observers believe this to be a deliberate reference, rather than because it was literally the same event.

The Trojan War
Actually the Crusades, and fought in an attempt to avenge the crucifixion.

The Anglo-Saxon kingdoms of the Early Middle Ages
These kingdoms (which make up some pretty large chunks of early English history) are, Fomenko claims, actually just the history of the Byzantine Empire – reflecting the fact that, after Constantinople fell to the Turks in 1453, its leaders fled to a cold, damp island on the other side of Europe, and also that both had some kings.

This is merely the barest of samples: the English translation of Fomenko's theories, *History: Fiction or Science?*, runs to seven thick volumes. Then again, I'd like to see you demonstrate that the entirety of human history is nonsense while also sticking to a strict word limit.

Who would do something so diabolical as to fabricate thousands upon thousands of years of world history? And what motive could they possibly have? The answers will take us to the heart of a conspiracy against the motherland, whose fiendishness is matched only by its non-existence.

The idea that everything we know about the distant past might be wrong is not, in itself, ridiculous. For one thing, just as in the case of the European Early Middle Ages, we have relatively few contemporary sources to tell us what was going on. Much of what we do know comes from later copies, which might have introduced mistakes; or later writers, who might not have known what was going on. And the further back we go, the less evidence we have from people who were actually there. On the face of it, there's plenty of room for errors or deliberate misinformation to have crept into the record.

Even when we do have first-hand evidence of events in ancient history, dating them isn't always easy. For reasons that should be obvious, any scroll that has, say, '15 March 44 BCE' written at its head can be dismissed as a forgery, but the calendar with which we're all familiar today wasn't developed until the sixth century CE, wasn't in common usage until the ninth, and has been reformed at different rates in different places since the sixteenth. Working out when events in the distant past really happened has historically been a laborious process involving, variously, messing around with astronomical data, poring over lists of rulers that may or may not contain gaps, and cross-referencing dating systems that may not even have years that are the same length.*

So how is it that history books today will confidently tell you that the Battle of Thermopylae happened in 480 BCE, or that Cyrus the Great of Persia captured Babylon and released the Jews from captivity in 539 BCE? Because, basically, other people have already done the legwork. A French Calvinist scholar called Joseph Scaliger, for example, spent much of the late sixteenth century comparing ancient calendars, placing

---

* The Islamic Lunar Calendar, still used in much of the Islamic world to determine the dates of religious festivals, is only 354–5 days long. Translating those dates into the Gregorian calendar is a delight.

Greek and Latin texts in order, calculating when eclipses happened, working out how to use coins as a tool in historical research, and generally expanding our notion of ancient history out from the Greek and Roman bit (with which every educated European was familiar) to include Persian, Babylonian, Egyptian and Jewish history, too. He and a few other thinkers worked out the basic chronology that made it possible to take the affairs of people who wouldn't know the Gregorian Calendar if it bit them, and attach them to dates that we'd all understand today.[5]

But it's in the nature of research conducted by specialists, using methods the rest of us can't easily grasp, that cynics are going to question it – if not dismiss it entirely in the hope of looking clever. One thinker who had his doubts over the orthodox timeline created by Scaliger was Sir Isaac Newton, whose posthumous work *The Chronology of Ancient Kingdoms Amended*[6] sifted various classical texts to propose alternative dates for the founding of Rome, the Trojan War, and (more surprising, this) the almost certainly mythical adventures of Jason and the Argonauts.[*]

Then there was Newton's French contemporary Jean Hardouin, a well-respected classical scholar in his day, who is nonetheless mostly remembered today for his crackpot theories. Notable among these was his fervent belief that – with the exception of Homer, Herodotus and Cicero, and selected

---

[*] The book also takes it as read that centaurs are real. If this seems like an odd flex from the founder of modern physics, it's worth remembering that Sir Isaac also spent much of his life trying to discover the secrets of alchemy, and once stuck a needle into the gap between his eyeball and eye socket just to see what would happen. Not all of his work would have passed peer review.

texts by Pliny, Virgil and Horace, which somehow won his seal of approval – the entire corpus of Greek and Roman literature had been forged by a bunch of thirteenth-century monks.[7]

Hardouin's theories are among those that inspired Fomenko's New Chronology. So are those of Nikolai Morozov, a Russian revolutionary, who was imprisoned from 1882 until 1905 for his political activities, but seems to have lost interest in the whole Revolution thing the moment the Tsar was overthrown.[*] Instead, he spent the last thirty years of his life studying science, astronomy and history, concluding – based on the descriptions of eclipses referred to in the New Testament – that the Scaligerian chronology was wrong, and that Jesus Christ had actually lived in the fifth century.[8] On top of that, he built a mountain of other conclusions, notably that Julius Caesar had never existed, that he was in fact the same person as the fourth-century emperor Julian the Apostate, and that, yes, large chunks of classical literature were just medieval forgeries.[†]

It was from Morovoz that Fomenko took the idea that Scaliger's chronology had been 'expanded arbitrarily' through 'repetition'[9] – holding that when the histories of one time and place seem reminiscent of those in another, it isn't simply

---

[*] There's another Nikolai Morozov who still sometimes makes the news today. He's a competitive figure skater, he performed in the 1998 Winter Olympics, and we have no reason to believe he subscribes to any strange views about when it was that the Romans were still moving about.

[†] Like *History: Fiction or Science?*, Morozov's magnum opus on this topic, which revels in the amazingly portentous title *Christ*, runs to seven volumes. Coincidence? You decide.

because human nature and the vicissitudes of fate cause certain patterns to repeat themselves. It's because they were literally the same events, accidentally copied and pasted over to a different setting.

Fomenko's attempts to 'prove' this involved a fair amount of time spent sifting the astronomical evidence – comparing ancient horoscopes or star catalogues with data about the movement of the heavens to work out when they might have been made; locating a real supernova that might have been the Star of Bethlehem so he could reassign the date of Jesus's birth; dating an eclipse that could have fallen over the crucifixion. (The possibility that biblical references such as these might, on occasion, simply be metaphors does not seem to have occurred to him.) From this, he built up a picture of when events plausibly might have occurred, if it wasn't at the time we've always thought.

But Fomenko is, by training, a mathematician, so his main tricks involve numbers. It's fairly intuitive that, when flicking through historic texts, you'd expect to find that eventful years (wars, riots, plagues, *etc.*) get a lot of pages, while quiet ones (no wars, no riots, no plagues, etc.) will get very few. Fomenko's theory is that by literally counting the number of pages each year in history has devoted to it, you can produce a unique historical fingerprint for any given period. So, for example, you might get few pages devoted to the first years of a century; then lots of pages about a war in years five and six; then a couple of pages on a plague in year twelve; then it goes quiet again for a while. What Fomenko argues is that if two texts about a place, supposedly from different eras, have roughly the same shape (spikes in years five and six, a smaller spike in year twelve, not a lot about the rest) then they are actually describing the same period of history. It's essentially dendrochronology again, only with book chapters instead of tree rings.

To 'prove' that this works, the mathematician compared two texts known to be about the same place in the same period – one a history of Rome written by Livy at the time of Augustus, the other a history of Rome written by a Russian historian in the twentieth century – and found they produced a graph of a similar shape. *Then* he compared texts about different places in different times and found they had radically different shapes. Then he compared a history of ancient Rome with one of medieval Rome, and found they *also* had the same shape. From this, he concluded that the events of ancient Rome actually took place in the Middle Ages*.

If you think this sounds a bit odd, wait until you hear his other trick, which is basically the same but concerns actual people: if two dynasties both follow the pattern of 'long-reigning but dull ruler who died in his bed, short-lived one stabbed to death by own bodyguards, extremely long-reigning successor seen as the father of the nation', then, well, they were probably the same dynasty, weren't they? Stands to reason.

In this way, Fomenko has 'proved', over many hundreds of pages and to his own satisfaction, that the ancient and medieval histories of the city of Rome were actually about the same period, that the ancient biblical kings of Judah and the fourth-century Western Roman Emperors were the same people, and so on.

He has not proved it to other people's satisfaction, however.

---

* Of course, there's a very good reason why modern histories of Rome might have a similar shape to that written by Livy: he's one of their best sources, so if Livy doesn't have anything much to say about certain years then his modern successors likely won't either.

In a much-cited essay from a 2001 edition of *Skeptic* magazine, Jason Colavito noted that Fomenko equated rulers that reigned for sixteen years with others that reigned for nine, or one that reigned for twenty-five with one that reigned for sixteen.[10] Fomenko also forced closer parallels by combining rulers, some of whom have similar names (Justin and Justinian), some of whom don't (Theodosius and Marcian).

Elsewhere, Colavito notes, Fomenko merged the early English king Edgar with his successor Edward the Martyr, on the grounds that their names are 'similar and consequently their union is natural'. This ignores quite how many of England's early kings were Edgars, Edwards, Edmunds, Eadwigs or Eadreds, plus Alfreds, Ethelreds, Ethelwulfs or Ethelberts; and that these were not, despite the shortage of vowels available in Anglo-Saxon England, the same man. What's more, notes Colavito with just a touch of sarcasm, 'the eleven Emperors Constantine (and the additional Emperors named Constans and Constantius) were apparently readily distinguished by the Barbarians'. Fomenko gives the impression of a man doing a jigsaw by tearing corners off pieces until they fit.

In some ways, of course, attempting to refute the New Chronology feels like a pretty strange exercise, since it basically amounts to attempting to prove that history happened: you might as well attempt to prove the sky is blue, or that two plus two equals four. But, for the record, while there may be some wriggle room about exactly how long ago specific events in the very ancient past took place – debate concerning the exact regnal dates of pharaohs from thousands of years ago, say – there is ample proof that these things happened a very long time ago. Quite apart from the fact that radiocarbon or dendrochronological dating backs up the existing chronology we all know and love, we have an almost unbroken series of coins, stretching from Republican Rome, several centuries BCE, all the way to the fall of Constantinople in 1453. The word 'Rome' is not a label that can be attached, as Fomenko suggests, to a series of civilisations based as far afield as Egypt and Moscow: it refers to a real city and the civilisation that grew out of it, whose history over more than two millennia we know in some detail. Fomenko is wrong.

That did not stop his English publisher from announcing, in 2004, a $10,000 prize for anyone who could prove that a human artefact dated from before the year 1000 CE.[11] The only catch was they were not allowed to use 'archaeological, dendrochronological, paleographical and carbon methods'. How exactly you are meant to prove that a pot dates from earlier than that without any of those methods is not exactly clear – produce a receipt, maybe? At any rate, the prize seems to remain unclaimed, but one suspects this says more about the terms of the contest than the existence or otherwise of artefacts from the ancient past.

Who, anyway, would want to rewrite human history to eliminate everything before the last millennium? The answer seems to be some combination of the Papacy, the Holy Roman Empire and the Romanov dynasty that ruled Russia from 1613 until the Revolution of 1917.* In other words, a coalition of Catholics (the main historic enemy of the

---

* We say 'seems': much of Fomenko's work is only available in Russian, so there's some debate about whether this explanation is Fomenko's own, or a gloss put over it by his supporters. Either way: this is how the theory has been widely interpreted, by both supporters and critics (see, for example, the work of Marlene Laruelle).

Orthodox Church), Germans (the main historic enemy of the Russian people) and the ruling house that sold Mother Russia down the river to its enemies. Because the New Chronology doesn't just rearrange history at random: it rearranges it to put Russia at the centre of everything.[12]

The notion that Moscow is the 'third Rome' has a long pedigree in Russian history. The second Rome, of course, was Constantinople, which continued to rule over a Roman Empire in the east for nearly a millennium after it vanished in the west. When that fell to the Ottoman Turks in 1453, the Grand Duchy of Moscow was the rising power in the Orthodox Christian world, and so naturally saw itself as the rightful successor. In 1547, Ivan the Terrible was crowned as the first Tsar of all the Russias: nearly 1,500 miles from Rome itself, and well over 500 from any territory ever claimed by the Empire, a Russian king was calling himself 'Caesar'.

Even though this idea has been floating around Russia for centuries, few outside the country – and essentially nobody outside the Orthodox world – have ever paid it much heed. This must have been intensely irritating, in exactly the way it would be if you knew you were the Messiah but nobody else believed you.

So, among all the stuff about copied-and-pasted dynasties, astronomical data and textual analysis based on page counts, is a literalisation of the notion that early modern Moscow was at the centre of a civilisation-defining empire. Fomenko posits the existence of a massive yet strangely forgotten land empire that he calls the 'Russian Horde'. This, in his telling, inherited both the grandeur of the earlier Romes (the first of which, oddly, was in Egypt), and their mission to spread civilisation and Christianity.

It also, conveniently, means that the surrounding

peoples – many of whom, by the time he was writing up his theories in the late 1980s, were scrambling to get out of the USSR – were actually also Russians, and part of a shared history. It even means that Genghis Khan's Mongol horde – the nomadic tribes that conquered much of Asia and eastern Europe in the thirteenth century, murdering and pillaging as they went, and traumatising medieval Russia into the bargain – were, in fact, tall, white, fair-haired, blue-eyed and thoroughly Russian-looking sort of chaps. How could Russia be humbled by foreign invaders, when those invaders were Russian, themselves? See, I'm not crying, I'm actually laughing.

Why don't we know any of this? Because Russia's enemies – and its traitorous leaders – suppressed the true history.

It's not hard to understand why, as the USSR collapsed and Russia looked weaker than it had done in decades, this might have been a comforting narrative: in Fomenko's telling, Russia wasn't merely at the heart of civilisation, it essentially *was* civilisation. The first political entity historians tend to recognise as Russia – Kievan Rus, in what is now Ukraine – emerged in the mid-ninth century. That is, you'll note, roughly when Fomenko's history starts. It's hard to avoid the suspicion these two facts are related.

Oh, and Jesus Christ? In Fomenko's telling, he was a twelfth-century Crimean. Or, from his point of view, a Russian. But you've probably guessed that by now.*

*   *   *

---

* He was also the Byzantine Emperor Andronikos I Komnenos, as well as possibly Pope Gregory VII, the Old Testament prophet Elisha, the eleventh-century Chinese Emperor Jingzong, and multiple others.

It's worth noting that Fomenko's theories have been all but universally dismissed as pseudohistory: no reputable historians have come even close to endorsing them. The chess grandmaster Garry Kasparov is sometimes listed as a supporter, but he has clarified – on several occasions, sometimes with the air of one who's regretting getting himself into this mess – that while he believes that Fomenko's work raises questions about traditional history, he does not buy into his replacement scheme.[13] Even the government of Vladimir Putin – which has not been shy of promoting narratives of Russian greatness, or of rewriting history when it comes to, say, Stalin – has not gone so far as to support the idea of the Russian Horde. The theory has no notable supporters.

Yet there are corners of the internet where ideas built on Fomenko's work have been enthusiastically embraced. There are, for example, several active subreddits concerned with the history of a vast, Eurasian empire known as Tartaria, which lasted into the nineteenth century but has now been wiped from the record books.[14] This was a multicultural and multi-ethnic polity covering much of what is now northern Asia, which specialised in grand architecture and had technology more advanced than anything western Europe could offer at the time. In some of the weirder versions, it may have been home to 'breatharians', a form of being who didn't need food or water but could draw energy directly from the air;[15] in the more pedestrian ones, it was populated simply by giants.

Much of the evidence for all this has disappeared beneath the ground thanks to a forgotten catastrophe known as the 'mud flood'. It's been hushed up by Western powers who didn't want to let on that another part of the world was more advanced than they were. Or possibly by a Russia that wanted to cover up its own historical atrocities towards a neighbour. The latter theory was helpfully promoted by a 1957 document from the CIA, of all things, leading exasperated historians to comment that, whatever its other qualities, the CIA was not the body you should go to for information on the medieval history of the Eurasian steppe.[16]

One reason all this has spread is simple Western ignorance about a region of the world we don't tend to hear much about. The word 'Tartary' does often appear on early modern maps of the region: some people have mistaken a geographical label for a political one, and merged it with half-remembered stuff about nomadic conquerors such as Ghengis Khan or the artist formerly known as Tamburlaine.*

But at the end of the day, a history you just don't know about is far less interesting than a secret one that's been deliberately hushed up. As with the Phantom Time Hypothesis – or the idea Paul McCartney has been dead since 1966 – it's simply more exciting to believe that everything you know is wrong. Although where the stuff about giants or breatharians comes from is anybody's guess.

Theories about flat Earth and Phantom Time are a reminder that, at the extremes of the conspiracy universe, the whole notion of consensus reality begins to break down. It's no longer discrete events that have been meddled with; history itself starts to seem like a lie.

This, as we'll see, is a theme that would come to dominate conspiracism in the twentieth century. It's time to finish the story of the Illuminati.

---

* Today he's more often called Timur Lek.

11

Who Runs the World? (Lizards)

From her earliest years, Nesta Helen Webster had an unquenchable sense of adventure and a restless, curious mind.

Sadly for her, she suffered the misfortune of being alive in a time when neither of those qualities was a good fit for the role women were expected to play in society. Born in 1876, she was the youngest child of fourteen in a well-off, deeply religious family (her mother was a bishop's daughter, her father a strict evangelical convert who was a big shot in Barclays). She received an expensive education, although her dream of attending Oxford or Cambridge was ruled out, as those universities were too liberal for her mother's tastes. As the nineteenth century began drawing towards its close, twenty-one-year-old Nesta said goodbye to Westfield College and set off on a grand tour of the world to expand her mind – traversing Africa, Asia and the Americas, and getting into Buddhism for a bit.

But on returning to the UK, Nesta became frustrated. She had grown to 'despise an idle life', and she chafed against the paucity of opportunities for a smart young lady such as herself.

'What careers were open to women at that date?' she would write later. She feared that marriage, the other option on offer, would be even worse, spelling 'the end of all adventure'.[1] She nonetheless wound up marrying a policeman who she'd met in India after a whirlwind courtship. But still, she wanted more; not for her the life of a schoolmistress or a nurse, and still less the stultifying existence of a society wife. She wanted to *do things*. Nesta Webster wanted to make her mark on the world.

So, she became a fascist.

And let's be clear about this: she did not become a *little bit* fascist. This isn't one of those 'Oooh, you can't say anything these days without someone calling you a fascist, it's political correctness gone mad' situations. No, Webster became really very fascist indeed. In the 1920s, she held a leadership position in the British Fascists, a group that would eventually merge into Oswald Mosley's British Union of Fascists. Her writing regularly appeared in far-right publications like the *Fascist Bulletin*, the *Patriot* and *British Lion*, and she was a key contributor to an infamous series of articles in the *Morning Post* titled 'The Jewish Peril'. So, yes. Definitely a fascist.

But her path from the open-minded, globe-trotting young woman – the one who developed a deep respect for the world's religions – to the enormous anti-Semite that she became isn't an entirely straightforward one. And the reason she features in our story is that the route she took would see Nesta Webster become perhaps the single most influential conspiracy theorist of the twentieth century. That route made her the wellspring of a huge range of modern conspiratorial ideas that say the world is controlled by a shadowy cabal of global elites, from the New World Order to the Bilderberg Group. And it's a route that runs through that old favourite, the French Revolution.

Webster's solution to the thorny question of how to blend her need for a meaningful career with her desire for new horizons was that she would become a writer. And she turned out to be a pretty good one: her first book was a well-received novel called *The Sheep Track*, in which she channelled her disdain for the enforced conformity and frivolity of women's lives, and gave voice to her desire for the less-travelled path.*
But it was when she tried her hand at non-fiction that things started to go a bit awry.

In 1916, she published a history of a Revolution-era romance between two French nobles, the Comtesse de Sabran and the Chevalier de Boufflers, which sparked in her a deep fascination for the period. Actually, that's perhaps an understatement; she seems to have come to believe on some level that she was actually a reincarnation of the Comtesse, and that she had personal memories of the Revolution. Not only did she become obsessed with the era, she developed a firm conviction that the Revolution had been a profound crime, and, moreover, that most of the histories of the period were wrong.

Much like many people who had actually lived through the Revolution, rather than merely imagining that they had, Webster went in search of an explanation for events that seemed inconceivable and monstrous to her. And she found her truth when she rediscovered the works of John Robison and the Abbé Augustin Barruel.

In 1920, she published *The French Revolution: A Study in Democracy*, in which she both came out as an opponent of democracy in general, and more specifically revived the Illuminati theory of the Revolution for a new age. What

---

* The history of conspiracy theorists calling people who don't agree with them 'sheep' is a long one, it turns out.

seemed to have faded into the obscurity of history was suddenly reborn. The Illuminati were *back*, baby.

But Webster wasn't content to leave Weishaupt's movement and its supposed plots in the 1700s. *A Study in Democracy* was just the first salvo in a period of astonishing productivity, in which she would update Barruel and Robison's beliefs to fit the anxieties of her age, and in doing so would play a pivotal role in defining the next century of Western conspiracy theories. A year after her book on the French Revolution, Webster published *World Revolution: The Plot Against Civilization*, in which she laid out her grand thesis: that 'Illuminised Freemasonry' was responsible for revolutions throughout the ages, and that such secret societies had long provided a 'terrible, unchanging, relentless, and wholly destructive' force shaping world events. She extended the Illuminati's brief lifespan both forward and back in time, insisting that it was still active in the twentieth century, but also that it had been around in some form since the twelfth century, bringing into the narrative groups like the Rosicrucians and the Knights Templar, which would become staples of the conspiracy view of history, and also of Dan Brown novels.*

This wasn't mere abstract historical speculation, but a

---

* Dan Brown's best-selling novel *The Da Vinci Code* owes a hefty debt to *The Holy Blood and the Holy Grail*, a 1982 book of conspiratorial pseudohistory whose three authors include Michael Baigent and Richard Leigh. The fact *The Da Vinci Code*'s villain is called 'Leigh Teabing' is probably not a coincidence, but may be a sign that Brown hasn't realised that other people can do anagrams, too. (The third author of *The Holy Blood and the Holy Grail*, Henry Lincoln, is sadly not recognised in the text of *The Da Vinci Code*. This is a shame, because he was one of the inventors of the Yeti in the Patrick Troughton era of *Doctor Who*.)

direct response to current events. Just as the French
Revolution had been a profound shock to the political establishment of the eighteenth century, so too had the Russian
Revolutions of 1917, which were followed by a flurry of
similar uprisings across much of Europe. In the Bolshevik
takeover in Moscow, Webster saw a clear parallel with the
horrors that had been inflicted on her beloved French nobles.
The leap she made was to conclude that they weren't just
thematically similar, but literally connected – with the exact
same group of villains responsible for both events, in a vast
conspiracy that spanned the centuries.

That Nesta Webster initially came to fascism through
anti-communism didn't mark her out as especially unusual:
many of her contemporaries followed the same road. Webster
abhorred the Bolsheviks and all they stood for, and saw
fascism as the best means to combat them. Not only that, but
she bought into a mythology that was rising across much of
Europe at the time – that of 'Judeo-Bolshevism', in which
communism was viewed as a specifically Jewish plot, and many
people 'looked at the revolution and saw only Jews at the
center of the action'.[2] In connecting this anti-Semitic
conspiracy theory with that of the Illuminati, Webster was
following in the footsteps of a mysterious Italian army captain
named Jean Baptiste Simonini, who back in 1806 had written
a letter to the Abbé Barruel suggesting that Jewish influence
was behind Weishaupt's group. Barruel ultimately rejected the
theory, but copies of Simonini's letter would circulate in
anti-Semitic circles throughout the nineteenth century.[3]

Once Webster was on board the fascism train, she went all
in. She defended *The Protocols of the Elders of Zion*, even while
acknowledging questions about their authenticity; she devoted
a large section of *World Revolution* to tenuous side-by-side

comparisons between Illuminati writings, the *Protocols*, and socialist and communist texts, in a not-terribly-convincing effort to prove they are one and the same. In 1924, she followed up *World Revolution* with the publication of *Secret Societies and Subversive Movements*, her most significant work, in which she both expanded on her theories and made it even more explicit that she thought the Jews were behind it all. '[The] immense problem of the Jewish Power,' she wrote, '[is] perhaps the most important problem with which the modern world is confronted.'

She would go on to publish further books and numerous articles expanding on her themes, including *The Socialist Network* in 1926, a lesser work largely notable for including a fold-out diagram of said network, which is an early example of the classic conspiracist belief that if you draw lines between a bunch of vaguely related things, you've proved they're a conspiracy. But *Secret Societies* would remain the high-water mark of her mainstream influence and celebrity, as once it became clear that her dreams of becoming a respected historian might have taken a bit of a knock, she increasingly focused her attention on real-world fascist organising.

Reaction to Webster's work was ... mixed, to say the least. Actual historians were deeply unimpressed. *The American Historical Review*, the premier history journal in the United States, opined that *A Study in Democracy* 'does not rise above the level of a reactionary pamphlet'. The review added: 'Mrs. Webster seems to be almost totally ignorant of the recent literature on the Revolution ... She has not the faintest idea of what proof means in historical research,' before concluding that it 'was a pure waste of time to write such a book, and it is unfortunate that it was ever published'. Furthermore, they warned, its publication 'may do much harm'.[4]

But at the same time, for a period, Webster found an appreciative audience on the right wing of politics. This was far from being limited to an extremist fringe: *A Study in Democracy* was praised in the *Spectator*, and she was invited to give talks on her theories to the British military. Webster's influence on the mainstream political thought of the day is perhaps best illustrated by a newspaper article published in London's *Illustrated Sunday Herald* in 1920. Titled 'Zionism vs Bolshevism: A Struggle for the Soul of the Jewish People', its purpose is to draw a line between what it describes as the 'good Jews' and the rest, of whom the worst are the 'International Jews'. It describes how 'from the days of Spartacus-Weishaupt to those of Karl Marx' there had been a 'world-wide conspiracy for the overthrow of civilisation' fuelled by an 'envious malevolence'. This, it claimed, had 'played, as … Mrs. Webster has so ably shown, a definitely recognisable part in the tragedy of the French Revolution'. This global conspiracy was, the article asserts, 'the mainspring of every subversive movement during the Nineteenth Century' – before culminating in Bolshevism, in which 'the majority of the leading figures are Jews'.[5]

The article wasn't dashed off by some forgotten tabloid hack. It was written by no less a figure than the Rt Hon Winston S. Churchill: future prime minister, regular occupant of the number-one slot on lists of greatest Britons, and at the time occupying the senior cabinet post of Secretary of State for War and Air.

Now, this isn't the place to re-litigate the 'Winston Churchill: good or bad?' question – oh *god*, please not that again – and Churchill himself held enough conflicting positions during his many decades of public life that you can paint just about any portrait of him you choose depending on what evidence you pick. Certainly there's little to suggest that a conspiracist mindset was a major driver of Churchill's beliefs over his career. But it does serve as a useful demonstration of how easily even long-debunked conspiracy theories can be adopted and amplified by political elites, as long as they flatter their preconceived view of the world.

While Webster herself saw her influence wane over the years, others were happy to pick up her theories and run with them. Foremost among these was Lady Queenborough, formerly Edith Starr Miller, a wealthy New York socialite possessed of abundant leisure time and a hatred of both Jews and Mormons. Miller had married the Baron Queenborough – a British industrialist and former Conservative MP for Cambridge, who would devote his later years to telling everyone how great Hitler and Franco were – and she would spend about a decade of her fascist-adjacent life 'researching' the history of secret societies. Lady Queenborough's *Occult Theocracy*, published in two volumes in 1931 and posthumously in 1933, is as much a classic of conspiracist literature as *Secret Societies*, helping to deepen the lore of the theory's mystical history as it bounced around from druids and witchcraft to Satanists, Templars and Rosicrucians.

Queenborough helped Webster's theories go transatlantic. They would gain a further foothold in the USA thanks to Gerald Winrod, a Baptist preacher, conspiracy theorist and committed anti-Semite who was commonly known as 'the Jayhawk Nazi', and who would be unsuccessfully tried for sedition in 1944 thanks to his public enthusiasm for Hitler. Winrod adopted Webster's analysis and her rediscovery of Barruel and Robison wholesale, citing all three extensively. He emphasised that 'the whole scheme was a Jewish plot to the core', and insisted that Karl Marx 'edited his teachings out of the writings of Adam Weishaupt'. His general attitude to the 'evil genius' and 'moral pervert' at the heart of his brief 1935 book can be inferred from the title – *Adam Weishaupt: A Human Devil.*[6]

This American link – embedding the notion of the conspiracy theory in the fringes of the anti-communist American right – is important, because it would be a few decades before the Illuminati conspiracy theories reared their head again. As the shock of the Bolshevik Revolution subsided and the threat of Nazism rose, the market for what Webster and her fellow fascists were selling diminished somewhat. But then, well, a bit more twentieth-century history happened, and before too long, the pendulum had swung back, so that anti-communism was a hot property once again.

First out of the gate this time was William Guy Carr, a former submariner who'd been born in Formby in Lancashire, but ended up serving beneath the waves with the Canadian Navy. After first getting into Illuminati theories when they'd been popular in the early thirties, he spent the next two decades, in time-honoured fashion, 'doing his own research' on the topics. The result was a series of books, beginning in 1955 with *Pawns in the Game* and *Red Fog Over America*, which drew from Webster, Queenborough and a slew of other influences to create a heady stew of only partly coherent conspiratorial beliefs, including blaming the conspiracy for the deaths of not just Abraham Lincoln, but also Charles I, Alexander Hamilton, President McKinley, Archduke Franz Ferdinand and – perhaps most notably – Jesus Christ.

Carr's influence was significant, both in his books' popularity (*Pawns in the Game* was reputed to have sold around half a million copies) and in how they adapted the Illuminati theories to fit the age. While maintaining the fervent anti-communism of his predecessors, Carr also drew in conspiratorial ideas from the left, and rendered the combination this created as a joint attack on America's religious traditions (as the publisher's blurb for *Pawns* read: 'The International Communists, and the International Capitalists ... have temporarily joined hands to defeat Christian democracy'). He presents the Illuminati as a front for Judaism – the group is frequently referred to as 'the Jewish Illuminati' – but then in turn portrays Judaism as a front for Satanism. *Pawns* also includes quite a lot of material on a supposed Satanic branch of Freemasonry known as 'Palladianism'; somewhat unfortunately for Carr, the Palladians had been invented wholesale in the 1880s by a French hoaxer named Léo Taxil – proving once again that you should never, ever make jokes.*

Notably, Carr's books were also among the first to use the phrase 'New World Order' to describe the conspiracy's supposed end goal of a single world government. That was a notion that would be taken to new heights by our next entrant in the Conspiracy Hall of Fame: enter Robert Welch.

Mr Welch was an American businessman, wealthy from candy sales and possessed of extremely powerful opinions on the matter of communism. In short, he did not like it one bit. In 1958, Welch founded the John Birch Society, named after an unfortunate US Army intelligence agent and former missionary, who was executed in a confrontation with communist troops in China in 1945. In Welch's Manichaean

---

* Lady Queenborough had also been big on Palladianism; Nesta Webster, to her minimal credit, doesn't seem to have been taken in, dismissing Taxil as a 'notorious romancer' in a footnote in *Secret Societies*.

view of the world, Birch's death made him the first American casualty in the great war against communism.

The John Birch Society was born following a long period of institutionalised conspiracism in the USA, in the form of the Red Scare and Senator McCarthy's anti-communist witch hunts. While both public opinion and mainstream politics had come round to the view that McCarthy's zealotry in rooting out communists – real and imaginary – had gone way too far, Welch was more of the view that things had not gone far enough. He was convinced that 'Communism … is wholly a conspiracy, a gigantic conspiracy to enslave mankind',[7] and determined that the John Birch Society would be on the frontline of the resistance.

But, as with many powerful drugs, eventually the buzz of feverish anti-communism wasn't quite enough. By the early sixties, Welch was becoming convinced that a vast communist conspiracy alone wasn't sufficient to explain what was going on in the world, and so … yep, you guessed it, he started to *do his own research*. In 1964, he revealed the new truth that he'd uncovered: that the communists were not at the top of the conspiracy pyramid. In fact, he wrote, 'the Communist movement is only a tool of the total conspiracy'.

Can you guess what that total conspiracy was?

Welch's revival of the Illuminati theory was mostly a straight update of Webster's work: the claim that communism was simply one offshoot of an Illuminati plot that stretched back nearly two centuries, a plot that had continued after the group supposedly collapsed, as was 'clearly proved in the detailed histories of Robison and the Abbé Barruel'. (In case you're wondering, Webster, Robison and Barruel are the only historical sources he cites to prove his case.) But Welch also started introducing his own terminology – he christened the modern inheritors of the Illuminati flame 'the INSIDERS', an 'inner core of conspiratorial power, able to direct and control subversive activities which were worldwide in their reach, incredibly cunning and ruthless in their nature, and brilliantly farsighted and patient in their strategy'.

Welch's revival of Webster's theory included plenty of his own additions, many of which would become mainstays of the right-wing conspiracy landscape in years to come. The ultimate goal of the INSIDERS (always capitalised, for unclear reasons) was 'surrendering all remaining American sovereignty to the United Nations, and enabling that Communist one-world government to "police" our country with foreign troops' – a state of affairs that the Birchers, following the lead of William Carr, would come to refer to as the New World Order. The INSIDERS became an amorphous but all-purpose enemy on whom Welch and his allies could hang any variety of their pet peeves, from the influential think tank the Council on Foreign Relations to the fluoridation of water – both still important parts of the conspiracy universe today.

At its peak, the John Birch Society had upwards of 100,000 members, and was seriously influential in Republican politics. But, as certain other groups had found in earlier times, growing influence also paints a target on your back. The Birchers' wild, scattershot paranoia, and willingness to accuse anybody – up to and including serving Republican presidents – of being part of the conspiracy, were traits that made them plenty of enemies. Most prominent was William F. Buckley, the intellectual daddy of the Republican party for many decades. Buckley went to war with the Birchers, determined to prevent them from turning his party into what he feared would become a fascist movement. By and large, he won; while the society remained active and influential throughout the seventies, it failed to become the dominant force in Republicanism, and eventually went into a period of sustained decline.

Despite this, the John Birch Society has long played an outsized role in the paranoid imagination of parts of the American left, sometimes coming close to taking on an almost Illuminati-like quality itself. Most notably, as mentioned in chapter 5, the evidence is pretty clear that Lee Harvey Oswald had attempted to assassinate senior Birch member Edwin Walker in his home some months before the Kennedy assassination (he missed). Fears of the Society's continued behind-the-scenes influence or possible resurgence have been commonplace down the years – every now and then, you could rely on articles appearing in the press with some variation on the theme of 'the John Birch Society is back'. This has been fuelled by the fact that Fred Koch – father of Charles and David Koch, the mega-donor funders of a suite of right-wing causes and long-time chief villains in the demonology of the American left – had been a prominent founding member of the Birchers.

Some of this has been a bit overstated, at least when it comes to the power of the actual Society, which has never returned to anything like its sixties heyday. The Trump administration was certainly ideologically aligned with the Birchers in many ways – the closest the US has come to a truly Birchist administration – and the conspiracy theories that Welch helped implant in sections of the American right were indeed a fundamental part of many Trump supporters' worldviews. But throughout this, the actual society has remained a shadow of its former self, with a fraction of the membership and limited direct influence. Its ideas may have grown in power, but it hasn't. And shared ideas aren't the same as a conspiracy, despite what Augustin Barruel would tell you.

Still, at their peak in the sixties, the Birchers were truly a force to be reckoned with. But then ... something unexpected happened.

This is where we need to address a different story you might have heard about the Illuminati, and how they came to be a byword for conspiracy: namely, it was all just a joke that got out of hand. That, in the words of one website, 'every Illuminati conspiracy theory is based on a hippie prank from the 1960s'[8] – but then people took the prank seriously, and things spiralled from there. This is a theory that's had some weight thrown behind it: it's been stated as a fact in a BBC article,[9] and the renowned documentary-maker Adam Curtis repeated it in his 2021 series, *Can't Get You Out of My Head: An Emotional History of the Modern World*.

It's not true, of course. As we've seen, there's an unbroken chain of influence from Barruel and Robison in the 1790s to Webster, Winrod and Welch – and that chain of influence carries on into the conspiracy theories of today. *That's* what all our modern conspiracy theories are based on, with all the important players at every stage taking it very seriously indeed.

But still, there is a nugget of truth here. A few years after Welch and the Birchers got heavily into beliefs about the Illuminati, they triggered a reaction that would transplant awareness of the conspiracy theory from the reactionary right to the left-wing counterculture, and from there into the mainstream. This reaction came in the form of something called 'Operation Mindfuck'.

The roots of this were in Discordianism, a sort of absurdist pseudo-religion dedicated to the worship of chaos, invented in the early sixties by counterculture writers Greg Hill and Kerry Thornley. It was Thornley who would team up in 1968 with a fellow Discordian, the writer and journalist Robert Anton Wilson, to create Operation Mindfuck – which is best summarised as an extended campaign of chaos manufacturing. The form this took was a series of spurious newspaper articles and hoax letters to the great and the good, in an attempt to spread the belief that just about every event in the United States was somehow connected to the Illuminati.

Wilson's interest in conspiracism originated from his role as an editor at *Playboy*, where he was in charge of the letters section, and was forced to read the Welch-inspired musings of the green-ink brigade, all furiously insisting that the Illuminati were real – or, as he would subsequently describe it, 'a lot of paranoid rantings from people imagining totally baroque conspiracies'. One day, he and his colleague Bob Shea were chatting when one of them idly suggested, 'Suppose all these nuts are right, and every single conspiracy they complain about really exists.'[10] And so the premise of Operation Mindfuck was born.

Thornley's interest in conspiracism, meanwhile, had a far more direct cause: he had known Lee Harvey Oswald well when they served in the military together, and had even written a book about Oswald in 1962 – almost certainly the only book written about Lee Harvey Oswald *before* he shot Kennedy. This had seen Thornley called to testify before the Warren Commission, and then subsequently dragged into Jim Garrison's conspiracist prosecution, which ended up with Garrison charging Thornley with perjury for insisting he'd not been in contact with Oswald after their military service. You can see how all that happening to you might stimulate some interest in the field of conspiracy theories, and why people believe them.*

There's not a huge amount of evidence that Operation Mindfuck in its initial iteration had any great success at spreading the Illuminati theory much further than the John Birch Society had already managed to (although Wilson did claim some victories in seeding some interest among radicals, writing in his autobiography that, 'New exposés of the Illuminati began to appear everywhere, in journals ranging from the extreme Right to the ultra-Left'). That would change when Wilson and Shea teamed up to turn the underlying premise of Mindfuck into a series of novels: *The Illuminatus! Trilogy*.

A sprawling work of gonzo sci-fi alt-history, *The Illuminatus! Trilogy* paints a hallucinatory world in which essentially every conspiracy theory is real at the same time, if anything can be considered 'real' at all. First published in 1975, it slowly worked its way up from being a cult hit, to a sleeper hit, to, eventually, a bona fide *hit* hit. It found an enthusiastic and diverse audience of what Wilson described as 'agnostic heretics' – a crowd of all-purpose non-believers and explanation-sceptics, who rejected mainstream narratives and thought they were being lied to on a grand scale, but who treated conspiracy theories with just as much scorn. Fans of the trilogy, he wrote, tended to 'doubt that anybody is shrewd enough to guess what the hell is really going on, or who is really in charge of this planet, or if anybody is in charge at all'.

---

* The charges against Thornley were eventually dropped by Garrison's successor, who was also Harry Connick Jr's dad. Thornley would decline in later life, and come to believe in a rather unusual Kennedy theory – which was that Thornley himself had done it.

From this point of view, it's not clear how many true believers in the Illuminati conspiracy, if any, Wilson's work actually spawned. But it certainly helped to usher awareness of the concept out of the fringes of the right and into the mainstream, and played a key role in making the Illuminati a pop-culture phenomenon as much as a genuine conspiratorial belief. And if nothing else, the trilogy – and especially the first volume, *The Eye in the Pyramid* – is almost certainly responsible for helping popularise the idea that the famous pyramid-eye imagery seen in the Great Seal of the United States is actually the logo of the Illuminati. It isn't! The 'Eye of Providence', as it's known, had nothing to do with the Bavarian Illuminati. It was just a popular depiction of the eternal presence of an interventionist God in early modern religious iconography, inspired by Egyptian hieroglyphs. There *was* an actual Illuminati logo, which was this: ⊙ – a 'circumpunct', a dot in the centre of a circle, possibly representing 'the sun radiating illumination to outer circles'.[11] Members would use this symbol instead of writing 'Illuminati' in their letters to each other, a super-secret code that completely failed to keep anything they were doing remotely secret.

But while Wilson and pals were busy satirising everybody and everything, the legacy of Welch's take on the Illuminati mythos continued to grow. Fuelled by political battles and culture wars, Welch's conspiracy theories proved to be a useful scaffolding on to which any and all topical bugbears could be attached – conspiracies within conspiracies, nested inside one another like a poorly evidenced matryoshka doll. The age of the superconspiracy was being born.

One of the most prominent early examples came straight from within the House of Birch: the 1971 book *None Dare Call*

It Conspiracy, written by Society members Gary Allen and Larry Abraham. This is notable for a couple of reasons. One, it sold an absolute *fuck-ton* – shifting somewhere in the region of four or five million copies during the 1972 presidential election campaign. It had a preface written by a sitting congressman, who warned that powerful forces would attempt to 'kill' the book and that 'the "experts" will try to ridicule you out of investigating for yourself as to whether or not the information in this book is true'.[12]

Another reason *None Dare Call It Conspiracy* is interesting is that it was ahead of its time in how it achieved its success, doing so in ways that set the stage for much of modern political campaigning. It was sold almost exclusively through mail order, and readers were encouraged to spread the word by ordering additional copies for people they knew. ('You may have received this book through the mail. It is a gift from a concerned American who has read the book,' says a note at the beginning.) It was an early example of what we'd call a viral hit today. Not only that, but Allen used those mail orders to build up an enormous mailing list, enabling him to continue to broadcast his message directly to those who'd shown they might be hooked by his theories.[13]

A final reason that *None Dare Call It Conspiracy* is an interesting milestone in the evolution of the Illuminati conspiracy theory is this: it barely mentions the Illuminati at all. As a Birchist publication, it takes Welch's terminology of 'the Insiders' and runs with that instead (although they drop the all-caps). The framework is identical – a conspiracy that has its origins in the run-up to the French Revolution, and uses communism as a tool to bring about its ultimate goals of a single world government – and you can see the connections if you know that Welch's use of 'the INSIDERS' was effectively synonymous with 'the Illuminati'. But the actual group only get mentioned a few times, mostly in the context of the claim that Karl Marx was simply copying the original Illuminati playbook when he wrote the *Communist Manifesto*, which he supposedly did on the orders of an Illuminati front group.

Allen and Abraham's book marks the point where Illuminati theories start to become almost entirely detached from the historical Illuminati, and it becomes possible to believe in theories that are clearly Illuminati-inspired without ever troubling yourself with the details of early modern Bavarian local politics. Instead, much of the book is concerned with a superconspiratorial universe of other, now familiar targets – income tax, central banks and national debt, the Council on Foreign Relations, the United Nations, the Rothschilds and the Rockefellers, the imminent plans for a 'New World Order', all of which are aspects of the Insiders' grand plot.*

A few years after Allen's book came out, another variant emerged from Des Griffin, whose 1976 *Fourth Reich of the Rich* took the basic ploy of extending the Illuminati's history backwards in time to its, er, logical conclusion: he sees the birth of the Illuminist conspiracy as ultimately originating with the fall of Lucifer from heaven. Much like William Carr's work before him, it's an explicitly religious interpretation of Illuminati lore, in which the Illuminati are a Satanic

---

* It's an interesting historical twist that Gary Allen's son is the political journalist Mike Allen, founder of the news organisation Axios and the original creator of *Politico*'s famous 'Playbook' newsletter – the ultimate 'insider' product, embracing all the tropes that *None Dare Call It Conspiracy* railed against (while still showing his father's appreciation of the power of building a good mailing list).

conspiracy founded in ancient Babylon by the biblical figure of Nimrod, and the Catholic Church is a continuation of the heretical ancient Babylonian religion. It combines the theories of Barruel and crew with those of an 1850s anti-Catholic conspiracist tract by a Scottish Presbyterian theologian named Alexander Hislop. Griffin didn't pioneer this combination himself – in fact, in the 1930s and 1940s it was a favourite of our old Nazi pal Gerald Winrod, whose monthly newspaper the *Defender* is filled with references to Babylon and Nimrod.* Nonetheless, Griffin's update of Winrod and Carr would help sow the seeds for a rich vein of conspiracy theories on the Christian right, in which political conspiracies merge with apocalyptic and millenarian interpretations of scripture, and you end up with people believing that proposals for universal healthcare are a harbinger of the End of Days.

This would reach a peak in the 1990s, when a conspiratorial and frequently apocalyptic form of political Christianity would come to play a major role in the radical right of American politics. At its extreme ends, this included figures like Texe Marrs, a former US Air Force officer whose take on Illuminati theories was almost completely divorced from their historical origins. For Marrs, the Illuminati simply represents the massed ranks of Luciferian forces that make up a super-conspiracy opposed to Christianity and determined to bring about the New World Order, which will itself fulfil the biblical prophecies and usher in the final battle between the forces of light and dark.

---

* If anyone has been inspired by this story to start their own conspiracy theory, the fact that Winrod is the same word as Nimrod only with the first syllable backwards and one letter turned upside down is right there.

But this movement also had a significant popular, almost mainstream, footprint. This is best illustrated by the televangelist and would-be Republican presidential candidate Pat Robertson, whose 1991 book *New World Order* was a *New York Times* best-seller, and introduced a sort of low-fat version of the conspiracy theory to a mass audience. Robertson doesn't indulge in some of the more extreme elements of the theory that the likes of Marrs do, but it still included many of the familiar touchpoints from the previous seventy years of the movement. The Illuminati were responsible for the French Revolution; communism was just the Illuminist manifesto lightly reworded; everything since then has been a continuation of the same core conspiracy, from the Rothschilds to the Bolsheviks to the Federal Reserve to the Council on Foreign Relations. For his history of the Illuminati and the subsequent world revolution, Robertson cites as evidence the works of John Robison and Nesta Webster.

Robertson was mainstream enough in the nineties that this all got him into quite a lot of trouble, with major articles in outlets like the *New York Times* and the *New York Review of Books* pointing out that he was quoting a fascist and that the theories were wildly anti-Semitic.

Robertson's work shows how the Illuminati theory had, in many ways, come full circle – but with a very different meaning after two centuries of social change. Both the Abbé Barruel and Robertson are arguing something very similar: that the natural order of society is the rule of Christian theology, and that the spread of any and all ideas that suggest otherwise amounts to a conspiracy. But where Barruel's conspiracy theory was an explicit defence of elites and an expression of anxiety about the rise of people-powered politics, Robertson's conspiracy theory is presented as a fear of elites plotting to suppress the liberties of the people. Barruel was fearful of the world to come; Robertson was looking back and wondering where it all went wrong. (Robertson was, of course, a millionaire with his own television network, which some might think makes his railing against elites just a shade hypocritical, but his audience didn't seem to mind.)

The Christian conservative branch of Illuminati theories was among the most influential in the years leading up to the millennium, but it wasn't the only one. Another branch would also incorporate the explicitly Satanic elements of Griffin, but add new features that would take the theory off into wild new directions – ones that would give it an audience that expanded far beyond the narrow ideological communities of the radical right.

While the 1970s had given us the first hints of how conspiracy theories from the political and religious spheres would begin to combine into superconspiracies, it also saw the beginnings of an ambitious crossover event that would massively expand the conspiracy cinematic universe. This wouldn't fully come to fruition until the 1980s; it would then go on to have a profound influence on the politics and the culture of the 1990s. The crossover was the merging of the Illuminati-inspired New World Order theories of the American right with a very different set of beliefs: ufology.

At first glance, you wouldn't think these would be natural bedfellows. The impulses that drive people to search for meaning in lights in the sky would seem to be far removed from those that fuel paranoid interpretations of the battle of ideas here on Earth; the existence of aliens would seem to be a particularly bad fit with the overtly biblical versions of the theory.

That wasn't going to stop them, obviously. UFO beliefs had always had elements of conspiracy, but from the late seventies onwards, the general accusations of a government cover-up blossomed into a more fully developed – and darker – conspiracy landscape, populated with cattle mutilations and abductions, mind-wiping men in black and elite collaboration with malign, otherworldly forces. The UFO community had independently created a framework for their conspiracy that shared many elements of (and was ripe for a crossover with) the by-now massively expanded Illuminati New World Order conspiracy universe.

The link-up between the two narratives had something to offer both groups, as Michael Barkun details in his book *A Culture of Conspiracy*. For the ufologists who bought into New World Order beliefs, they gained a more fully worked-out plot, replete with an extensive backstory and a wide cast of characters. For the conspiracists of the radical right and the USA's burgeoning militia movements, they gained potential access to a much larger audience for their ideas – as we saw in chapter 6, UFO beliefs are shared to some degree by a large percentage of the population.

The prime exponent of this fertile crossover was a gentleman named Milton William Cooper, the conspiracy theorist who, more than anybody, helped to extricate the Illuminati theory from the confines of the extreme right and bring it to a dazzlingly broad set of audiences. His 1991 book, *Behold a Pale Rider*, was certainly still popular on the right – it became a key text for many militia groups. Timothy McVeigh, the white nationalist who killed 168 people in the 1995 bombing of the Alfred P. Murrah Federal Building in Oklahoma City, was a fan. But Cooper's influence reached much further than that. His book first rose to popularity among prison inmates, for whom the worldview of an implacable system out to get them had obvious resonance. The book was later said to have become one of the most shoplifted items in the history of Barnes & Noble. He also found a devoted audience in some Black communities, and became a touchstone for many of the greatest names in hip-hop, with Public Enemy, Wu-Tang, Tupac, Nas and Jay-Z just some of the famous names who have referenced his work in their lyrics. Cooper's influence on popular culture didn't stop there, either: significant chunks of the plot of *The X-Files* are lifted straight from Cooper's worldview.

The theory that underpins *Behold a Pale Rider* is ... well, it's quite complicated. Cooper's thesis drew freely from every branch of twentieth-century Illuminati beliefs. It incorporates Webster and Queenborough's backward projection of the Illuminati to the Knights Templar. It follows Carr and Griffin in explicitly linking the historical plot to Satanic influence; it also buys into an assertion that Griffin made that the *Protocols* are in fact an Illuminati text. Like Welch, Allen and the Birchers, it folds in groups representative of internationalist politics like the Bilderberg Group and the Council on Foreign Relations. And, crucially, it brings in the world of UFO theories – claiming that the Illuminati have been plotting since the early years of the twentieth century to fake an extra-terrestrial threat in order to bring about the New World Order, but also that, *at the same time*, there really are aliens, and the Illuminati are in league with them. Oh, and it claims the reason Kennedy was killed is that he was about to blow the whistle on the alien cover-up (that's one of the bits *The X-Files* borrowed).

One of the key components of Cooper's UFO theories was something called '*Alternative 3*', which offers perhaps the most impressive example yet of why it's basically impossible to produce a hoax that *someone* won't believe. *Alternative 3* presents the theory that the elites of Earth are already far along with their plan to abandon the planet – and most of its population – in the face of looming environmental disaster. Colonies on the moon and Mars are already underway, and any day now, the political leaders and super-rich will climb into their spacecraft and leave us to our fate. (It doesn't actually mention aliens at all, but you can see how it would fit well with UFO theories about governments working together with little grey men.)

The thing about this is: *Alternative 3* was a British TV drama, broadcast on ITV in 1977. It really wasn't intended to fool anybody into thinking it was real. It was part of an enjoyable, if somewhat curtailed, tradition of deadpan British TV hoaxes, presented as non-fiction and fronted by trusted news and documentary presenters. Richard Dimbleby's infamous 'spaghetti trees' April Fool's joke from 1957 began it; they largely petered out after the BBC's 1992 Halloween broadcast of *Ghostwatch*, a supposedly live paranormal investigation that traumatised an entire generation of British children* and caused a press outcry after it was claimed that at least one viewer died of a heart attack.

Part of the problem was that, like the spaghetti trees, *Alternative 3* was originally supposed to be broadcast on 1 April. But, regrettably for everybody involved, its broadcast was delayed, meaning that it ended up going out on 20 June: not a date generally recognised as one on which national TV channels broadcast hoaxes.

There may also have been a degree of cultural confusion at play in the drama's move from fiction to supposed fact. That it wasn't actually a documentary should have been relatively

---

* Including one of the authors of this book.

obvious from the fact that many of the 'scientists' in it were
played by actors familiar from UK TV (indeed, they were
named in a cast list in the closing credits). By the time *Behold
a Pale Rider* was published in 1991, most British viewers would
have looked at footage of the scheme's mastermind – one 'Dr
Carl Gerstein' – and gone, 'Oh look, that's Colonel Von
Strohm from the bawdy Nazi-themed sitcom *'Allo 'Allo!*'* But
for our transatlantic cousins, this crucial piece of information
was sadly lacking. Which may be why Cooper was able to
state unambiguously in the book that: '*Alternative 3* is a reality.
It is not science fiction.' (It was science fiction.)

Cooper's theories are, as they say, a *lot*. That's only the
UFO and Illuminati-adjacent bits, by the way. We haven't
even mentioned the stuff about HIV being a plot to wipe out
minority communities, which also found its own audience, at
one point rather unfortunately including a serving Minister of
Health in South Africa.

The success of Cooper's work likely came, not in spite of,
but because of exactly this scattershot approach: plucking
different strands of conspiracy from a wide range of theories,
without much care for either logical or ideological consistency.
There really was something for everyone in his work; people
from all walks of life and all sides of the political spectrum
could read it and find *something* that resonated. As a result, he
almost certainly did more than anybody since Robert Anton
Wilson and *The Illuminatus! Trilogy* to bring the broad
conspiracy universe to mainstream attention.

(In one of those historical coincidences that would strike
someone more conspiracy-minded as too good to be true, in

---

* It remains unclear whether *The Fallen Madonna with the Big Boobies*
was intended to be relocated to Mars.

November 1991 Cooper ended up on the bill at a convention in Atlanta where Wilson was the guest of honour. According to those present, Cooper profoundly lost his shit at Wilson, screaming, 'You think everything is a joke, don't you?' – which, fair play, was an accurate assessment – before adding, 'Laugh all you want. You'll soon see how funny it is.')[14]

Cooper's skill at harvesting disparate aspects from a century of conspiracist traditions and crafting them into an attention-grabbing (if not entirely coherent) whole, with an appeal to people of all political stripes, is one that's shared by our final stop on this tour of the Illuminati's strange journey from Bavarian scandal to world domination. And, like *Alternative 3*, this one begins on British television.

The transformation of David Icke from a reassuring BBC sport presenter to a messianic conspiracy theorist is one of those aspects of pre-millennium British culture that – like Jimmy Savile, or indeed the bawdy Nazi-themed sitcom *'Allo 'Allo!* – is tricky to explain to Americans or people under the age of twenty-five.

Today, of course, if you want to see a famous face from the television losing their grip on reality in real time, you simply have to log on to Twitter, where you'll be confronted with more examples than you could possibly wish for. But in April 1991, when Icke appeared on Terry Wogan's BBC1 chat show in front of a baffled, laughing audience, it simply wasn't how these things happened. If celebrities had wobbly episodes, they tended to have them behind closed doors. They didn't go on prime-time television to clarify that, while they were not claiming to be the son of God *per se*, they were indeed a manifestation of the Godhead in much the same way that Jesus Christ had been. Which is exactly what Icke did.

The late eighties and early nineties had been a turbulent time for Icke. He had left his job at the BBC over his plans to refuse to pay the poll tax; he had risen rapidly to become one of the leading spokespeople for the Green Party, which was enjoying a surge in popularity as environmental issues made their way on to the mainstream political agenda; he had also got really into spiritualism, and was temporarily living in a throuple with his wife and a psychic who he'd got pregnant. He had taken to wearing only turquoise clothes, on the grounds that the energy of the colour turquoise was at the same frequency as the energy of love and wisdom, and he had begun to speak of prophecies delivered to him by other-worldly beings, which predicted great geological catastrophes that would soon befall the nation.

As all this suggests, Icke came from a very different part of the political spectrum to the likes of Webster, Welch or Robertson. In the early years of his transformation from snooker presenter to non-conventional thinker, he was most definitely from somewhere on the left – concerned about poverty and the environment; anti-war and opposed to organised religion.* He was very much an adherent of what were commonly termed 'New Age' philosophies, a loose movement that was as much about ~vibes~ as it was a

---

* Icke's outlook at the time is captured well in one of his comments to Wogan: 'When a child dies in this world of preventable disease every two seconds; when the economic system of the world must destroy the Earth, simply for that system to survive; when you see all the wars and when you see all the pain and when you see all the suffering, is it a force of love and wisdom and tolerance that is in control of this planet? Or is it a force that wishes to bring about the very hate, the very aggression, the very suffering?'

coherent set of beliefs, as likely to focus on crystals and healing as it was UFOs and global cover-ups. The first books that Icke would publish after coming out as a manifestation of the Godhead were very much in this mould, with titles like *The Truth Vibrations* and *Love Changes Everything*; they were far more focused on matters spiritual, paranormal and crop-circular than they were anything from the conspiracy world.*

But while he may have started from a different political worldview from the right-wing conspiracy theorists, that didn't stop Icke adopting the theories they'd promulgated wholesale. His first book venturing into full-on conspiracism, 1994's *The Robots' Rebellion*, entirely buys into and expands the narrative developed by Webster, Welch and their successors. The book explains that history has long been controlled by secret societies, and the Illuminati are at the heart of everything, the elite of the elite, sitting at the top of a vast pyramid of interlinked conspiracies that Icke terms 'the Brotherhood'. In setting this out, he provides a useful summary of the superconspiracy worldview: 'At that Illuminati level,' he writes, 'all the secret societies become the SAME organisation.'[15]

Like theorists from Webster onwards, he extends the Illuminati's existence back in time, tracing their origin to the fourteenth century, and crediting them for events such as the Protestant Reformation (all designed to create conflict, of course). And also like Webster, he promotes *The Protocols of the*

---

* Crop circles, he revealed in *The Truth Vibrations*, were created by the Earth herself, in order to 'send out energy to help the polluted skies and ozone layer, to draw in other healing energy for the Earth, to boost flagging ley-lines, and to use symbols to awaken the memory of the soul.'

Elders of Zion as an accurate guide to what's been happening in the world – although initially, at least, he attempts to dodge accusations of anti-Semitism by, in the tradition of Griffin and Cooper, ascribing the authorship of the *Protocols* to the Illuminati (he refers to them as the 'Illuminati Protocols'). What he was describing was 'not, repeat not, a conspiracy by the Jewish people', he insisted.[16] In later years, this distancing would fall away, and his work would include increasingly explicit anti-Semitic content.[*]

Perhaps the most famous element of Icke's beliefs – the one most people have heard of – is that the world is controlled by shape-shifting reptilian aliens from the fourth dimension. This didn't really form a major part of his theories until the publication of *The Biggest Secret* in 1999, a dizzying work that attempted to unite a huge range of conspiracy beliefs into one whole. It brings together a grand sweep of history, from the Assyrian Empire to the 'murder' of Princess Diana (who was 'killed on an ancient Merovingian sacrificial site to the goddess Diana'), via the French Revolution (arranged by the Illuminati), the assassination of Lincoln (ordered by Edwin Stanton), and vaccines being used as population control in preparation for a world government (pushed by the UN).

But most importantly, Icke reveals that the world is run by

---

* Icke has consistently denied being anti-Semitic. The alien race of mind-controlling lizards who rule the world's political and financial systems is not, he insists, a metaphor for the Jewish people: he literally does mean lizards. But even if you grant that, his work still features a plethora of undeniably anti-Semitic tropes, from Rothschild conspiracy theories to his promotion of the teaching of Holocaust denial.

mind-controlling reptilian aliens from the constellation of Draco.* The Illuminati are now reconfigured as an elite bloodline of human-reptilian hybrids who do the bidding of the pure-breed alien reptiles, and almost every famous person you can think of throughout history was secretly an Illuminati-reptilian. Also, the reptiles drink the blood of children. 'The Brotherhood hierarchy today are seriously into Satanic ritual, child sacrifice, blood-drinking and other abominations,' he writes, echoing the toxic myths of blood libel that began in Norwich 850 years earlier. He suggests many elites are addicted to blood-drinking because of a substance called 'adrenalchrome', which is produced by the pineal gland 'during periods of terror', and so is released into the victim's blood just before a sacrifice is conducted.

Most celebrities are either reptilians, or are mind-controlled by them (he lists Madonna, Elvis and Barbra Streisand as mind-slaves; and Frank Sinatra, Bob Hope and Kris Kristofferson as controllers). Every American president, Icke claims, has been an Illuminati-reptilian. He describes Hillary Clinton as 'a sixth-degree Illuminati witch and slave handler', while Tony Blair is named as a 'Brotherhood frontman' who attended an Illuminati human sacrifice in Belgium in the 1980s with the Queen Mother, Mohamed Al-Fayed and the Rothschilds; the date of his election (1 May 1997) was, Icke says, chosen as a nod to the date the Illuminati was founded.[17]

Very little of what Icke wrote was originated by him – most aspects of it were cribbed from other sources in the

---

* Constellations don't have any physical existence – they're simply collections of stars that appear in recognisable patterns when viewed specifically from Earth. But given all the giant lizards stuff, this feels like a relatively minor problem.

existing conspiracist subculture. But just like Cooper, Icke showed a talent for curating, synthesising and promoting the most compelling elements from different strands of the conspiracy-verse; his work has a pick-'n'-mix, something-for-everyone quality that's given him an appeal that stretches from the New Age left to the reactionary right. His fans range from radio host and conspiracy nexus Alex Jones, on whose shows Icke has regularly appeared over the years, to Pulitzer Prize-winning author and social-justice activist Alice Walker. His books have sold hundreds of thousands of copies, his live events draw serious crowds at major venues, and he has proven adept at using current affairs to attract more fans – most notably in recent years with Covid-19, where he was an early and influential promoter of 5G conspiracy theories and anti-vaccination fears.

We preferred him when he was on *Grandstand*, to be honest.

These examples are just some of the more influential ones from the great explosion of conspiracy culture that ramped up over the closing decades of the twentieth century. While not every major conspiracist belief had been fully integrated into the superconspiracy worldview by this point, many were on their way. And almost every major branch of the superconspiracy world – even if they didn't name the Illuminati outright – owed some debt to the lineage of theories derived from the backlash to one overreaching academic in eighteenth-century Bavaria.

By the turn of the millennium, conspiracism was no longer just a mindset, but a movement. It was a sprawling, interconnected series of established subcultures, which fed off and nourished each other, even when they had very different motivations and straddled much of the political spectrum. But it was also more than that: it had become an *industry*. People were able to make a living off the production of conspiracy theories, and there was an eager and growing audience, always hungry for more twists and turns in the narrative of global control. What had started in the local politics of the Counter-Enlightenment was now a worldview, a community and a business model all rolled into one.

And then in 2001, on a crisp September morning in New York City, two planes flew out of a clear blue sky.

12

The Age of Conspiracy

The first plane to reach its target in the 9/11 attacks hit the North Tower at 8.46am Eastern Time. Within two hours, nearly 3,000 people were dead. Within seven, the conspiracy theories had begun.[1]

It is perfectly true to say that jet fuel cannot, in fact, melt steel beams. That fact on its own should be fairly uncontroversial. Steel generally melts at temperatures somewhere above 1,500°C; jet fuels mostly burn in the 1,000–1,200°C range. The maths is straightforward. Case closed.

But of course, when somebody says that jet fuel can't melt steel beams, the chances are they're not simply an innocent metallurgist regaling you with some fun facts, because this claim became a central pillar of the conspiracy theory that the September 11 attacks were not actually caused by al-Qaeda operatives flying hijacked planes into the World Trade Center and the Pentagon. Instead, the theory goes, the Twin Towers were brought down by a series of controlled explosions, set in advance by conspirators plotting to fake a terrorist atrocity.

This was the theory that began to emerge in those first few hours. At 3.12pm on the day of the attacks, a software consultant named David Rostcheck posted a message on an internet forum that may have been the first claim of a 9/11 conspiracy. 'Look at the footage,' he wrote. 'Those buildings were *demolished*'. In the years that followed, this belief would be expanded by others into a detailed theory that led to 'steel beams' becoming an article of faith for some, and a meme for others.

The obvious point is that, while true, the steel beams thing is also somewhat irrelevant, because the 'official narrative' is not that the towers of the World Trade Center *melted*. As the magazine *Popular Mechanics* pointed out as early as 2005, in a lengthy feature examining the various 9/11 conspiracies, you don't have to melt steel to rob it of its structural integrity – you just need to heat it up. The hotter it gets, the weaker it gets. It starts to degrade at just over 400°C; by 600°C, it's already lost close to half its strength; at 1,000°C, the temperature the hottest fires of the World Trade Center burned at, that strength has reduced to a feeble ten per cent. Add to that the severe damage caused by the initial impact of the planes, which took out several load-bearing columns, plus further distortion from the metal expanding, and the collapse is the polar opposite of inexplicable.[2]

There is no single '9/11 conspiracy theory': instead, there are many of them, often mutually contradictory. A few of them aren't inherently implausible, like the claim that Flight 93 wasn't brought down by a passenger revolt, but was shot down by the US military. (It's not true, but it could have happened: jets had been scrambled to do just that if needed.) An awful lot are wild fantasies, however, like the claim that there were no planes involved, and all the footage of planes in contemporary news reports was either CGI or the result of 'missiles surrounded by holograms' that made them 'look like planes'.[3]

Like the steel beams theory, many of these rest on supposed inconsistencies in the mainstream story that turn out to be nothing of the sort. For example: the notion that the wreckage of Flight 93 was scattered over too wide an area for a simple plane crash, suggesting it had been hit with a missile (the wreckage area was actually consistent with other high-velocity crashes – most aviation accidents happen at slower speeds, because they occur close to take-off or landing). Or the theory that the visual appearance of the damage to the Pentagon proves that it could not have been hit by a plane (which seems to stem from the belief that a crashing plane will leave a precisely plane-shaped hole, like Wile E. Coyote going through the side of a cliff).

And, as with many conspiracy theories, the attempt to construct an alternative narrative from a patchwork of supposed gaps in the mainstream version only leaves you with much, much bigger plot holes than the ones you're supposed to be fixing. Like, it's never been entirely clear why, if the CIA had gone to the trouble of planting enough explosives in multiple skyscrapers to demolish them, they also needed to then fly planes into them in order to convincingly fake a terrorist attack. Why not just ... fake a bombing? (This was something David Rostcheck pondered in his original demolition theory on the day of the attacks: 'If you're going to demolish the building, what's the point of the flashy display?')[4]

Lots of these attempts to pick holes in the official narrative are flawed because – much like Bertrand Russell's questions about the Kennedy assassination decades earlier – they expand the definition of 'official narrative' to include any and all media reports from the panicked and confusing hours after the incident. If you've ever been inside a newsroom during a breaking news event (a terrorist attack, a mass shooting, a natural disaster), you'll know that much of the information that emerges in those early stages is completely wrong, a baffling mixture of rumour, crossed wires and dead ends. Sifting the small nuggets of truth from the river of confusion is easier said than done. Even the most diligent reporters can get it wrong.

But for conspiracists, no mistake can ever be just a mistake – it's always evidence of the conspirators letting a vital clue slip. 'I was the only person updating the website until about noon that day, and things were crazier than they'd ever been,' explained one poor journalist with WCPO Cincinnati in 2006, after she'd inadvertently become a central figure in the theory that Flight 93 never crashed at all, and instead landed safely at Cleveland airport before the passengers were mysteriously 'disappeared'.[5] In reality, this was based on a mistaken Associated Press report that misidentified a different plane; it was corrected within minutes, but the hassled WCPO staffer forgot to delete the original story, leaving it as the internet's only evidence of an event that never occurred.

Naturally, on the blog post the journalist wrote some years later explaining all this, the very first comment accuses her of being in the pay of the Bush administration. This was a familiar experience for anybody who tried to push back against the theories – the editor-in-chief of Popular Mechanics recalled getting death threats, and being told that the magazine must have published their work 'on orders from a cabal of Masons and Illuminati'.[6]

The 9/11 attacks were almost the perfect example of an event so dramatic that even a simple conspiracy ('it was a terrorist plot') doesn't feel sufficient to explain it. But it's notable that the conspiracy theories about it came in two distinct waves – and that the notion of 9/11 as a grand conspiracy didn't break through into the mainstream until years after the event. Despite the shocking nature of the atrocity, even many people who would eventually become 'truthers' didn't immediately reach for conspiracy as an explanation.

Initially, the theories were largely confined to the existing conspiracy culture – the people who already had their fixed beliefs, who viewed the whole world as dominated by conspiracies, and for whom every major news event needed to be integrated into the overarching super-conspiracy narrative. So, the UFO enthusiasts insisted they saw a UFO in the footage from New York. Alex Jones blamed the New World Order (and rapidly got dropped by a majority of the radio stations that carried his show). Milton Cooper blamed 'the defense industrial complex'.[7] Texe Marrs blamed 'the notorious men of Satan's Washington, D.C. Illuminati brotherhood'.[8]

David Icke initially blamed the Illuminati as well, but later moved on to a more complex theory that involved (among other things) the Bundesbank, Mohamed Al-Fayed, genetically engineered zombie celebrities, and George Bush and Tony Blair having some form of psychic link.[9] A smattering of websites were set up devoted to cataloguing the supposed flaws in the official story, but they initially had limited impact. The closest the conspiracy theories got to the mainstream was outside the English-language world, notably in the book 9/11: *The Big Lie* by the left-wing French journalist

Thierry Meyssan – but even that was a widely criticised fringe publication in its country of origin.

It wasn't until around 2004 that these theories started to gain a significant following outside the realms of the conspiracist true believers. The most famous example of this second wave was the amateur documentary *Loose Change*, which was released in multiple updated editions between 2005 and 2009. It was this film above all else that brought 9/11 conspiracy theories to a mass audience, becoming the 'seminal text' of the burgeoning truther movement.[10] This film didn't originate most of its theories – they were largely cribbed from the websites, books and documentaries produced by the existing conspiracy industry. What *Loose Change* did do, and very successfully, was translate and repackage these for a wider audience who weren't already embedded in conspiracy culture. And in doing so, it offered a preview of the conspiracy landscape in the decades ahead – a viral hit produced by amateur creators, remixing and re-contextualising an existing trove of conspiracy lore. (All of this with the figure of Alex Jones looming large in the background – Jones was both an inspiration for the first editions of the film, and a financial backer of later editions.)

Why did it take several years for 9/11 conspiracies to crack the mainstream? It's impossible to disentangle the explosion of popularity that they suddenly achieved around 2005 from two major developments in the years since the attacks. The first is that the internet of 2005 was quite different from the internet of 2001. It had far more users (two thirds of the US population, up from just under half); the rise of blogging had opened up the power of publishing to more people than ever before; and perhaps most importantly, the internet finally had video better than a postage-stamp-sized RealPlayer file that took two hours to download. This was essential for the spread of *Loose Change*, which was originally distributed on DVD, but first gained widespread attention when someone uploaded it to the nascent Google Video.

The other factor is that, in late 2004, after fifteen months of fruitless searching, the US government had officially admitted that maybe Iraq didn't have any weapons of mass destruction (WMD) after all.

The theory that 9/11 was staged by the government in order to justify a war probably seemed fairly implausible to most people.* But it certainly seemed *more* plausible now that many people believed that the US, the UK and their allies really had fabricated a different justification for war. The revelation that Iraq II had been fought on a false premise opened up a huge space in which conspiracy theories could flourish. Indeed, one of the team behind *Loose Change* had served in Operation Iraqi Freedom, and had gone from initially supporting the war to becoming profoundly disillusioned with it.

It's still something of an open question as to what extent the misleading case for war was due to deliberate deceit – an actual conspiracy, in other words – as opposed to a shoddy intelligence operation and a ton of politically motivated

---

* It's worth noting what we might call the 'weak' version of the theory, which is that the failure of the US government to act on warnings that an attack was being planned was – at least partly – due to some of the administration's more bellicose elements being okay with it happening. (In conspiracy world, these are known as MIHOP and LIHOP – Made It Happen On Purpose and Let It Happen On Purpose.) LIHOP is not quite as implausible, but remains entirely speculative.

groupthink. Probably a little from column A, a little from column B.

In fact, you could make a decent argument that the claim of an active Iraqi WMD programme *itself* counts as a conspiracy theory. 'These people are secretly working together to produce and conceal deadly weapons' certainly *sounds* like a conspiracy. Moreover, the political and intelligence communities of multiple countries approached the question in almost exactly the way many conspiracy theorists do: cherry-picking evidence that supported a predetermined conclusion, ignoring evidence that didn't, and massaging, manipulating and distorting the evidence that remained until it fitted more neatly into the desired narrative.

And, like many conspiracy theories, this one has proved to be weirdly resilient, even as the evidence piled up against it: one poll in 2015 found that forty-two per cent of Americans, including a majority of Republicans, still believed that US forces *had* found an active WMD programme in Iraq.

When George W. Bush won re-election in 2004 by a narrow margin, many Democrats found it hard to accept the result. Very soon after election night, when promising early signs for John Kerry had ebbed away as crucial swing states were belatedly called, theories began to circulate alleging that widespread fraud using rigged voting machines had stolen the election. When lawmakers gathered in the Senate Chamber on 6 January 2005 to certify the results, some Democrats lodged objections to key results, delaying the count. Stop us if this sounds familiar.

However, in this case, the theory of a stolen election didn't take over the party. John Kerry swiftly conceded, the majority of elected officials accepted the result, and by and large, the

Democratic party decided to move on with its life. But still, thirty-one members of the House and one Senator voted against recognising the result. And there remained a small but persistent group of theorists who never recognised the legitimacy of the election, and continued to spend years digging into the evidence. Their arguments about the security of American elections – some of them perfectly reasonable, some overblown – would resurface sixteen years later, and the group would split over whether to support Donald Trump's claims of fraud. [11]

Divisive national votes have, unsurprisingly, been a consistent source of conspiracy theories throughout recent decades. In July 2014, a few weeks before Scotland voted on whether to leave the United Kingdom, then-British Prime Minister David Cameron flew to the Shetland Islands in the North Sea. This was widely seen as an odd move from a Prime Minister who at least had the self-awareness to know that his presence in Scotland in the weeks before the referendum might not help the unionist cause.

So why had he done it? Soon enough, rumours began to circulate that he had gone to visit a massive oil field – one valuable enough to turn an independent Scotland into a sort of tartan Norway. Viral Facebook posts alleged that workers on the Clair Ridge oil field had been stood down and asked to sign NDAs to keep the existence of the store of black gold secret until after the vote.

As the campaign dragged bitterly on, some pro-independence activists accused both unionist politicians and journalists of hushing up the truth. Their theory was that the forces of unionism were keeping the oil wealth quiet in order to weaken the case for independence. Once Scotland had voted to remain within the UK, the London government could announce the field's existence, safe in the knowledge it could continue shipping the wealth it generated down to England.

Now, there certainly is an oil field at Clair Ridge – one which oil companies had been trying to work out how to access since the 1970s with limited success. But the Clair Ridge was no more accessible in the run-up to the referendum than it had been decades earlier. At time of writing, drilling has yet to begin, and Scotland is still in the union (for now). It's fairly clear that the belief in secret Scottish wealth in 2014 was serving as an outlet for the widespread feeling that the union had been draining Scotland of its oil over decades: that an independent Scotland could have grown rich on the proceeds of a resource that instead had been poorly spent in a country twelve times the size. Norway built a massive sovereign wealth fund with its oil revenues; the Thatcher government used it to fund tax cuts.

Speaking of divisive referendums that spawned conspiracy theories: let's talk about Brexit. This produced no end of the things – from the belief among some Leave supporters that their votes would be rubbed out if they used a pencil to mark their ballot, to the idea common among Remainers that the real motivation for leaving was so hedge funds could short the market, or so that offshore account holders could avoid imminent EU legislation. (None of these are true.) But perhaps the biggest conspiracy theory to stem from it was one that suggested we were being manipulated on a far deeper level than any of us realised.

The narrative runs something like this: Cambridge Analytica, a shadowy political consultancy, used vast troves of personal data illicitly harvested from Facebook to power a frightening leap forward in political campaigning. The new science of 'psychographics' enabled them to use this data to micro-target individual voters with adverts fine-tuned to their personalities, manipulating their deepest fears in order to change their votes. This dark psychological power was at the heart of the shock victories for both the Leave campaign in Britain's EU Referendum and Donald Trump in the US Presidential Election, which were linked efforts to subvert democracy by the same group of puppet-masters (either the Russians, or the sinister rich people, or possibly both).

The thing is, it turns out that almost none of this is true. Cambridge Analytica *did* buy a large trove of personal Facebook data (such as profile information and likes) on millions of people, which had been gathered without explicit permission. And, as the *Guardian*'s Harry Davies revealed in 2015, they *did* use this in Ted Cruz's primary campaign for the 2016 Republican nomination.[12] But the grand claims for what they were able to do with it, and their supposed influence on the voters of two countries, seem completely overblown.

Despite a ton of hype around psychographics – using information about people's interests and lifestyle to build a psychological picture of them, and target ads based on their personality traits – there's no evidence that anyone has actually got it to work in real-life political campaigning. There's barely any evidence it even works for retail ads (and it's *much* easier to get someone to switch their detergent preference than their political worldview). For now, it's nowhere near as effective as more tried-and-tested techniques. The fact that Cambridge Analytica supposedly only got into data in 2013, when data had played a huge role in US elections for a decade or more, is a clue that they were hardly at the cutting edge of the industry.[13] Insiders from Cruz's failed campaign said that Cambridge Analytica never delivered what they promised, despite millions of dollars in payment (it was 'like an internal Ponzi scheme', one staffer reportedly said).[14]

Throughout the whole affair, the people who most whole-heartedly bought the firm's marketing spiel were its critics; everybody who actually worked with them was less impressed by their skills. Cambridge Analytica did do some work for the Trump campaign, but the reaction from campaign insiders there was roughly the same as the Cruz campaign: that Cambridge Analytica were full of shit and rather too fond of taking credit for other people's work. There's no evidence that they even used their psychographic data on the presidential campaign – the company's own internal documents suggest they stuck to traditional approaches that had nothing to do with micro-targeting, such as running ads in swing states, or buying Google ads so that people who searched 'Trump economic plan' would get a link to ... Donald Trump's economic plan.[15]

As for Brexit, an investigation by the UK's Information Commissioner revealed that Cambridge Analytica had effectively no involvement in the campaign at all, beyond some early exploratory emails with the unofficial pro-Brexit campaign Leave.EU. They weren't the all-powerful dark wizards of a terrifying new digital dystopia. They were a low-rent, old-school, dirty-tricks operation with a crappy industry reputation, who were woefully behind the curve on data and, as a result, bet the house on a speculative, unproven technique. Their main achievement during this time was helping Ted Cruz, the living avatar of the American Christian right, somehow lose the evangelical vote to a foul-mouthed, twice-divorced New York libertine who couldn't name a single Bible verse. They had nothing to do with Brexit, and their contribution to the Trump campaign could have been replicated by anybody who'd glanced at FiveThirtyEight in the previous six months. The whole affair was an object lesson in why you don't take a snake-oil salesman's pitch at face value, and then act like you've uncovered some great hidden truth about snakes.

It's not surprising that people who were shocked and horrified by these election results would look for explanations, and would gravitate to ones that portrayed the results as illegitimate. But does either really need an extraordinary explanation? 'UK not keen on Europe' and 'America prone to racial tensions and bouts of populism' are not earth-shattering revelations. Like every other theory through the ages that casts its bad guys as devious, skilled manipulators of public opinion – from eighteenth-century fears of 'impious pamphlets' onwards – the Cambridge Analytica theory saw the hidden hand of a malign intelligence at work in the basic fact that *some people just disagree with you.*

Even in cases where there almost certainly was some sort of conspiracy going on, people still managed to see grander conspiracies at work. That there was a Russian influence operation trying to put their thumb on the scale of the 2016 presidential race, hacking emails from the Democratic National Committee and spreading disinformation via fake social media accounts, is hard to deny. How much actual impact this had on the election, and to what extent the Trump camp was involved, are far less clear – but the attempt was certainly real.

This, in itself, shouldn't be entirely surprising. 'Interfering in another country's election' was standard operating practice for both the USA and the Soviet Union during the Cold War era. One academic study found that between 1946 and 2000, America and the USSR 'intervened in about one of every nine competitive national-level executive elections' around the world.[16] When various US senators declared that Russia's meddling in their election amounted to an 'act of war', it would have been understandable if large sections of the world's population raised an eyebrow and asked, 'Oh really?'

But in the face of this real conspiracy, quite a lot of people still spent several years imagining a far grander conspiracy than the one we actually have evidence for, and seeing Russian influence in every shadow. Nowhere was this more apparent than in the thorny issue of Russian 'bots'.

'Bots' is kind of a misnomer, as most fake accounts of the kind we're interested in aren't purely automated, but rather authored by humans using semi-automated tools to help them run large numbers of high-frequency accounts. But they are a real phenomenon, and their use is far from limited to Russia. The truth, though, is that they're often not particularly effective. A few we know of managed to amass a large following and had a degree of influence, but most of them had hardly any followers. They weren't doing much more than shouting into the void.

The real problem with the bot panic wasn't how effective they were – it was identifying them in the first place. It's really, *really* hard to accurately identify an account as a bot. And that's not really because the bots are incredibly skilled at pretending to be human; it's more that actual humans, especially ones with strong political convictions and a lot of free time, are really weird and often seem like bots.

And so, for several years, we had a string of stories about the discovery of supposed bot networks trying to influence our politics, many of which crumbled once you looked into them a bit more deeply. One enterprising journalist for the website Byline wrote an article about how he'd identified 'a foreign-based troll pushing Russian messaging', only for the *Scotsman* to reveal two days later that the account actually belonged to a perfectly human security guard from Glasgow. ('People might not agree with my opinions,' he said, 'but that doesn't make me a Russian troll.')[17]

Meanwhile, an academic study from City, University of London supposedly identified a network of 13,000 pro-Brexit bots, based on the fact that they tweeted a lot during the referendum and then went dormant soon after. The study, along with its accompanying press release, named as one of the five most active 'bots' an actual, human UKIP parliamentary candidate.[18] The reason he stopped tweeting shortly after the referendum – as a quick Google search would show – was that *he died of cancer*.

It's hard not to conclude that the most effective outcome of the actual Russian influence operation might not have been the election of their preferred candidate for president; it might have been convincing a large swathe of otherwise reasonable people that anybody disagreeing with them on the internet wasn't even human.

Meanwhile, those emails that the Russians hacked – from Democrat strategist and long-time Clinton aide John Podesta, which were released by WikiLeaks in the run-up to the 2016 election – would also provide the inspiration for a little thing called 'Pizzagate'. Which is possibly the dumbest conspiracy theory in a book full of them.

While the emails had all the trappings of a genuine scandal – private emails leaked! Secrets uncovered! – most of the actual contents were little more than mundane office email blah-blah. Outside of a few intra-party dirty tricks, they didn't actually include anything terribly bad, unless you counted Podesta's insistence to his sceptical colleagues that walnut sauce was a great pizza topping.[*]

This wasn't going to stop people finding scandal in them, though. The walnut sauce, it would turn out, was the key to everything. Based on a previous unfounded rumour from a white supremacist Twitter account, the notion of a paedophile ring in the Democratic hierarchy was already floating around the ether. And so all this food chitchat, the internet decided, was a *code*. If you simply substitute the word 'pizza' for 'girl', 'pasta' for 'little boy', and 'sauce' for 'orgy', for example, then the emails actually revealed a paedophile cabal operating in the heart of Washington.

That's it. That's literally the entire basis for the whole thing. I mean, you could equally point out that if you substitute the word 'pizza' for 'fissile material', 'pasta' for 'kidnapped nuclear scientist', and 'sauce' for 'blast radius', then the emails indicate that you need to evacuate a twenty-five-mile zone around D.C. *right now*, but I'm not sure what the point would be.

Anyway, as a result of this nonsense, on 4 December 2016, a man with an AR-15-style semi-automatic rifle stormed a pizza restaurant in D.C., firing shots in an attempt to rescue the children whom he firmly believed were being held captive in the basement. The restaurant he attacked doesn't even have a basement.

This was a sudden and shocking demonstration that what has started in the online world – and consequently been dismissed as fringe nonsense by many commentators – may not always stay there. But it wasn't entirely unprecedented.

---

[*] We've not tried it. Maybe it's delicious? But life is too short.

In a remarkably similar incident in 2002, an armed man was arrested after breaking into Bohemian Grove, the location of the exclusive male-only gatherings of the global elite that conspiracist literature had for several decades linked with the Illuminati, the occult and other shady goings-on. The man, Richard McCaslin, was armed with several guns, a sword, a crossbow and bomb equipment, and was dressed in a skull mask as his superhero alter-ego, 'the Phantom Patriot'. He told police he was there to put a stop to the child abuse and human sacrifices that supposedly took place on the grounds. He added that he was prepared to kill to achieve this; a goal he was thwarted in by the fact that no guests were actually in the venue at the time, because it was the middle of winter.

Although no one was hurt, McCaslin was nonetheless convicted on charges including arson, burglary and brandishing a weapon at a police officer,[19] and spent the next six years in jail, writing comic books about the Phantom Patriot's adventures. There are also photos of him in his costume (boiler suit, bandana, skull mask) looking like a rejected character from Alan Moore's *Watchmen*. He died in 2018.

Where did McCaslin get the idea that Bohemian Grove hosted human sacrifices? It turns out it was from a film made by Alex Jones – an odd, rambling work full of blurry footage, in which the writer and journalist Jon Ronson has a cameo (he was making a documentary about Jones at the time). Texe Marrs turns up at the end of the film to explain how this all links back to the Bavarian Illuminati.

Having expanded from radio to embrace the internet, Jones had spent much of the 2010s using his website Infowars to push right-wing conspiracy theories about the government's weather weapons ('We had floods in Texas like fifteen years ago, killed thirty-something people in one night. Turned out it was the Air

Force') and how Robert Mueller was evil ('The word is he doesn't have sex with kids, he just controls it all. Can you imagine being a monster like that?').[20] Having built up a substantial audience for this stuff, he then tried to sell them dietary supplements with names like 'Super Male Vitality'; in 2014, he reported revenues of over $20 million a year.[21]

Jones was sometimes seen merely as a kook, famous for his evidence-free 2017 claim that 'the majority of frogs in most areas of the United States are now gay'. (It's unclear how he checked this.) But people quickly came to realise that his theories were far from harmless fun. Notoriously, he claimed the 2012 Sandy Hook Elementary School massacre – which left twenty-six people dead, including twenty six- and seven-year-olds – was staged. The shooting was 'completely fake', Jones said, a hoax using 'crisis actors' to increase support for gun-control policies.[22]

The idea that governments would stage events to clear the path for particular policies – 'false flags' – is obviously not entirely baseless. There are plenty of examples in history, done in the hope of excusing wars or provoking coups in foreign lands. But the ubiquity of the concept in conspiracy circles goes far beyond the reality, to the point that it becomes an attempt to deny reality itself – any event that dominates the news but doesn't fit with your worldview can simply be dismissed. In the last few years, the words 'false flag' have been attached to everything from the 2013 Boston bombing to the 2015 Paris attacks. The concept of 'crisis actors' was introduced to explain why, in those cases in which conspirac-ists believed there had been no real attacks, there were all those survivors and grieving relatives on their TV screens saying otherwise. Once again, it's an attempt to use a bigger conspiracy to cover up a plot hole.

For the grieving families at Sandy Hook, being accused of not being real people was a nightmare piled upon trauma, so eight of them ended up suing Jones over his comments. (After that, he switched his story to a claim that the attacks had happened, but were really the work of agents of the Democratic party.) In 2018, assorted social media channels finally banned him; in 2021, a judge ruled that he was liable for damages in the Sandy Hook lawsuit.

The 2010s also saw the revival of a dark, old conspiracy theory that has existed in various forms for almost two centuries. The 'Great Replacement' theory, in its modern form, stems from a 2011 book by the French author Renaud Camus, *Le Grand Remplacement*, in which he argued that political elites ('replacists') were deliberately overseeing the replacement of the white population in France, and Europe more broadly, with Muslim populations from Africa and the Middle East.

The country and the populations involved may have changed, but this is identifiably from the same lineage of immigration panic theories that Samuel Morse was promoting in 1835 and Charles Chiniquy was pushing in 1886, when they claimed that the Catholic Church was trying to seize power in America through immigration. It forms a subset of the broader category of theories usually termed 'white genocide', which have been around for generations, in which fears over immigration, birth rates and the possibility of non-white populations holding a degree of political or economic power are combined into a conspiracy theory that this is all being directed by some unseen cabal. Jews are frequently suggested to be the ones behind it; when torch-carrying marchers in Charlottesville, Virginia chanted 'Jews will not replace us' in 2017, that's what they were talking about.

An explicitly white nationalist concept, you might hope that the Great Replacement theory would be confined to the fringes, but naturally it wasn't: it's been welcomed into the political mainstream in many countries. Across Europe, politicians have adopted more or less explicit versions of Great Replacement into their rhetoric and platforms, and politely disguised versions of it are printed in serious news outlets; in the United States, it's become a mainstay of one section of the right, with Fox News presenter Tucker Carlson explicitly defending the theory, stating that it's a goal of the Democratic party to 'replace the current electorate' with 'more obedient voters from the Third World'.

The theory has also led to violence and deaths: in at least three mass shootings around the world, including the attack on the Tree of Life synagogue in Pittsburgh and that on the Al Noor Mosque in Christchurch, the shooters referenced their belief in the Great Replacement as a motivation.

But for perhaps the most disturbing and most impactful conspiracy theory of the modern age, we need to look to the sprawling web of interconnected conspiracies that became known as QAnon. This was what brought Jake Angeli to the Senate on 6 January 2021 in his furry hat and tattoos. It was also, in many ways, the logical conclusion of how conspiracy theories have developed over time. A gigantic, confusing and frequently contradictory superconspiracy, QAnon didn't just lead to the Capitol invasion, but also saw multiple adherents elected to Congress in the US, while simultaneously spreading internationally and growing far beyond its origins in US politics.

Given what it became, it's worth going back to the beginning to see how QAnon started. Because it did not begin as an all-encompassing worldview – it began with a small group of extremely online Trump fans trying to convince themselves that things weren't going badly for their favourite President.

In October 2017, the still-young Trump presidency was ... not going well. The man who hired only 'the best and most serious people' had seen his administration suffer a string of high-profile scandals, firings and resignations. His signature policies – the Wall, the Muslim immigration ban – were being blocked, either by the courts or by a Congress his own party controlled. The self-inflicted wound of the Mueller investigation was eating away at his administration and its hangers-on, providing a distraction for some and a risk of jail time for others. It wasn't simply that Trump was a bad president from the vantage point of smug liberals; it's that he was failing to deliver the things his actual supporters had elected him to do. For some of those supporters – the very online ones in particular – this was hard to reconcile with the hopes they'd invested in him. They thought they'd elected a commanding God Emperor who would rule through force of will and punish their enemies. Instead, they got a baffled old man moaning at the television.

This was the context in which QAnon emerged: a politician's fans trying to rationalise the gap between their expectations and reality. The poster on the anonymous 4chan message boards who would become known as 'Q' didn't invent the most popular rationalisation the crowd had settled on – it was already in place.

What was this rationalisation, this more comforting interpretation of events, that Q played into? It was that Trump, the grandmaster of five-dimensional chess, was actually playing a long game. What we saw publicly was all distraction, sleight of hand: the smoke over the horizon that indicates a great battle is being fought just out of sight. That battle was over another unfulfilled promise: that Trump would 'lock her up' and bring Hillary Clinton and her coterie of evildoers to justice over the ill-defined but terrible crimes that Trump had accused her of throughout the campaign. This was the one true goal of his presidency, the crowd had decided; everything else was just a means to an end. In this interpretation, the image of the feckless playboy billionaire was a facade, a game that had to be played in order to disguise his real purpose – which was fighting crime and bringing villains to justice.

Essentially, it cast Trump as Batman, pretending to be Bruce Wayne.

So when, on 28 October 2017, news broke that the first indictments stemming from the Mueller investigation would be coming down imminently, the Trump fans on 4chan's '/pol/' board (short for 'politically incorrect') were primed to believe that it would not in fact be a figure from Trumpworld in the firing line, but someone from the other side.* This was the moment the mask would come off, the true plan would be revealed, and the lamentations of the vanquished enemies would be great.

The first 'Qdrop' played into this belief. 'HRC extradition already in motion effective yesterday with several countries in case of cross border run,' it read. 'Passport approved to be flagged effective 10/30 @ 12:01am. Expect massive riots organized in defiance and others fleeing the US to occur.' It didn't make a huge impression when it first landed. People pretending to have inside knowledge and using the anonymity of the 4chan boards to cosplay as senior military or

---

* It would turn out to be Trump's former campaign chief Paul Manafort.

intelligence figures was commonplace, a sort of mutually agreed game of 'let's pretend'. 'Q' wasn't even the only one doing it on that original thread. But the poster in question was persistent – they kept the identity up, continuing to drop tantalising hints of secret knowledge over the coming weeks.

Of course, within a few days, it was quite apparent that the original prediction of Hillary Clinton's arrest on 30 October hadn't come to pass – only the first of many blown predictions from Q. But every time a prophecy failed, it could be explained away by the fact that, behind the scenes, the plot was growing ever more complex. New enemies would rise, and new information would emerge that proved the conspiracy ran even deeper than previously expected. In order to sustain the narrative, every time the theory failed to match up to reality, another element needed to be bolted on.

This meant that, in an inversion of the way these things usually go, QAnon was a theory in search of a conspiracy. That Trump was fighting an evil plot was clear; what that plot actually was had considerably more flexibility. As a result, QAnon became a ravenous consumer and assimilator of just about every conspiracy theory that already existed. Any belief that could be useful in explaining why the moment of reckoning still hadn't arrived, and why the President was still pretending to be incompetent, would be gleefully brought into the fold.

The person behind it all, the mysterious Q,* didn't even need to come up with the theories themselves. Possibly stung by their repeated failed predictions, they took to posting

---

* It's likely that the person in control of the 'Q' account actually changed at one point, with new authors hijacking the account once it had become apparent that it had a large following.

increasingly obscure and incomprehensible messages. These would then be 'interpreted' by the community that had grown up around the account, with followers competing to read meaning into the meaningless. If an interpretation became popular among the community, it would be accepted into the canon, and could be referenced in subsequent Qdrops; if it didn't catch on, everybody would simply move on to the next thing. The feedback loops that had informed the multiple versions of *Loose Change* in the 2000s had been sped up and scaled up; processes that had taken months back then, and years in previous decades, now happened in days and hours.

Not only that, but those feedback loops included the subject of the theory itself. Trump got his information from the same fever swamps and client media that incubated these theories, then fed them right back to his supporters – who took it as confirmation that they had been on the right track. As we've seen, political elites throughout history have interpreted things not going their way as evidence of conspiracy. Now, the porous boundaries between elite opinion and fringe theories collapsed completely when faced with a president whose worldview was shaped by cable news and Twitter, and who was so used to absolute rule in his own personal fiefdoms – and so unaware of how America is actually governed – that he interpreted basic things like 'the separation of powers' or 'free elections' as a Deep State conspiracy against him personally.

All this meant QAnon became one of the first truly crowd-sourced conspiracy theories – and as its adherents searched for explanations for the latest plot twists and gnomic pronouncements, they had centuries' worth of ready-made conspiracy lore to draw from.

And so Pizzagate morphed to incorporate more elements of

previous Satanic panics and child abuse theories, folding in Illuminati ceremonies and myths about elites addicted to the fear hormone 'adrenochrome' (the spelling had changed slightly, but it was the same theory David Icke had been pushing years before). The New World Order merged with the Deep State to provide an overarching framework by which to understand the plots. New Age theories about alternative medicine sat alongside white-supremacist theories about the Great Replacement. As new events happened, they could be incorporated into the QAnon pantheon with ease – Covid saw anti-vaccination and 5G theories brought into the fold; the 2020 election would see long-stoked Republican theories about illegal voters combined with the Bush-era Democrat beliefs about rigged voting machines. In narrative terms, it was less a straightforward story, and more the Marvel Cinematic Universe.

The result was something that, from the outside, looked like an incoherent mess. If you search online, you can find 'maps' produced by believers illustrating the QAnon world-view. They are baffling, hyperdense network diagrams of interlinked people, institutions, events and belief systems – massive fractal images in which zooming in on any node in the network reveals another conspiracy theory. Princess Diana sits alongside the North American Free Trade Agreement; the Trilateral Commission is just over from ley lines; Black Lives Matter, fluoridation, cattle mutilations and the 1973 oil crisis are all part of the same masterplan. The overwhelming feeling you get is that this conspiracy must be an absolute nightmare to organise. It would be a logistical feat just to get sign-off on any decision when the stakeholders include Halliburton, CERN, George Soros, Pope Francis, the Martian Slave Colony, the reptilians from Draco, and the secret race of builders who made the pyramids.

But while it doesn't make sense in the traditionally understood manner, everything included in the superconspiracy has proven its ability to explain some part of the world to some people, in a way that is emotionally satisfying to them and flatters their fears. It may not be coherent, but every aspect of it has been tested, at the kind of scale only the internet allows. As a result, it offers the ultimate 'something-for-everyone' conspiracy experience, with numerous points of entry that can entice people with questions and concerns into the community.

That's something that has been deliberately exploited by its followers as they proselytise for it: rather than hit potential converts with the full theory right from the off, they will focus on one aspect – fear of child abuse is a common one – that will appeal to potential new followers. This has allowed QAnon to spread far beyond its origins in the Trump fandom and become almost entirely detached from the US domestic politics that spawned it, as it spreads to other countries and latches on to their pre-existing cultural anxieties and conspiracy beliefs. In the UK, arriving just a few years after a series of revelations (many genuine, some not) about high-profile paedophiles, QAnon found particularly fertile ground in which to grow. The result was a surge in conspiratorial beliefs about child abuse grouped under the slogan 'Save The Children',* in which many participants seem to not have even realised that they were promoting one branch of a vast conspiracy theory that was implicitly linked to the declining fortunes of an American president.

It remains to be seen what will happen to QAnon in the

---

* Nothing to do with the charity of the same name, who must have been really rather annoyed about the whole thing.

long term. Is it dependent on Trump's political fortunes? Will it fade away over time? Will it split into different factions, or mutate into new variants? Are we witnessing the early stages of a new religion? Whatever QAnon becomes as time goes on, it seems likely that this is what conspiracy theories will look like in the future: increasingly decentralised, crowd-created conspiracy universes, greedily gobbling up and regurgitating the theories of the previous centuries to feed our narrative desire for new twists.

In March 2017, the *Guardian* published a piece headlined, 'Are we entering a golden age of the conspiracy theory?' In June 2020, Politico answered the question, telling us, 'You're living in the golden age of conspiracy theories'. Four months later, it was CNN's turn: 'How the pandemic and politics gave us a golden age of conspiracy theories'.[23] Between YouTube, Covid and Donald Trump, the world's media seemed to agree, the world had entered what might possibly be referred to as – you've guessed it – a golden age of conspiracy theories.

But if you've learned anything at all from this book, it should be to question that assumption. Sure, conspiracism is having a bit of a moment, but it isn't its first. In the US of the late sixties and seventies, with trust in government at a low thanks to war, assassinations and Watergate, interest in conspiracy theories went nuclear. It was even higher in the 1950s thanks to the Red Scare; in the 1890s, it was stoked by racial tensions and fears of overmighty corporations.[24] Conspiracism is like the economy, political extremism and the tides: it ebbs and flows, even if, as is true of all those things with the possible exception of the tides, we keep being surprised when the cycles repeat.

So is there something else about this particular wave of

conspiracism that's unique? The last few years have seen politicians like Donald Trump or Jair Bolsonaro push conspiracy theories for their own political ends, and much of our political discourse – from all sides of politics – has a distinctly conspiratorial edge. Adam Enders, an assistant professor at the University of Louisville who researches how conspiracy theories affect politics, told Politico: 'Entrepreneurial politicians have realized that they can tap into these conspiratorial, populist sentiments ... "I know you feel this way. Let me remind you that you feel this way. And then let me connect that to important things that are happening, like this upcoming vote, or this policy."'[25]

Again, though, that's hardly new. In 1964's *The Paranoid Style in American Politics*, Richard Hofstadter highlighted examples of conspiracist thinking in Barry Goldwater's campaign for the presidency. And in Joseph McCarthy's attempts to discredit his opponents as communists in the previous decade. And in the populism of the 1890s. And in the anti-Catholicism of the 1850s. Beyond the US, the idea that the Reichstag Fire was the work of a secret communist cabal active inside Germany (rather than, as actually seems to have been the case, a single angry Dutchman) gave Hitler the pretext he needed to found the Nazi state. The importance of this event has led the historian Richard Evans to argue that the Third Reich was 'founded on a conspiracy theory'.[26]

So, even if we are living in a golden age of conspiracy theories, it isn't the first, and it's depressingly unlikely to be the last. The best we can probably hope for is that recent events represent a genuine peak – rather than one of those miniature peaks that is actually hiding another whole stretch of mountain range.

But if what we're living through isn't unprecedented, it

nonetheless feels like it might be *different*. The superconspiracies of our age may draw upon the theories of the past centuries, but they're radically different in size, in form, and in their level of detachment from reality.

The politics of recent decades might be one reason. The seismic shocks of 9/11, the War on Terror, and then the financial crisis contributed to instability, polarisation and a general sense of permanent rolling panic. Not only that, but they surely fuelled our sense that the world is shaped by forces beyond our control. That's understandable, when someone in a bank in Reykjavik making a couple of bad bets on the Florida housing market means that suddenly you no longer have a job and your local library shuts down.

At the same time, changes in the economy have pushed us to sort ourselves into in-groups that fuel polarisation. The shift to a service economy has meant more and more 'good' jobs congregating in fewer and fewer places, which means we've become ever more divided by geography – former industrial centres become older and more reactionary; big cities and university towns younger, more diverse and more liberal.

But of course, the biggest change is the internet. For the first time in human history, most of us carry devices in our pockets through which we can talk to the rest of humanity, get politically radicalised and look at pictures of cats, all from the convenience of our own homes, or the supermarket queue, or wherever we happen to be.

The rise of living online has driven us out of our collective mind in about as many ways as there are people on the internet. But as to why it's driven us specifically towards conspiracism, there are a few major reasons:

It gave us a machine for generating conspiracy theorists

The algorithms social media use when determining which content to show you were designed by Silicon Valley's best and brightest to keep viewers watching or clicking for as long as possible. But it turns out the best way to optimise how much you engage usually involves promoting material that provokes conflict and has a sense of narrative urgency, while maximising the time you spend on the site usually involves promoting material that leads people down rabbit holes. Both of these, you'll be shocked to learn, favour conspiracy theories (along with a whole host of other nonsense).

The result? Sites like YouTube became conveyor belts for transforming people who had expressed mild curiosity about the details of 9/11 into people who sat on Facebook all day saying things like: 'Jet fuel can't melt steel beams.'

These algorithms get a lot of blame for our current mess, and with good reason. But they're not the only reason why the internet has put a rocket under the conspiracy world. They can't be – think about WhatsApp, for example, which, as the pandemic proved, is a potent vector for misinformation, and which doesn't have *any* content recommendation algorithms. What you see is just what you're sent by your friends, family and colleagues. The only algorithm is *us*. We are our own rabbit hole.

It reinforces our existing beliefs

Tweet an opinion on a controversial topic, and you're likely to get likes and retweets from people who agree, and – Twitter being Twitter – anger and abuse from people who don't. Both responses are likely to make you double down; neither to make it more likely your follow-up tweet will be, 'Hey guys, is it possible that I'm actually wrong about this?'

The 'social' bit of social media might as well have been designed to entrench you further into whatever view you held in the first place. And some of your views, we're sorry to say, are probably pretty unhinged. Some of them might even count as conspiracy theories.

It industrialised trolling

There have always been people making things up, to see how gullible everyone else is – remember Operation Mindfuck from chapter 11? – but the internet has massively ramped up the scale of such material. As a result, some conspiracy theories have begun with hoax videos or posts made as sort of fishing exercises, intended to see whether anyone would be dumb enough to believe them, but have then taken on a life of their own.

What's more, some of the platforms that have been the best petri dishes for such theories – 4chan; 8kun, previously known as 8chan – are anonymous sites where posts vanish after a period of time, leading to a culture in which people show they're part of the in-group by conducting, essentially, the most offensive acts of trolling possible. It is not a coincidence that this was where QAnon emerged.

At any rate, people on the internet may not always believe what they say. But what matters is whether other people start believing it.

It broke the media

Once upon a time, most print news coverage came in packages called 'newspapers', in which domestic news, foreign news, sports and so on were all bundled up together and you'd pay one fee to get the lot. Once the internet arrived, though, it turned out that wasn't quite as sustainable a model

as people had hoped. At the same time, producing and distrib-
uting content to a roughly professional standard has become
easier than ever.

As a result, with advertising revenues plummeting and the
competition for eyeballs increasingly fierce, many news organisations abandoned expensive, unpopular things like 'foreign
reporting' or 'fact-checking'. Instead, they found their solution
in cheap but popular hot takes and culture-war content that
keep viewers clicking. New outlets sprang up that targeted
niche groups and discovered a route to success through feeding
them a diet of exactly what they wanted to hear.

Of course, it's not like the media was never a driver of
conspiracy theories before. If there was a golden age of media
when it was scrupulously honest and non-partisan and good at
examining its own biases, then it was – how to put this – a very
short golden age. But still, recent changes haven't exactly helped.

It made everything findable

Once upon a time, to have a hope of reviving an old
conspiracy theory, you'd need the right fascist to randomly
stumble across the right centuries-old book by the right
French priest. Now, though, basically every conspiracy theory
that has ever existed can be found with a quick Google or
Bing search. People looking for any explanations about what's
gone wrong in the world can find the story that best fits
them, more easily than ever before.

It helped conspiracists meet each other

Compounding that is something that's built into the very
fabric of both the web and social media: networking.
Conspiracies no longer need to be siloed in their own little
subcultures: it's much easier for them to cross over and mix

with others, and to infiltrate non-conspiratorial spaces. Just look at the way anti-vax and anti-5G conspiracies started merging with both the New World Order and New Age lifestyle communities. In the pre-internet age, it took decades for ufology to crossover with Illuminati beliefs: thanks to the efficiency of modern communications technology, now it could happen in a matter of weeks.

It gave us valuable feedback

The rapid speed of online publishing also means that theories can go through a rapid process of feedback and iteration – being adapted on the fly in response to suggestions from the conspiracy community. That's what happened with *Loose Change*, and even faster with QAnon. It's a process akin to natural selection: the unpopular theories will fade away; those that grab attention will thrive and multiply. The modern conspiracist doesn't need to be Thomas of Monmouth, labouring away on his book for two decades and hoping that someone will like it. Now they can find out in real time which parts of their theory people like best and focus on those. You don't even need to have a single author: the crowd can craft narratives all by itself.

Put these things together, and what you get is a massive acceleration of the same processes that have produced conspiracism in the past. In the old model, someone would come up with a conspiracy theory and write a book about it, then see if it resonated with people. A rumour might spread from town to town, before fading away without ever being recorded. A belief might become the received wisdom in a single community, without anyone from outside that community ever hearing of it.

In our brave new world, however, they can now go

through a process of crowdsourcing, remixing and A/B testing on a massive scale, incorporating the most popular elements and jettisoning those that don't resonate. All of it is searchable, all of it can be easily spread between communities, and all of it is juiced by platforms that optimise for engagement and our own tendencies to double down on our worst instincts. Run that long enough, and what you get is QAnon: a superconspiracy theory that may seem scattershot and incoherent, but which is fine-tuned to recruit more conspiracists, and which absorbs all other theories like the Blob.

The result is a world where we swim in a sea of conspiracism, where nothing is as it seems, and everything is connected. Even if you're pretty sure that you are the sort of level-headed and sensible person who would *never* believe a conspiracy theory in your life, someone you know will. There will almost certainly be a theory somewhere in this chapter that people who share your politics – people you'd instinctively think of as being on your side – have bought into.

And somewhere out there, just through the result of these processes happening over and over again – without anybody planning it, but simply as a consequence of a certain propensity in human nature – there's a conspiracy that's tailor-made for you. We are all conspiracists now.

Conclusion

I f conspiracy theories are all around us, and none of us are immune from believing in them; if, sometimes, the conspiracies are real, and reality can seem just as unhinged as the YouTube commenter's wildest fever dreams – then how can you know if you're looking at a made-up conspiracy theory or a real conspiracy?

We can't tell you for sure. (Obviously, even if we could, we wouldn't, because we're probably in on it, too.) But we can offer some questions it might be worth asking yourself. They're not a fool-proof set of rules for how to spot bullshit, but they are a handy guide on how to check your own thinking, and hopefully avoid falling into the rabbit hole.

Could anything disprove it?
Scientific enquiry works by testing ideas and seeing if they're wrong. So: what would it take to prove this theory false? What facts would make you think, 'Oh, well, that doesn't fit with the theory'? What does the theory predict will happen next?

If those things exist, cool – let's honestly check if the theory holds up as new facts emerge, or if predictions don't pan out. But if there is literally no information that could demonstrate that, say, the Illuminati are not behind this, then we have to acknowledge that now we're working on faith alone.

By the same token:

How does it deal with contradictory evidence?

Any decent theory, conspiracy or otherwise, has to confront the fact that not all the evidence will back it up. Reality is messy and complicated, and we dealt with loads of the simpler questions – gravity, where babies come from, the shape of the Earth – ages ago.* People honestly trying to work out what's true will acknowledge inconvenient facts that might undermine their thesis, and make an attempt to explain them away that's a bit more sophisticated than, 'Well they would say that, wouldn't they?'. If what you're looking at consistently ignores contrary evidence, or dismisses it all as being part of the conspiracy, that's a red flag.

While you're at it, check that the evidence people cite actually says what they claim it does. A lot of conspiracist 'research' has something of the cargo cult about it: it *looks* like good science or history, with its mountains of evidence and references and footnotes. But often, as we've seen many times, when you look a bit closer, the individual pieces of evidence don't actually stand up. And if the bricks crumble, so does the house.[1]

---

* A load of physicists probably just shouted 'gravity isn't simple!' in unison, which is fair. We were talking more about the 'apple goes down' side of things rather than the 'gravitational time dilation' or 'three-body problem' aspects.

It's also worth asking, as you read those dozens of strangely irrelevant footnotes:

Does it exist in a bubble?

If, in the endless YouTube videos and thesis-length web pages on a particular topic, all the copious footnotes lead to other, suspiciously similar YouTube videos and thesis-length web pages ... well, then you can probably draw your own conclusions. A closed loop where a small number of people just cite each other's work over and over isn't healthy. (This applies equally to conspiracy subcultures, media outlets and university departments.)

Are you applying the same standards to the conspiracy theory as you do to the official narrative?

As we've seen, lots of conspiracy theories rely on picking holes in mainstream or official explanations for events. Which is cool: official narratives *should* have holes picked in them. But there are two things to be careful of.

One, as we've said before, is avoiding hindsight bias: not reading too much into supposed inconsistencies, and demanding narratives where everything is meaningful, and nothing is random. But another is that, if you're going to subject mainstream narratives to that sort of detailed scrutiny, you have to do the same for the theory with which you're proposing to replace them. Yes, you might find the official story implausible – but is the conspiracy any *more* plausible?

With that in mind, we can also ask some practical questions about the supposed conspiracy:

How many people would this conspiracy need to involve? And what's keeping them in line?

We know that groups of people can keep a secret, and even lie in a coordinated way: just consider the actions of, say, a police force after any scandal involving that police force. But we also know that it's *hard*. Things leak. People blow the whistle. They tell their spouse about the rough day they had at work. Sometimes they write detailed notes about the crimes they are doing, or take pictures of the crime and send them to all their mates. In a world where fitness apps give away the layout of secret military bases, or Instagram uploads unmask covert incursions, it's harder than ever to keep things truly secret.[2]

So it's always worth asking how many people this conspiracy would have to involve in order to work. How much would each of them need to know? Is it really plausible that only a few people have full knowledge? Is nobody outside the circle of trust likely to get, you know, suspicious?

And what's keeping them inside the tent? Did they all sign up for this in the first place? Or is the idea that every new hire at Omnicorp gets an induction session where they're told that they've accepted a job with an *evil* organisation – and somehow none of them quit?*

More than that, can you guarantee nobody has an incentive to defect? If, say, the world's big pharma companies are all in on the microchips-in-vaccines plot, why wouldn't one of them have an incentive to break trust, blow the whistle, drive all their competitors to bankruptcy and prison and emerge as a global monopoly?

---

* To be fair, the package of benefits at Omnicorp is fantastic. They have free pizza on dress-down Fridays!

Does it ascribe a ridiculous level of competence to the conspirators?

We have plenty of evidence for how competent governments, corporations and powerful people in general actually are. The answer is 'not very'. Which rather raises the question of why they suddenly become almost infallible as soon as they're doing conspiracies.

Equally, if your conspirators really are geniuses, it's worth asking if those talents wouldn't be much more valuable if used for regular, non-evil purposes. Take 5G: you don't need sinister motives to explain why people are installing an *extremely popular consumer technology*. If every phone network is making it a central part of their marketing, maybe it isn't a secret plot.

Does this plan rely on everything going right?

Conspiracy theories often work backwards: they take a series of events and draw a narrative that explains them. But does it work the other way round, if you start from the beginning? If you were a conspirator, and you wanted to achieve a specific goal, is *this* really how you'd go about it? Or does it involve nobody screwing up, and a ridiculous number of unpredictable things all going your way?

If it's one of those plans where Event A leads to Government Policy B, which provokes Public Backlash C, opening up Power Vacuum D, etc., then it really feels like there must be alternative plans that would be easier, more reliable and less likely to put you in jail. This kind of story might slide by in a movie when there are also cool explosions, but it's less useful if you're trying to explain how the world works.

Has the conspiracy been kept completely secret, apart from a coded clue to the entire plot that the conspirators have deliberately placed in plain sight, like printing it on banknotes or something, as if they're a serial killer taunting Mister Police?

Nobody does this. Next.

Does the motivation behind the conspiracy even make sense?

The most implausible part of 9/11 conspiracy theories is the idea that it would take an unprecedented atrocity to give Western countries sufficient pretext for military action in the Middle East. To put it bluntly, history doesn't suggest that reticence about meddling in the Middle East has ever been a major feature of Western foreign policy.[3] At the very least, doesn't it seem like ... well, overkill? Could you not have just assassinated an ambassador, or something? Many wars have been fought over far, far less.

In other words, when thinking about the supposed motive of the conspirators, ask yourself whether it really is something they want, and whether the conspiracy is actually a necessary or proportionate plan to achieve the goal.

On a similar note, 'who benefits?' is a common question in conspiracy thinking: identify the beneficiaries of any particular event, the logic runs, and you have your prime suspects. The trouble is, the world isn't that simple. Random things happen all the time, and sometimes people get lucky and benefit. It doesn't mean that, for example, a cartel of delivery firms, video-conferencing platforms, outdoor heating manufacturers and alcohol-gel suppliers caused the pandemic.

Is it really likely that these people are working together?
We've noted from the start the tendency of conspiracy
theories to lump together everybody they don't like and
assume they're all secretly in league. Additionally, a lot of
conspiracy thinking seems to operate on what you might call
the Professional Wrestling Model of Public Discourse – in
which everything is a performance and supposed enemies are
just following a script. In front of a crowd, you'll see people
hitting each other over the head with chairs. But really, this
was all planned in advance, and after the show's over they'll
congratulate each other on a job well done.

Obviously, versions of this can certainly happen in spheres
other than WWE. Supposedly competing businesses can form
cartels. Authoritarian leaders might create puppet opposition
parties to siphon discontent into controllable channels. And
much of our media and politics *can* seem like a cosy backslap-
ping club, where pundits perform furious arguments for the
cameras before sharing a laugh in the green room afterwards.

But a sensible rule of thumb is still that, usually, there is a
lot less unity than is displayed publicly. If there's one thing
the bulk of human history teaches us, it's that it's hard
enough to get people in the same room wearing forced smiles
for the time it takes to snap a picture, never mind getting
them to abandon their short-term self-interest, their ideological differences, or their personal grudges for long enough to
work towards a common goal. Those politicians at the press
conference *may* genuinely have reached an agreement that will
usher in a new era of harmony and cooperation; far more
likely, however, is that at least some of them are already
plotting how to stab the others in the back.

And it's those micro-plots that probably make up the bulk
of genuine conspiracies in the world: small, petty, driven by

personal ambition, and frequently based on little more than who fucked or fucked-over whom at Oxford.

How does it make you feel?

The economist Tim Harford suggests asking this question as a first step when thinking about statistics you see in the news.[4] It applies here too. Does reading something provoke a strong emotional response in you – fear, anger, disgust? That's when you should be cautious. Not because that means it's not true, but because it brings your guard down. When something stirs our emotions, we're less good at judging its accuracy, less likely to think about it critically. (Scammers of all kinds know this, and use it to play us.)

That's when it might be time to take a breath, go for a walk, and then come back and look at it again with a clear head. It's also worth asking yourself: is it *narratively satisfying*? Again, that's a reason for caution – because reality often isn't.

While we're asking questions, it's worth considering: does any of this really matter? Okay, so you've got this one friend who thinks the CIA killed Kennedy, or a weird cousin who thinks the Earth is flat. Are they really doing any harm?

Perhaps not. But often, as we've seen over and over again, conspiracy theories tend to escalate. A quick peek into the rabbit hole can soon enough mean someone gets pulled inside – and once you're in, it can be hard to find the way out again. Recent years have been full of heartbreaking stories of the effects this can have: relationships destroyed, families pulled apart, lives ruined.

Beyond personal tragedy, some conspiracy theories are genuinely damaging to society. It matters when people believe Covid vaccines are a tool of population control, rather than a public health measure. It matters when people believe minority groups are part of a plot to undermine society. And it matters when people try to prevent the inauguration of a president because they believe a free and fair election was stolen.

But there's another reason why conspiracy theories are a serious business: they distract us from the real issues. Many problems in the world today aren't the result of a small group controlling events (if they ever were). They're broader and more deeply embedded than that: they're 'us' problems, not 'them' problems.

Take climate change. Pretty much every reputable scientific organisation in the world agrees that the planet is getting hotter, and that human action is the cause. As of July 2021, a third of Americans denied that human-made climate change exists[5] – and while it's not inherently conspiratorial to believe the climate isn't changing, or that humanity isn't to blame, it is kind of necessary to explain why 97% of all climate scientists might be engaged in a cover up.* But even among those who believe in it, there's a temptation to view it as a problem that stems from the actions of a few malign companies, rather than the impersonal forces of global economic demand.†

---

* It's also not entirely clear what's in it for the scientists, given that presumably any climatologist willing to blow the whistle on the sham would have made an absolute mint from oil companies.

† There's a frequently cited report – the 2017 Carbon Majors Report – which said that just 100 companies had been responsible for over 70% of all carbon emissions over the previous three decades. This is accurate, as far as it goes, but there's a crucial bit of context you need: those companies are the ones extracting the fossil fuels, not the ones consuming them.

If we fool ourselves into thinking that all we need to do to solve complex social issues is to find the small group of bad guys responsible and bring them to justice, we're in for a nasty shock. As such, if you care about the issues that underpin any conspiracy theory, then you should care enough to find out what the real situation is, and how we can improve it.

When the physician John Snow was confronted with a devastating cholera outbreak in London's Soho in 1854, he saw the same patterns of poverty and disease that had been fuelling conspiracy theories and riots for decades. His diligent work – mapping every victim of the outbreak, seeing how they clustered around one location, and identifying the source as a single pump that had been sunk too near a cesspit – didn't just help to stop that outbreak. It helped kickstart the fightback against the disease worldwide, revolutionised public health, and helped found the science of epidemiology.

It didn't happen overnight, because people are always unwilling to abandon their pet beliefs, but gradually germ theory began to be accepted. Authorities came to understand the importance of sanitation; modern sewage systems were installed in London, then in other cities. Eventually, the disease that had rampaged across the globe for the best part of a century began to recede. We still haven't managed to truly fix it – every year, tens of thousands around the world still die from a disease that's both treatable and preventable – but at least now we know what we need to do. And we're not blaming doctors anymore – at least, not for spreading cholera.

And that's why we should take conspiracy theories seriously, and make sure we can recognise and counter them, both in others and in ourselves. Because if we let ourselves get distracted by easy narratives, tricked into seeing false patterns, and convinced that sinister evildoers are behind every misfortune, then we can't do what John Snow did: the careful work of uncovering the true patterns in the invisible forces that shape our lives. And if we don't do that, then we can't make things better.

If we understand conspiracy theories, then maybe – just maybe – we might make it out of the rabbit hole.

Acknowledgements

Writing a book can be a solitary existence at the best of times. Writing a book during a sodding pandemic only multiplies that – even if you're not writing the book on your own, you are, in fact, writing the book on your own. Our thanks go to everybody who helped make it a little less solitary, in ways large and small; that gratitude extends much further than the limited list of names we're able to provide here.

We want to thank the whole team at Wildfire, Headline and beyond, including Alex Clarke, Serena Arthur, Tara O'Sullivan for a swift and perceptive copy edit, and above all Ella Gordon for her enthusiasm, dedication and good humour in shepherding this book towards existence. None of this would have happened without our agent, Antony Topping, who suggested we write this book together in the first place, and to whom we are extremely grateful.

This book draws on the original work of a huge number of scholars and journalists, and we must express our deep gratitude for their diligence and insight. While some are mentioned by name in the text, that by itself is an incomplete guide to the works that have helped shape this book: we would strongly encourage readers to explore further the books and articles referenced in the endnotes. Of course, any errors, misinterpretations or overenthusiastic extrapolations of their work are ours alone.

Jonn would like to thank his mum Kim and her partner Alan; assorted friends and colleagues including Scot, Manu, Rachel, Brad, James, Jasper, Tom (not that one), Jim (who isn't the same as James), Matt and Lance; his editors at the *New Statesman*; and anyone on Twitter who was kind enough to help out when he needed a good, cleansing fight, with the noteworthy exception of the anti-vax people; Henry Scampi, who is quite simply the best dog in the world, yes he is, yes he is, yes he IS; and Agnes, who is quite simply the best.

Tom would like to thank his family – Don, Colette, Ben and Ellie – for their support and tolerance; the friends who provided encouragement and stimulating conversations, both on and off-topic, in particular James, Maha, Chris, Damian, Holly, Sian, Agnes and above all Kate, who was a lifeline; and his former colleagues at Full Fact, who helped shape his thinking on these topics and are lovely people. Given the circumstances of the book's writing, he would also like to thank his houseplants: Ken, Lily, Spidey, Spidey II, Lil' Bertie and Dead Gareth. Gareth, I am so sorry.

We would like to thank the staff of the White Bear, Fugitive Motel and the Dog House, who definitely helped, at least during the periods when it was legal to work there.

Finally, Jonn and Tom would like to thank each other: for patience and morale-boosting, for sharing both the times of hard work and the times of procrastination, and above all for invaluable friendship. Contrary to some predictions, we did not murder each other even a little bit, for which we are both profoundly grateful.

Notes

Introduction

1   Tweet from Donald J. Trump, 4 November, 2020 (since deleted);
     quoted in Aaron Rupar, 'Trump signals he's counting on the
     Supreme Court to help him steal the election', *Vox*, 4 November
     2020

2   Li Cohen, '6 conspiracy theories about the 2020 election –
     debunked', CBS News, 15 January 2021; Sam Levine, 'Arizona
     Republicans hunt for bamboo-laced China ballots in 2020 "audit"
     effort', *Guardian*, 6 May 2021.

3   Marshall Cohen, '"Things could get very ugly": Experts fear
     post-election crisis as Trump sets the stage to dispute the results
     in November', CNN, 21 July 2020; David A. Graham, 'The "Blue
     Shift" Will Decide the Election', *The Atlantic*, 10 August 2020.

4   Ipsos, 'Over half of Republicans believe Donald Trump is the
     actual President of the United States', ipsos.com, 21 May 2021.

5   Jonathan Swan, 'Scoop: Trump's plan to declare premature
     victory', Axios, 1 November 2020.

6   Amy Sherman and Miriam Valverde, 'Joe Biden is right that
     more than 60 of Trump's election lawsuits lacked merit',
     Politifact, 8 January 2021; Michael D. Shear and Stephanie Saul,
     'Trump, in Taped Call, Pressured Georgia Official to "Find" Votes
     to Overturn Election', *New York Times*, 3 January 2021.

7   Joseph Roisman, *The Rhetoric of Conspiracy in Ancient Athens*,

University of California Press, 2006; Victoria Emma Pagán, 'Conspiracy Theories in the Roman Empire', *Routledge Handbook of Conspiracy Theories*, Routledge, 2020.

8   Greg Miller, 'The enduring allure of conspiracies', *Knowable Magazine*, 14 January 2021; NPR, 'American Shadows', *Throughline*, 7 March 2019; Joseph E. Uscinski and Joseph M. Parent, *American Conspiracy Theories*, Oxford University Press, 2014, pp. 1–3.

9   Adam Smith, *The Wealth of Nations: Books 1–3*, Penguin Books, 1999, p. 12.

1 What Is a Conspiracy Theory?

1   Much of the description of William's murder and the aftermath are from E. M. Rose, *The Murder of William of Norwich: The Origins of the Blood Libel in Medieval Europe*, Oxford University Press, 2015.

2   Michael Butter, 'There's a conspiracy theory that the CIA invented the term "conspiracy theory" – here's why', *The Conversation*, 16 March 2020.

3   Andrew McKenzie-McHarg, 'Conceptual History and Conspiracy Theory', *Routledge Handbook of Conspiracy Theories*, Routledge, 2020, p. 23.

4   Thomas of Monmouth, *The Life and Passion of William of Norwich*, Penguin Classics (Kindle edition), 2014.

5   Gavin I. Langmuir, 'Thomas of Monmouth: Detector of Ritual Murder', *Speculum*, Vol. 59, No. 4, October 1984, pp. 820–46.

6   Richard Hofstadter, 'The Paranoid Style in American Politics', Knopf Doubleday Publishing Group, 2008, p. 29.

7   Hofstadter, 'The Paranoid Style in American Politics', p. 36.

8   Rose, *The Murder of William of Norwich*, p. 206.

2 Psyche!

1   Mimi Swartz, 'The Witness', *Texas Monthly*, November 2003.

2   Arthur Goldwag, *Cults, Conspiracies & Secret Societies*, Vintage Books, 2009.

3   'What Aren't They Telling Us? Chapman University Survey of American Fears', blogs.chapman.edu, 11 October 2016.

4   'Democrats and Republicans differ on conspiracy theory beliefs', publicpolicypolling.com, 2 April 2013.

5   Art Swift, 'Majority in U.S. Still Believe JFK Killed in a Conspiracy', news.gallup. com, 15 November 2013.

6   Joel Rogers de Waal, 'Brexit and Trump voters are more likely to believe in conspiracy theories', YouGov.co.uk, 14 December 2018.

7   Joseph E. Uscinski and Joseph M. Parent, *American Conspiracy Theories*, Oxford University Press, 2014.

8   Mick West, *Escaping the Rabbit Hole*, Skyhorse, August 2020; Michael Shermer, *Conspiracies & Conspiracy Theories*, Audible, September 2019; David Robson 'Why smart people are more likely to believe fake news', *Guardian*, 1 April 2019.

9   Joseph E. Uscinski, 'How playing on conspiracy theories can be key to electoral success', blogs.lse.ac.uk, 7 June 2016.

10   Sharon Parsons, William Simmons, Frankie Shinhoster and John Kilburn, 'A Test Of The Grapevine: An Empirical Examination Of Conspiracy Theories Among African Americans', *Sociological Spectrum*, Vol. 19, No. 2, 1999, pp. 201–22.

11   Sam Jackson, *Conspiracy Theories in the Patriot/Militia Movement*, extremism.gwu.edu, May 2017.

12   Michael Shermer, 'Why Do People Believe in Conspiracy Theories?', scientificamerican.com, 1 December 2014.

13   Uscinski and Parent, *American Conspiracy Theories*; Shermer, 'Why Do People Believe in Conspiracy Theories?'; Michail Zontos, 'Book Review: *American Conspiracy Theories* by Joseph E. Uscinski and Joseph M. Parent', blogs.lse.ac.uk, 25 February 2015.

14   Jan-Willem van Prooijen, 'Voters on the extreme left and right are far more likely to believe in conspiracy theories', blogs.lse. ac.uk, 24 February 2015.

15   'What Aren't They Telling Us?', blogs.chapman.edu.

16   Robert Brotherton, Christopher C. French and Alan D. Pickering, Goldsmiths University of London, 'Measuring belief in conspiracy theories: the generic conspiracist beliefs scale', *Frontiers in Psychology*, Vol. 4, 2013.

17   Much of the discussion of cognitive biases, and how they relate

to conspiracy theories, was drawn from: Shermer, *Conspiracies & Conspiracy Theories*.

18   An oft-repeated paraphrase of the central thesis of: Michael Barkun, *A Culture of Conspiracy*, *(Comparative Studies in Religion and Society)*, University of California Press, 2013.

19   Goldwag, *Cults, Conspiracies, & Secret Societies*.

20   Shermer, *Conspiracies & Conspiracy Theories*.

21   Tamotsu Shibutani, *Improvised News: A Sociological Study of Rumor*, The Bobbs-Merrill Company, 1966, p. 57.

22   Felix Light, 'Coronavirus Conspiracy Theories Flourish in Russia's Republic of North Ossetia', *Moscow Times*, 22 May 2020.

23   Joseph Melnyk, Sophia Pink, James Druckman and Robb Willer, 'Correcting Inaccurate Metaperceptions Reduces Americans' Support for Partisan Violence', OSF Preprints, 20 September 2021.

24   West, *Escaping the Rabbit Hole*.

25   David Robarge, 'DCI John McCone and the Assassination of President John F. Kennedy', *Studies In Intelligence*, Vol. 51, No. 3, September 2013, p. 13.

3 Panic! At the Discourse

1   Jérôme Jamin, 'Cultural Marxism: A survey', *Religion Compass*, Vol. 12, January–February 2018.

2   Leopold Engel, *Geschichte des Illuminatenordens*, 1906, p. 102, quoted in Klaus Epstein, *The Genesis of German Conservatism*, Princeton University Press, 1966, p. 91.

3   'Einmal gefalt mir sein Gang nicht: seine Manieren sind roh un ungesh-liffen ...' from Reinhard Markner, Monika Neugebauer-Wölk and Hermann Schüttler, *Die Korrespondenz des Illuminatenordens, Band I: 1776-1781*, De Gruyter, 2011, p. 8.

4   Adam Weishaupt, *A Brief Justification of My Intentions*, Justice Publications, 2014. Kindle edition.

5   Weishaupt, *A Brief Justification*.

6   Sisko Haikala, 'Denouncing the Enlightenment by Means of a Conspiracy Thesis: Göchhausen's *Enthullung der Weltburgerrepublik*', *Finnish Yearbook of Political Thought*, Vol. 4, No. 1, 2000, pp. 96–125.

7   Epstein, *The Genesis of German Conservatism*, p. 521.

8   Epstein, *The Genesis of German Conservatism*, p. 526.

9   Epstein, *The Genesis of German Conservatism*, p. 537.

10   Amos Hofman, 'The Origins of the Theory of the Philosophe Conspiracy', *French History*, Vol. 2, No. 2, 1988, pp. 152–172.

11   Amos Hofman, 'Opinion, Illusion, and the Illusion of Opinion: Barruel's Theory of Conspiracy', *Eighteenth-Century Studies*, Vol. 27, No. 1, Autumn 1993, pp. 27–60.

12   Augustin Barruel, *Memoirs Illustrating the History of Jacobinism*, Real View Books, 1995, p. 410, p. 68, p. 72.

13   John Playfair, 'Biographical Account of the Late John Robison, LL.D', *The Works of John Playfair, Vol IV*, A. Constable & Co, 1822, p. 163.

14   Elizabeth Wynne Fremantle, *The Wynne Diaries, 1789–1820*, (ed. Anne Freemantle), Oxford University Press, 1952, p. 168; Mark Dilworth, 'Horn, Alexander [name in religion Maurus] (1762–1820), Benedictine monk and political agent', *Oxford Dictionary of National Biography*, 23 September 2004.

15   Playfair, *The Works of John Playfair*, p. 161.

16   Kim A. Wagner, *The Great Fear of 1857: Rumours, Conspiracies and the Making of the Indian Uprising*, Peter Lang, 2010.

17   Aisha K. Finch, *Rethinking Slave Rebellion in Cuba*, University of North Carolina Press, 2015.

18   Tom Zoellner, 'How a wild conspiracy theory hastened the end of Texas independence', *Washington Post*, 14 May 2020.

19   Michael Taylor, 'British Conservatism, the Illuminati, and the Conspiracy Theory of the French Revolution, 1797–1802', *Eighteenth-Century Studies*, Vol. 47, No. 3, Spring 2014, pp. 293–312.

20   Edmund Burke, in Barbara Lowe, P. J. Marshall & John A. Woods (eds), *The Correspondence of Edmund Burke, Vol. X*, Cambridge University Press, 1978, pp. 38–39.

21   J. M. Roberts, *The Mythology of the Secret Societies*, 3rd ed., Watkins, 2008, p. 207.

22   Hofman, 'Opinion, Illusion, and the Illusion of Opinion: Barruel's Theory of Conspiracy'.

23   Jean Joseph Mournier, *On the Influence Attributed to Philosophers,*

Free-masons, and to the Illuminati, on the Revolution of France, W. and C. Spilsbury, 1801, p. v.

24   Andrew McKenzie-McHarg, 'How to Sabotage a Secret Society: The Demise of Carl Friedrich Bahrdt's German Union In 1789', *The Historical Journal*, Vol. 61, No. 2, 2018, pp. 379–402.

25   Thomas Jefferson, 'From Thomas Jefferson to Bishop James Madison, 31 January 1800', *Founders Online*, National Archives (Original source: *The Papers of Thomas Jefferson*, Vol. 31, 1 February 1799–31 May 1800, ed. Barbara B. Oberg, Princeton University Press, 2004, pp. 349–352).

26   Vernon Stauffer, *New England and the Bavarian Illuminati*, Good Press, 2019.

4 The Faults in Our Stars

1   Matt Thompson, 'Paul is Dead', BBC Radio 4, first broadcast October 2014; Rob Sheffield, '"Paul Is Dead": The Bizarre Story of Music's Most Notorious Conspiracy Theory', *Rolling Stone*, 11 October 2019; Dorothy Bacon, 'Paul Is Still With Us', *Life*, 7 November 1969 (available online via the Paul McCartney Project: the-paulmccartney-project.com/interview/the-case-of-the-missing-beatles-paul-is-still-with-us/); Avery Gregurich, 'Pop star's death rumor begins at Drake', *Times-Delphic*, April 2013.

2   Dorothy Bacon, 'Paul Is Still With Us'.

3   Rob Sheffield, '"Paul Is Dead"'.

4   Marina Hyde, 'Whoever hacked Rebekah Vardy's Insta was obviously never at Baden-Baden', *Guardian*, 10 October 2019.

5   Ovid, *Metamorphoses XV*, 840.

6   Greg Jenner, *Dead Famous: An Unexpected History of Celebrity from Bronze Age to Silver Screen*, Weidenfeld & Nicolson, 2020.

7   Michelle Ruiz, 'A Deep Dive Into Brad Pitt and Jennifer Aniston's Relationship – and Our Obsession With It', *Vogue*, 21 January 2020.

8   'Paul is Dead,' BBC Radio 4.

9   'Celebrity Doppelgangers', doppels.proboards.com.

10   Larry Bartleet, 'Imposter alert! Nine ridiculous conspiracy theories about celebrity changelings', *NME*, May 2017.

11 Ryan Broderick, 'Here's How I Accidentally Made an Old Avril Lavigne Death Hoax Go Viral', buzzfeed.com, 2 October 2015.

12 'Avril Lavigne morreu e foi substituída por uma sósia?', Avril Esta Morta: A Teoria Da Conspiracao, avrilestamorta-blogspot-com, May 2011.

13 Ashley Feinberg, 'Did Avril Lavigne Die in 2003?: An Internet Conspiracy, Explained', blackbag.gawker.com, 2 October 2015; Ryan Bassil, 'Investigating the Conspiracy that Says Avril Lavigne was Killed Off and Replaced with an Actress', *Vice*, 1 October 2015.

14 Kenneth Partridge, 'Suspicious Minds: The Bizarre, 40-year History of Elvis Presley Sightings', mentalfloss.com, 14 August 2017; Patrick Lacy, '1977 International Flight of Fancy', elvisde-coded.blogspot.com, 26 February 2012.

15 BuzzFeed Unsolved Network, 'The Mysterious Death of Tupac Shakur: Part 1', youtube.com.

16 Sources for this section include: Arit John, 'All the Illuminati References in Katy Perry's Dark Horse Video', *The Atlantic*, 20 February 2014; 'Katy Perry: I Want to Join the Illuminati!', *Rolling Stone*, August 2014.

17 Lindsay Grace, 'Games blamed for moral decline and addiction throughout history', theconversation.com, 9 October 2019.

18 Tess Barker and Barbara Gray, '"Me Time" :)', *Britney's Gram*, 4 April 2019.

19 'Britney Spears Checks in to Mental Health Facility ... Distraught Over Dad's Illness', TMZ, 3 April 2019.

20 Tess Barker and Barbara Gray, '#FREEBRITNEY', *Britney's Gram*, 16 April 2019.

21 *When Louis Met ... Jimmy*, director Will Yapp, writer Louis Theroux, BBC Two, 13 April 2000.

5 Assassin Screed

1 William Hanchett, *The Lincoln Murder Conspiracies*, University of Illinois Press, 1986, p. 234.

2 Charles Chiniquy, *Fifty Years in the Church of Rome*, Craig & Barlow, 1885, p. 5, p. 668-669.

3   Hanchett, *The Lincoln Murder Conspiracies*, p. 164.

4   Jonn Elledge, 'The most dangerous job in America? US presidents
        have a fatality rate roughly 27 times that of lumberjacks', *New
        Statesman*, 25 October 2016.

5   John Smith Dye, *The Adder's Den, or, Secrets of the Great Conspiracy
        to Overthrow Liberty in America*, 1864, p. 91.

6   Manuel Eisner, 'Killing Kings: Patterns of Regicide in Europe,
        AD 600–1800', *The British Journal of Criminology*, Vol. 51, No. 3,
        2011, pp. 556–577.

7   R. G. Hoffman, 'The Age of Assassination: Monarchy and
        Nation in Nineteenth-century Europe' in J. Rüger & N.
        Wachsmann (eds), *Rewriting German History*, Palgrave Macmillan,
        2015.

8   Emma Graham-Harrison, Andreas Rocksen and Mads Brügger,
        'Man accused of shooting down UN chief: "Sometimes you have
        to do things you don't want to ..."', *Guardian*, 12 January, 2019

9   'Excerpts: Israeli security cabinet statement', news.bbc.co.uk, 11
        September 2003.

10   Harry Enten, 'Most People Believe In JFK Conspiracy Theories',
        fivethirtyeight.com, 23 October 2017.

11   Bertrand Russell, *The Autobiography of Bertrand Russell*, Taylor and
        Francis, 2000, Kindle edition, pp. 663 and 699.

12   Karen Barlow, 'Holt disappearance theories resurrected online',
        abc.net.au, 25 September 2007.

13   Bridget Judd, 'Inside the disappearance of Harold Holt – one of
        the largest search operations in Australian history', abc.net.au, 31
        October 2020.

14   Tom Frame, *The Life and Death of Harold Holt*, Allen and Unwin,
        2005, p. 273.

15   I. R. Hancock, 'Holt, Harold Edward (1908–1967)', *Australian
        Dictionary of Biography*, National Centre of Biography, Australian
        National University, first published 1996, accessed online 2
        March 2021.

6 Unidentified Lying Objects

1   John Winthrop, *The Journal of John Winthrop, 1630–1649*, Laetitia

Yeandle and Richard Dunn (eds), Belknap Press of Harvard University Press, 2009, p. 284.

2 Michael Barkun, *A Culture of Conspiracy (Comparative Studies in Religion and Society)*, University of California Press, 2013, p. 81; and Lydia Saad, 'Do Americans Believe in UFOs?', gallup. com, 20 May 2021

3 Barkun, *A Culture of Conspiracy*, 2013, p. 81; and Lydia Saad, 'Americans Skeptical of UFOs, but Say Government Knows More', gallup. com, 6 September 2019

4 For example: Helene Cooper, Ralph Blumenthal and Leslie Kean, '"Wow, What Is That?" Navy Pilots Report Unexplained Flying Objects', *New York Times*, 26 May 2019.

5 Daniel Drezner, 'UFOs exist and everyone needs to adjust to that fact', *The Washington Post*, 28 May 2019.

6 'Preliminary Assessment: Unidentified Aerial Phenomena', Office of the Director of National Intelligence, dni.gov, 25 June 2021.

7 John Winthrop, *The Journal of John Winthrop, 1630–1649*, p. 493.

8 Cotton Mather, *Magnalia Christi Americana*, Thomas Parkhurst, 1702, p. 25–26.

9 Jason Colavito, 'The UFO Battle over Nuremberg', jasoncolavito. com, 12 December 2012.

10 William J. Birnes, *The Everything UFO Book*, Everything, 2011, pp. 21–2.

11 Han Dae-gwang, 'UFO incident in the Joseon Dynasty', khan. co.kr, 18 July 2016.

12 Tomas Blahuta, 'Ufologist: Slovak fighters have already chased UFOs, the inter-dimensional gate is not far from the nuclear powerplant in Jaslovské Bohunice (Interview), refresher.sk, 15 February 2019.

13 Richard Stothers, 'Unidentified Flying Objects in Classical Antiquity', *The Classical Journal*, Vol. 103, No. 1, Oct–Nov 2007.

14 Stothers, 'Unidentified Flying Objects in Classical Antiquity'.

15 Donald R. Prothero and Timothy D. Callahan, *UFOs, Chemtrails, and Aliens: What Science Says*, Indiana University Press, 2017, p. xii.

16 Gregory L. Reece, *UFO Religion: Inside Flying Saucer Cults and Culture*, Bloomsbury, 2007, p. 213

17 'Science: Martians over France', *Time*, 25 October, 1954.

18   Megan Garber, 'The Man Who Introduced the World to Flying Saucers', *The Atlantic*, 15 June 2014; Quotation from the *Spokane Daily Chronicle*, 27 June 1947.

19   Story related in: Goldwag, *Cults, Conspiracies, & Secret Societies*.

20   Pew Research Centre, 'Beyond Distrust: How Americans View Their Government', pewresearch.org, 23 November 2015.

21   Lily Rothman, 'How the Roswell UFO Theory Got Started' *Time*, 7 July 2015.

22   'Top 10 literary hoaxes', *Guardian*, 15 November 2001.

23   Goldwag, *Cults, Conspiracies, & Secret Societies*.

24   Gideon Lewis-Kraus, 'How The Pentagon Started Taking UFOs Seriously', *New Yorker*, 30 April 2021.

25   Helene Cooper, Ralph Blumenthal and Leslie Kean, 'Glowing Auras and "Black Money"', *New York Times*, 16 December 2017.

26   Timothy Egan, 'Terror In Oklahoma, In Congress: Trying to Explain Contacts With Paramilitary Groups', *New York Times*, 2 May 1995.

27   Patricia Sullivan, 'Militia-friendly Idaho Rep. Helen Chenoweth-Hage (Obituary), *Washington Post*, 4 October 2006.

28   Rose Eveleth, 'Even Astronauts Have Accidents', *Smithsonian Magazine*, 11 June 2013.

29   James Ball, 'Alex Gibney on Kubrick and the Moon Landing', *The New Conspiracist*, season 2, episode 1, 23 April 2021.

30   Richard Godwin, 'One giant … lie? Why so many people still think the moon landings were faked', *Guardian*, 10 July 2019.

31   David Crookes, 'Yuri Gagarin: How the first man in space sparked a conspiracy theory', *All About Space* magazine/livescience. com, 12 April 2021.

32   Available via Wikimedia Commons (en.wikipedia.org/wiki/ Mowing-Devil#/media/File:Diablefaucheur.jpg)

33   Jeremy Northcote, *Spatial distribution of England's crop circles: Using GIS to investigate a geo-spatial mystery*, Edith Cowan University Australia, sieu.edu.

34   William Tuohoy, '"Crop Circles" Their Prank, 2 Britons Say', *Los Angeles Times*, 10 September 1991; Leon Jaroff, 'It Happens in the Best Circles', *Time*, 23 September 1991.

35   This section draws heavily on an article Jonn wrote for the *New*

Statesman in 2018 (he was going through a very difficult period personally at the time): Jonn Elledge, 'What if the same force that created civilisation is the thing most likely to destroy it?', *New Statesman*, 3 August 2018.

7 Viral Misinformation

1   Richard J. Evans, 'Epidemics And Revolutions: Cholera In Nineteenth-Century Europe', *Past & Present*, Vol. 120, No. 1, 1988, p. 129.

2   Heinrich Heine, *French Affairs: Letters from Paris (Vol. I)*, W. Heinemann, 1893, p. 169.

3   Alexandre Dumas, *My Memoirs (Vol. VI)*, trans. E. M. Waller, Methuen, 1907, p. 119.

4   Alexandre Boumard, 'Du choléra-morbus, ou De l'asthénie des organes gastriques', 1832, quoted in François Delaporte, *Disease and Civilization: The Cholera in Paris, 1832*, trans. Arthur Goldhammer, MIT Press, 1986, p. 48.

5   Dumas, *My Memoirs*, p. 119; Heine, *French Affairs*, p. 171.

6   Delaporte, *Disease and Civilization*, p. 56.

7   Quoted in Delaporte, *Disease and Civilization*, p. 53.

8   Heine, *French Affairs*, p. 170.

9   Samuel K. Cohn Jr, 'Cholera revolts: a class struggle we may not like', *Social History*, Vol. 42, No. 2, 2017, pp. 162–180.

10   Cohn, 'Cholera revolts'.

11   Samuel K. Cohn, Jr., *Epidemics: Hate and Compassion from the Plague of Athens to AIDS*, Oxford University Press, 2018, pp. 169 and 172; John Puntis, '1832 Cholera Riots' (letter), *Lancet*, Vol. 358, Issue 9288, 6 October 2001.

12   Cohn, *Epidemics*, p. 166.

13   Sean Burrell and Geoffrey Gill, 'The Liverpool Cholera Epidemic of 1832 and Anatomical Dissection – Medical Mistrust and Civil Unrest', *Journal of the History of Medicine and Allied Sciences*, Vol. 60, No. 4, October 2005, pp. 478–98; Geoffrey Gill, Sean Burrell and Jody Brown, 'Fear and frustration: the Liverpool cholera riots of 1832', *Lancet*, Vol. 358, Issue 2001, pp. 233–7.

14   Cohn, *Epidemics*, p. 172.

15   R. J. Morris, *Cholera 1832 – The Social Response to an Epidemic*, Holm & Meier, 1976, quoted in Burrell and Gill, 'The Liverpool Cholera Epidemic'; C. R. Goring, M.D., 'Cholera or No Cholera – Tricks of Some Governments' (letter), *Lancet*, Vol. 17, Issue 432, 10 December 1831, p. 377.

16   Alessandro Manzoni, *I Promessi Sposi*, Cosimo Inc, 2010, p. 534.

17   *The New York Herald*, European edition, 31 January 1890.

18   See, for example, *Richmond Palladium*, Vol. 43, No. 284, 11 October 1918, p. 2.

19   *New York Times*, 19 September 1918, p. 11.

20   Cohn, *Epidemics*, p. 546.

21   Pam Belluck, 'Red Cross Faces Attacks at Ebola Victims' Funerals', *New York Times*, 12 February 2015; Cohn, *Epidemics*, p. 261.

22   'The Epidemic of Plague in Hong Kong', *British Medical Journal*, Vol. 1, No. 1326, 16 June 1894.

23   E. Pryor, 'The Great Plague of Hong Kong', *Journal of the Hong Kong Branch of the Royal Asiatic Society*, Vol. 15, 1975, pp. 61–70.

24   Srilata Chatterjee, 'Plague and Politics in Bengal 1896 to 1898', *Proceedings of the Indian History Congress*, Vol. 66, 2005–2006, pp. 1194–1201; Natasha Sarkar, 'Plague in Bombay: Response of Britain's Indian Subjects to Colonial Intervention', *Proceedings of the Indian History Congress*, Vol. 62, 2001, pp. 442–9; Anita Prakash, 'Plague Riot In Kanpur – Perspectives on Colonial Public Health Policy', *Proceedings of the Indian History Congress*, Vol. 69, 2008, pp. 839–846; Ira Klein, 'Plague, Policy and Popular Unrest in British India', *Modern Asian Studies*, Vol. 22, No. 4, 1988, pp. 723–755

25   Margot Minardi, 'The Boston Inoculation Controversy of 1721–1722: An Incident in the History of Race', *William and Mary Quarterly*, Third Series, Vol. 61, No. 1, January 2004, pp. 47–76.

26   Mark Best, Duncan Neuhauser and L. Slavin, '"Cotton Mather, you dog, dam you! I'l inoculate you with this; with a pox to you": smallpox inoculation, Boston, 1721', *Quality & Safety In Health Care*, Vol. 13, No. 1, 2004, pp. 82–83; Matthew Niederhuber, 'The Fight Over Inoculation During the 1721

Boston Smallpox Epidemic', *Science in the News (Harvard University)*, 31 December 2014.

27   John B. Blake, 'The Inoculation Controversy in Boston: 1721–1722', *New England Quarterly*, Vol. 25, No. 4, December 1952, pp. 489–506; Amalie M. Kass, 'Boston's Historic Smallpox Epidemic', *Massachusetts Historical Review*, Vol. 14, 2012, pp. 1–51.

28   Robert M. Wolfe and Lisa K. Sharp, 'Anti-Vaccinationists Past And Present', *British Medical Journal*, Vol. 325, No. 7361, 24 August 2002, pp. 430–2; Aaron Rothstein, 'Vaccines and their Critics, Then and Now', *New Atlantis*, No. 44, Winter 2015, pp. 3–27.

29   Dale L. Ross, 'Leicester and the anti-vaccination movement, 1853–1889', *Transactions – The Leicestershire Archaeological and Historical Society*, Vol. 43, 1967, pp. 35–44; S. C. McFarland, 'The vaccination controversy at Leicester'/'The vaccination controversy at Leicester – Continued', *Public Health Reports (1896–1970)*, Vol. 15, No. 10, 9 March 1900, pp. 551–5.

30   Robert Bartholomew and Hilary Evans, *Panic Attacks: Media Manipulation and Mass Delusion*, The History Press, 2013.

31   Jesse Hicks, 'Pipe Dreams: America's Fluoride Controversy', *Distillations (Science History Institute)*, 24 June 2011.

32   A. R. Mushegian, 'Are There 10^{31} Virus Particles on Earth, or More, or Fewer?', *Journal of Bacteriology*, Vol. 202, No. 9, 9 April 2020.

8 2020 Hindsight

1   Katie Shepherd, 'A man thought aquarium cleaner with the same name as the anti-viral drug chloroquine would prevent coronavirus. It killed him', *Washington Post*, 24 March 2020; Mohammad Delirrad and Ali Banagozar Mohammadi, 'New Methanol Poisoning Outbreaks in Iran Following Covid-19 Pandemic', *Alcohol and Alcoholism*, Vol. 55, Issue 4, July 2020, pp. 347–8; Dickens Olewe, 'John Magufuli: The cautionary tale of the president who denied coronavirus', news.bbc.co.uk, 18 March 2021.

2   Leo Benedictus, 'There is no plan to combat the new coronavirus with helicopters spraying disinfectant', fullfact.org, 1 April 2020.

3   Jim Waterson and Alex Hern, 'At least 20 UK phone masts
     vandalised over false 5G coronavirus claims', *Guardian*, 6 April
     2020; James Vincent, '5G coronavirus conspiracy theorists are
     endangering the workers who keep networks running', *The Verge*,
     3 June 2020.

4   Facebook post subsequently deleted; archived image in Victoria
     Bell, 'Facebook brands post linking Wuhan coronavirus to 5G
     "false information"', Yahoo! News, 31 January 2020.

5   Quinn T. Ostrom, Stephen S. Francis and Jill S. Barnholtz-Sloan,
     'Epidemiology of Brain and Other CNS Tumors', *Current
     Neurology and Neuroscience Reports*, Vol. 21, Article 68, 24
     November 2021; SSM's Scientific Council on Electromagnetic
     Fields, 'Recent Research on EMF and Health Risk: Fifteenth
     report from SSM's Scientific Council on Electromagnetic Fields,
     2020', *Strålsäkerhetsmyndigheten* (Swedish Radiation Safety
     Authority), ssm.se, 25 April 2021.

6   Grace Rahman, 'Here's where those 5G and coronavirus
     conspiracy theories came from', fullfact.org, 9 April 2020.

7   Graeme Wearden, '3G rollout threatened by mast protests',
     ZDNet, 19 April 2002; 'Mast pulled down by vandals', news.bbc.
     co.uk, 17 March 2003; 'Mobile mast protest in second week',
     news.bbc.co.uk, 14 November 2003; 'Controversial village mast
     hit in £40,000 vandal attack', yorkpress.co.uk, 22 November
     2007.

8   Frances Drake, 'Mobile phone masts: protesting the scientific
     evidence', *Public Understanding of Science*, Vol. 15, No. 4, 2006,
     pp. 387–410.

9   Dennis K. Flaherty, 'The vaccine–autism connection: a public
     health crisis caused by unethical medical practices and fraudulent
     science', *The Annals of Pharmacotherapy*, Vol. 45, Issue 10, 2011,
     pp. 1302–4; Luke E. Taylor, Amy L. Swerdfeger and Guy D.
     Eslick, 'Vaccines are not associated with autism: an evidence-
     based meta-analysis of case-control and cohort studies', *Vaccine*,
     Vol. 32, Issue 29, 2014, pp. 3623–9.

10   Maddy Savage, 'Thousands of Swedes are Inserting
     Microchips Under Their Skin', *All Things Considered*, NPR, 22
     October 2018.

11   Lauren Chadwick and Ric Wasserman, 'Will microchip implants be the next big thing in Europe?', euronews.com, 1 June 2021.

12   Deloitte, 'Mobile Consumer Survey 2019: UK', deloitte.com, 2019

13   Edward C. Holmes, Stephen A. Goldstein, Angela L. Rasmussen, David L. Robertson, Alexander Crits-Christoph, Joel O. Wertheim, Simon J. Anthony, Wendy S. Barclay, Maciej F. Boni, Peter C. Doherty, Jeremy Farrar, Jemma L. Geoghegan, Xiaowei Jiang, Julian L. Leibowitz, Stuart J. D. Neil, Tim Skern, Susan R. Weiss, Michael Worobey, Kristian G. Andersen, Robert F. Garry and Andrew Rambaut, 'The origins of SARS-CoV-2: A critical review', *Cell*, Vol. 184, Issue 19, 2021, pp. 4848–56.

14   Kangpeng Xiao, Junqiong Zhai, Yaoyu Feng, Niu Zhou, Xu Zhang, Jie-Jian Zou, Na Li, Yaqiong Guo, Xiaobing Li, Xuejuan Shen, Zhipeng Zhang, Fanfan Shu, Wanyi Huang, Yu Li, Ziding Zhang, Rui-Ai Chen, Ya-Jiang Wu, Shi-Ming Peng, Mian Huang, Wei-Jun Xie, Qin-Hui Cai, Fang-Hui Hou, Wu Chen, Lihua Xiao and Yongyi Shen, 'Isolation of SARS-CoV-2-related coronavirus from Malayan pangolins', *Nature*, Vol. 583, 2020, pp. 286–9.

15   Kristian G. Andersen, Andrew Rambaut, W. Ian Lipkin, Edward C. Holmes and Robert F. Garry, 'The proximal origin of SARS-CoV-2', *Nature Medicine*, Vol. 26, 2020, pp. 450–452.

16   Kate E. Jones, Nikkita G. Patel, Marc A. Levy, Adam Storeygard, Deborah Balk, John L. Gittleman and Peter Daszak, 'Global trends in emerging infectious diseases', *Nature*, Vol. 451, 2008, pp. 990–993; D. Grace, F. Mutua, P. Ochungo, R. Kruska, K. Jones, L. Brierley, L. Lapar, M. Said, M. Herrero, P. M. Phuc, N. B. Thao, I. Akuku and F. Ogutu, 'Mapping of poverty and likely zoonoses hotspots (Zoonoses Project 4, Report to the UK Department for International Development)', International Livestock Research Institute, 2012.

17   Rachael Krishna, 'This is not a vaccine for the 2019 coronavirus', fullfact.org, 10 March 2020; Grace Rahman, 'The makers of Dettol did not know about the new Wuhan coronavirus before the rest of us', fullfact.org, 30 January 2020.

18   David Quammen, *Spillover*, Vintage, 2012, p. 512.

9 Plots of Land

1   Christine Garwood, *Flat Earth: The History of an Infamous Idea*, Pan, 2007; Donald R. Prothero, *Weird Earth: Debunking Strange Ideas About Our Planet*, Red Lightning Books, 2020; Bob Schadewald, *The Plane Truth*, 2015, incomplete manuscript available at www.cantab.net/users/michael.behrend/ebooks/PlaneTruth/pages/index.html

2   Stephanie Pappas, '7 Ways to Prove the Earth Is Round (Without Launching a Satellite)', livescience.com, 28 September 2017.

3   Alfred Russel Wallace, *My Life: A Record of Events and Opinions*, Vol. 2, Chapman & Hall, 1905, p. 370.

4   Garwood, *Flat Earth*, p. 112.

5   Tony Reichhardt, 'The First Photo From Space', airspacemag.com, 24 October 2006.

6   Al Reinert, 'The Blue Marble Shot: Our First Complete Photograph of Earth', *The Atlantic*, 12 April 2011.

7   For example, in: Prothero, *Weird Earth*.

8   David Yanofsky, 'The guy who created the iPhone's Earth image explains why he needed to fake it', qz.com, 27 March 2014.

9   Interview with Jonn Elledge, February 2021.

10   Rob Picheta, 'The flat-Earth conspiracy is spreading around the globe. Does it hide a darker core?', edition.cnn.com, 18 November 2019.

11   Richard Sprenger, James Bullock, Alex Healey, Tom Silverstone and Katie Lamborn, 'Flat Earth rising: meet the people casting aside 2,500 years of science' (video), *Guardian*, 5 February 2019.

12   SciJinks, 'Why Does the Atmosphere Not Drift off Into Space?', scijinks.gov. (It's a measure of how basic this science is that our reference is to a US government science website aimed at children.)

13   Michael Vollmer, 'Below the horizon – the physics of extreme visual ranges', *Applied Optics*, Vol. 59, Issue 21, July 2020.

14   NASA, 'The Deadly Van Allen Belts?', nasa.gov.

15   Mack Lamoureux, 'This Dude Accidentally Convinced the
      Internet That Finland Doesn't Exist', *Vice*, 12 August 2016.

16   [u/Raregan], 'What did your parents show you to do that you
      assumed was completely normal, only to discover later that it
      was not normal at all?' [online forum post], reddit.com.

17   [u/PM_ME_NICE_MESSAGES], 'The Finland Conspiracy and
      all you need to know about it.' [online forum post], reddit.com.

18   Jack May, 'The city that doesn't exist, and when Angela Merkel
      made a joke – the story of Bielefeld', Jack May, citymonitor.ai, 9
      January 2017.

19   Kate Connolly, 'German city offers €1m for proof it doesn't
      exist', *Guardian*, 5 September 2019.

20   '"Bielefeld exists!": How a German city debunked an old
      conspiracy', thelocal.de, 18 September 2019.

21   Brad Esposito, 'Everything You Need to Know about the
      Conspiracy Theory that Australia Does Not Exist, buzzfeed.com,
      23 March 2017.

22   Tom Smith, 'Some People Think Australia Doesn't Exist —
      Here's Why', theculturetrip. com, 19 April 2018.

23   [Masterchef], 'Australia doesn't exist' [online forum post],
      theflatearthsociety.org, 10 November 2006.

24   Quoted in Lamoureux, 'This Dude Accidentally Convinced the
      Internet That Finland Doesn't Exist'.

25   E. G. R. Taylor and Mercator, 'A Letter Dated 1577 from
      Mercator to John Dee', *Imago Mundi*, vol. 13, 1956, p. 60.

26   John Dunmore, *Chasing a Dream: The Exploration of the Imaginary
      Pacific*, Upstart Press, 2016.

27   'The Phantom Isles of the Pacific; Cruiser Tacoma is Looking for
      Mysterious "Dangers to Navigation" – Hundreds of Illusions
      Charted as Land', *New York Times*, May 1904.

28   This story is told in: Malachy Tallack, *The Un-Discovered Islands:
      An Archipelago of Myths and Mysteries, Phantoms and Fakes*, Polygon,
      2016.

10 In Search of Lost Time

1   This section is drawn from a number of sources, including: Katie
     Serena, 'Bizarre Phantom Time Hypothesis Theory Says it's
     Actually the Year 1720 Because the Early Middle Ages were
     Faked', allthat'sinteresting.com, 6 October 2017; 'Martin Belam,
     'J.K. Rowling doesn't exist: conspiracy theories the internet can't
     resist', *Guardian*, 27 October 2017; James Felton, 'The
     "Historians" that Believe We're Currently Living in the Year
     1724', iflscience.com, 27 January 2021.

2   Dr. Hans-Ulrich Niemitz, 'Did the Early Middle Ages Really
     Exist?', 10 February 1995.

3   Brian Koberlein, 'Astronomy, Charlemagne and the Mystery of
     Phantom Time', *Forbes*, 12 December 2016.

4   Anatoly Fomenko, *History: Fiction or Science? Chronology 1:
     Introducing the Problem*, Mithec, 2006.

5   Anthoney T. Grafton, 'Joseph Scaliger and Historical
     Chronology: The Rise and Fall of a Discipline', *History and Theory*,
     Vol. 14, No. 2, May 1975.

6   Isaac Newton, *The Chronology of Ancient Kingdoms Amended*, 1728
     (available at gutenberg.org).

7   *Encyclopedia Britannica*, 'Jean Hardouin, French scholar', britannica.
     com.

8   Stephen Sorenson, 'Nikolai Alexandrovich Morozov', ctruth.
     today, 4 April 2019.

9   Fomenko, *History: Fiction or Science? Chronology 1*, p. 16.

10   Jason Colavito, 'Who Lost the Middle Ages?', jcolavito.tripod.
     com/ *Skeptic* magazine, Vol. 11, Issue 2, summer 2004, pp. 66–70.

11   Franck Tamdu, 'Publisher announces 10,000 USD cash reward
     for the solid scientific refutation of the New Chronology. Have a
     look at the advertising spot that History Channel TV refused to
     air', prweb.com, 14 January 2004.

12   Marlene Laruelle, 'Conspiracy and Alternate History in Russia: A
     Nationalist Equation for Success?', *The Russian Review*, Vol. 71,
     No. 4, October 2012, pp. 565–80.

13   Kasparov's support has been mentioned by various sources, including: a number of reports by the *Telegraph*'s Moscow correspondent Marcus Warren in 2001; Anatoly Fomenko and Gleb. V Nosovsky, 'History of New Chronology' introductory essay to Fomenko, *History: Fiction or Science?* Vol. 1, 2003; Edward Winter, 'Garry Kasparov and New Chronology', chesshistory. com, 2014. Garry Kasparov [u/Kasparov63], 'Hello Reddit, I'm Garry Kasparov, former world chess champion, tech optimist, and an advocate both of AI and digital human rights. AMA!' [online forum thread], reddit.com, 18 May 2021.

14   Zach Mortice, 'Inside the "Tartarian Empire", the QAnon of Architecture', bloomberg.com, Bloomberg CityLab, 27 April 2021.

15   Theory outlined in various places, including: Gorgi Shepentulevski, 'Part 14: Tartaria was One Nation, One Country, One Race, One Language!', Tartaria Facebook group, facebook. com, 20 June 2021.

16   'National Cultural Development Under Communism', General CIA Records, June 1957 (available at cia.gov.uk).

11 Who Runs the World? (Lizards)

1   Nesta Webster, *Spacious Days*, Hutchinson, 1950, quoted in Martha F. Lee, 'Nesta Webster: The Voice of Conspiracy', *Journal of Women's History*, Vol. 17, No. 3, Fall 2005, p. 85.

2   Paul Hanebrink, *A Specter Haunting Europe: The Myth of Judeo-Bolshevism*, Harvard University Press, 2018, p. 15.

3   Claus Oberhauser, 'Simonini's letter: the 19th century text that influenced antisemitic conspiracy theories about the Illuminati', *The Conversation*, 31 March 2020.

4   Fred Morrow Fling, 'The French Revolution: A Study in Democracy by Nesta H. Webster', *The American Historical Review*, Vol. 25, No. 4, July 1920, pp. 714–715.

5   Rt. Hon. Winston S. Churchill, 'ZIONISM versus BOLSHEVISM: A STRUGGLE FOR THE SOUL OF THE JEWISH PEOPLE', *Illustrated Sunday Herald* (London), 8 February 1920, p. 5.

6   Gerald Burton Winrod, *Adam Weishaupt: A Human Devil*, Defender
        Publishers, 1935.

7   Robert Welch, *The Blue Book of The John Birch Society*, The John
        Birch Society, 2017, Kindle edition.

8   'Every Illuminati conspiracy theory is based on a hippie prank
        from the 1960s', wearethemighty.com, 9 February 2021.

9   Sophia Smith Galer, 'The accidental invention of the Illuminati
        conspiracy', BBC Future, 11 July 2020.

10   Robert Anton Wilson, 'The Illuminatus Saga stumbles along',
        first published in *Mystery Scene Magazine*, No. 27, October 1990,
        reprinted in *Prometheus: The Journal of the Libertarian Futurist Society*,
        Vol. 13, No. 2, Spring 1995.

11   James H. Billington, *Fire in the Minds of Men: Origins of the
        Revolutionary Faith*, Basic Books Inc., 1980, pp. 94–5, quoted in
        Terry Melanson, *Perfectibilists: The 18th Century Bavarian Order of
        the Illuminati*, Trine Day, 2008, Kindle edition.

12   John G. Schmitz, Introduction to Gary Allen and Larry
        Abraham, *None Dare Call It Conspiracy*, Dauphin Publications,
        1971, p. 3.

13   Associated Press, 'Gary Allen, 50, Dies in West; Spread
        Conservatives' View', *New York Times*, 2 December 1986.

14   Mark Jacobson, *Pale Horse Rider: William Cooper, the Rise of
        Conspiracy, and the Fall of Trust in America*, Penguin Publishing
        Group, 2018, p. 164.

15   David Icke, *The Robots' Rebellion – The Story of Spiritual Renaissance*,
        Gill & Macmillan, 2013, p. 176.

16   Icke, *The Robots' Rebellion*, p. 175.

17   David Icke, *The Biggest Secret: The Book that will Change the World*,
        Ickonic Enterprises, 1999, Kindle edition.

12 The Age of Conspiracy

1   Anthony Summers and Robbyn Swan, *The Eleventh Day*,
        Transworld, 2011, p. 113.

2   David Dunbar and Brad Reagan (eds), *Debunking 9/11 Myths: Why
        Conspiracy Theories Can't Stand Up to the Facts (USA Edition)*, Hearst,
        2011.

3   Former MI5 officer David Shayler, quoted in Brendan O'Neill, 'Meet the No Planers', *New Statesman*, 11 September 2006.

4   David Rostcheck, 'WTC bombing', USAttacked@topica.com [online forum], 11 September 2001, reproduced at serendipity.li/wot/davidr.html, retrieved on 16 December 2021.

5   Liz Foreman, 'WCPO.com's Flight 93 Story', Inside WCPO Blog, 8 February 2006, archived at Internet Archive Wayback Machine, bit.ly/3KUidKp.

6   James B. Meigs, in Dunbar and Reagan (eds), *Debunking 9/11 Myths*, 2011.

7   Quoted in Barkun, *A Culture of Conspiracy*, p. 165.

8   Texe Marrs, 'The Mysterious Riddle of Chandra Levy', texe-marrs.com, 29 January 2002.

9   David Icke, 'An Other-Dimensional View of the American Catastrophe from a Source They Cannot Silence', davidicke.com, 8 March 2002, archived at Internet Archive Wayback Machine, bit.ly/3KPmHlj.

10   John McDermott, 'A Comprehensive History of "Loose Change" – and the Seeds it Planted in Our Politics', *Esquire*, 10 September 2020.

11   Joanna Weiss, 'What Happened to the Democrats Who Never Accepted Bush's Election?', politico.com, 19 December 2020.

12   Harry Davies, 'Ted Cruz using firm that harvested data on millions of unwitting Facebook users', *Guardian*, 11 December 2015.

13   Carole Cadwalladr, 'The great British Brexit robbery: how our democracy was hijacked', *Observer*, 7 May 2017.

14   Andy Kroll, 'Cloak and Data: The Real Story Behind Cambridge Analytica's Rise and Fall', *Mother Jones*, May/June 2018.

15   Paul Lewis and Paul Hilder, 'Leaked: Cambridge Analytica's blueprint for Trump victory', *Guardian*, 23 March 2018.

16   Dov H. Levin, 'Partisan electoral interventions by the great powers: Introducing the PEIG Dataset', *Conflict Management and Peace Science*, Vol. 36, Issue 1, 1 January 2019, pp. 88–106.

17   J. J. Patrick, 'We need to talk about identifying trolls ...', byline.com, 13 November 2017; 'I'm not a Russian troll – I'm a security guard from Glasgow', *Scotsman*, 15 November 2017.

18   Marco T. Bastos and Dan Mercea, 'The Brexit Botnet and User-Generated Hyperpartisan News', *Social Science Computer Review*, Vol. 37, Issue 1, 1 February 2019, pp. 38–54; '13,500-strong Twitter bot army disappeared shortly after EU referendum, research reveals' (press release), city.ac.uk, 20 October 2017.

19   'Man Convicted of Crimes at Bohemian Grove', *Los Angeles Times*, 18 April 2002.

20   Tucker Higgins, 'Alex Jones' 5 most disturbing and ridiculous conspiracy theories', cnbc.com, 14 September 2018.

21   Elizabeth Williamson and Emily Steel, 'Conspiracy Theories Made Alex Jones Very Rich. They May Bring Him Down.' *New York Times*, 7 September 2018.

22   Higgins, 'Alex Jones' 5 most disturbing and ridiculous conspiracy theories'.

23   Daniel Freeman and Jason Freeman, 'Are we entering a golden age of the conspiracy theory?', *Guardian*, 28 March 2017; Zack Stanton, 'You're Living in the Golden Age of Conspiracy Theories', politico.com, 17 June 2020; A. J. Willingham, 'How the pandemic and politics gave us a golden age of conspiracy theories', edition.cnn.com, 3 October 2020.

24   Uscinski and Parent, *American Conspiracy Theories*.

25   Quoted in Stanton, 'You're Living in the Golden Age of Conspiracy Theories'.

26   Richard J. Evans, 'The Conspiracists', *London Review of Books*, Vol. 36, No. 9, 8 May 2014.

Conclusion

1   This endnote was just to see if anybody took us at our word and followed up *our* references. Well done you! You should check out the rest of the notes, there's some cracking reads in here.

2   Alex Hern, 'Fitness tracking app Strava gives away location of secret US army bases', *Guardian*, 28 January 2018; Max Seddon, 'Does This Soldier's Instagram Account Prove Russia is Covertly Operating in Ukraine?', buzzfeednews.com, 30 July 2014.

3   'Iraq War (disambiguation)', en.wikipedia.org, retrieved 15 December 2021.

4   Tim Harford, *How to Make the World Add Up: Ten Rules for Thinking Differently About Numbers*, Bridge Street Press, 2020, chapter 1.
5   'A third of Americans deny human-caused climate change exists', *Economist*, 8 July 2021.